THE STOCK
SELECTOR SYSTEM

THE STOCK SELECTOR SYSTEM

How to Build a Stock Portfolio for Profits in Any Market

Michael D. Sheimo

John Wiley & Sons, Inc.

New York · Chichester · Brisbane · Toronto · Singapore

Copyright © 1995 by Michael D. Sheimo
Published by John Wiley & Sons, Inc.

This publication is designed to provide accurate and authoritative
information in regard to the subject matter covered. It is sold
with the understanding that the publisher is not engaged in
rendering legal, accounting, or other professional services. If
legal advice or other expert assistance is required, the services
of a competent professional person should be sought. FROM A
DECLARATION OF PRINCIPLES JOINTLY ADOPTED BY A
COMMITTEE OF THE AMERICAN BAR ASSOCIATION AND
A COMMITTEE OF PUBLISHERS.

Library of Congress Cataloging-in-Publication Data:

Sheimo, Michael D., 1944–
     The stock selector system : how to build a stock portfolio for
profits in any market / Michael D. Sheimo.
        p.   cm.
     ISBN 0-471-57113-X (cloth)
     1. Stocks.   2. Portfolio management.   I. Title.
HG4661.S43   1995
332.63'22—dc20   94-13212

Printed in the United States of America

10 9 8 7 6 5 4 3 2 1

TO
Linda Sheimo
My best selection ever . . .

Acknowledgments

We often presume that writing is an individual sport, but this is not the case. There are so many friends and associates who gave of their time and patience for my book. Whether I asked them to read a new chapter or story, allow time for essential phone calls, or just to listen, these actions placed a demand on others that must be recognized.

First I thank my wife Linda for her patience, valuable assistance, and accurate insights. I'd also like to acknowledge my downtown Minneapolis friends. Thanks to Linda Cullen and Chip Delaney at Pillsbury for their steady understanding, and to Lynda Kamps for her reassurance. Additional thanks to Shelly Welch and Kris Baker of A. C. Nielsen Team as well as to Tom Kraack, Jane Ohl, and Mary Owen at Norwest Bank for their encouragement. Also a special thanks to Barb Roche of Smith Barney, for her confidence and support of my writing.

Contents

Introduction

Within limitations, the future can be foreseen. The present is always tending toward the future and there are always in existing conditions signals of danger or encouragement for those who read with care.

—Charles Henry Dow
(Founder of The Wall Street Journal)

Buying stock is about looking toward the future. You buy stock to increase your wealth through the return on your investment. If the economic outlook is bright, the stock market—and your chosen stocks—should increase in price and value in the coming years. If a company continues a pattern of growth, its stock price can ascend accordingly. But how do investors plan and take advantage of such events?

Because investors cannot know the future, they must depend on available information to ascertain what might occur. We can use information from the immediate past to make a simple forecast:

That stock went up $10 in the past week.

I believe it will go up another $10 this week.

You can also take a broader and deeper look at past events to create a more specific and longer-term vision:

The stock has grown 20 percent annually for the past five years. I believe it will continue to grow at this rate or better for the next five years. The growth will come from newly developed products and the recent acquisition of a well-established distribution company.

Here we have experience on our side, with a track record that illustrates precisely how the present is tending toward the future.

Understanding Market Forces— The Impact of Here and Now

The forecast can be refined even further with an understanding of the overall market. Experts say that the stock market always discounts economic changes six months to a year in advance. While that may be true in steady, less volatile markets, it is usually not the case when things heat up. In a fast-moving market, major investors are more concerned with the next few minutes than they are with the next six months. The present is indeed always tending toward the future, but at a variable speed.

If the Dow Jones Industrial Average is down 50 points at noon on heavy volume, you can be assured that the market is reacting to what might happen in the next few minutes. Since the market reacts to the here and now as well as what might happen several months from now, the key is to understand crowd psychology. Are the masses of investors overreacting to emotionalism?

Long-term investing requires solid reasoning to determine why a stock should increase in value over a measured period of time. That kind of investing takes analysis, planning, and examination of results.

How Much Information Is Necessary?

But how much information do you actually need to know? Enough business and investing information is created each day to fill a good-size library. Deciding how much of that information is actually useful and using those facts while they are still relevant are learned skills of the successful investor.

I've know investors who read and collect volumes of information to support their own special analysis techniques. Some of them spend most of their lives in a futile attempt to come up with totally accurate analyses. While doing some research in a public library, I once encountered a man wearing a torn raincoat and an old fedora, who guarded a stack of *Wall Street Journals* as he spoke on a public telephone. I learned from others that this man was in fact an active investment adviser with several clients. With an office consisting of a chair and a pay phone at the library, he obviously had low overhead expenses as well!

As he talked on the phone, he pulled a newspaper from the stack, looked up some bit of information, then hastily made a few scribbled notes in his large, spiral-bound notebook. He looked a slave to data, that stack of papers being his ball and chain.

The simple, timesaving forms in this book can help you free yourself from the slavery of too much information because they retain only the most important investment facts. A manageable level of information makes the data more comprehensible and thus generally more useful.

Three Important Concepts

This book is primarily concerned with three concepts in common stock investing:

1. Setting specific objectives.
2. Selecting stock to meet the objectives.
3. Evaluating performance in terms of the objectives.

The central concept in this book—setting objectives—controls the other two. If investors set specific objectives effectively, the second and third concepts are merely follow-up activities. An *objective* here is a material goal that an investor strives for, not in terms of emotions or beliefs, but rather as an end based on observable results. It is the most important concept of any investment activity.

To establish realistic objectives, the book will first focus on the type of stock that will best serve a stated interest. Investors who know the type of stock they are looking for can gain a specific, though tentative, idea of their prospects. We will develop a list of prospect stocks that have shown the ability to meet an established gain objective. Then the analysis will look at past growth results in earnings and prices of stocks that are the better prospects.

Tightening the focus in the final selection will allow us to choose only those stocks that are most likely to achieve our objective over a set period of time. When the stocks have been selected and purchased, it will be a simple matter to identify the ones that are achieving the objective and those that are not.

Learning how to set specific objectives is essential to any endeavor. This book establishes a tight set of criteria for a good objective. Setting specific investment objectives is not difficult. If you work closely with a stock broker or investment adviser, this system can help you both understand exactly what is to be achieved. The stock selecting system can also help you double-check the suitability of an investment proposed by your adviser or broker.

Get That Broker off Your Back

When you receive a phone call about stock that sounds interesting, tell the broker to call you back with five-year figures on sales growth, earnings growth, and price growth. Also ask for the annual average P/E (price–earnings) ratio for each of the five years. For good measure, explain to the broker that you are interested only if there are solid reasons to believe the next five-year price growth will be in line with your investment objective. In other words, where is the stock's growth coming from?

The broker's return phone call should supply most of the information you need to reach a decision. The majority of the basic research will have been done. It's always prudent to do some checking and verifying, but you won't waste your time with a broker who twists your arm to buy a stock that doesn't line up with your objective. You will have real information on which to base an informed decision.

Making the Stocks Come to You

Because selecting the best stocks in the market is a desirable, but often futile exercise, it is not our concern. The aim is not to select the best companies. Some of the best run, financially sound companies can also be the worst possible investments. Rather, we want to select good stocks that meet well-defined objectives. Our only concern will be to select stocks that are likely to achieve strong objectives. Rather than chasing after this good stock or that fast-track company, you want to make the stocks come to you.

Results Analysis Is Essential

Even though this is not intended to be a "trading book," which recommends buys and sells of different stocks, an update of results is useful. The total figures quoted here include all dividends and are based on the assumption that no new stocks are being added to the portfolios. Sells have been made as stocks showed weakening earnings and lower prices. The best analysis cannot predict the future sales or earnings of a company with absolute reliability. Since the only certainty in life is change, it is essential to watch and actively manage any stock portfolio. Results here are based on selling underperforming stock and reinvesting the proceeds in the good performers. It is a strategy based on the concept of "sell the losers and let the winners run."

Results through 1993

If you had used the Stock Selector System and had selected the stocks in this book in March 1991, your results at the end of 1993 look like this:

Stock Portfolio Category	Annual Dividend Income (%)	Price Gain with Dividends (%)	Price Gain Annualized (%)	Annual Objective (%)
Income	7.0	43,0	14.3	7.0
Growth	.5	67.9	22.6	20.0
Total return	4.3	42.0	14.0	12.0
Speculation	0.0	34.2	34.2	30.0

* Objective is for dividend income only.
** Speculation stocks were all sold in the first year.

The Dow Industrials show a 29% (average 9.7% annual) increase for the same time period through 1993. Every portfolio met or exceeded its objective and was well ahead of the market. The original fourteen stocks were trimmed to eight of the best.

Analysis Enhancement with Computer Programs

As computer prices continue to drop, their popularity reaches new heights. Computers are excellent tools for keeping track of numbers and other analytical information. This book gives a detailed explanation on how to set up the Stock Selector System, in a Lotus 1-2-3 spreadsheet. In fact, with only a few adjustments for style and procedure, it should be compatible with any spreadsheet format. Once set up, the numbers are easy to keep track of, without all that extra paper. Spreadsheet software will also graph trends, making any progression of numbers easier to read.

Appendix A explains how to configure this analysis system into Lotus 1-2-3 and WordPerfect formats. The suggested setup is not complex; it was designed for anyone with minimal computer spreadsheet experience. If you already have considerable spreadsheet experience, this information can help you achieve a more sophisticated, interactive analysis system.

The basic informational format shown in Appendix A was first designed for the Lotus 1-2-3 spreadsheet and then adjusted only slightly to a WordPerfect Tables spreadsheet.

These forms and the Stock Selector System are tools to help you stay in control of your stock market investing. They will help you maintain consistent success by fulfilling the following requirements:

- Concise objectives, based on factual information.
- Basic understanding of how the stock market works.
- Action based on conclusions drawn from analysis.
- Evaluation of objective achievement, with adjustment when conclusions change.

If you are a beginning stock investor or a seasoned veteran looking for a more consistent approach, this book is for you. Whether your objective involves income, growth, total return, or speculation, this book can help you be consistently successful with your stock investing.

Analysis

Keep Analyses Brief

Analyses can be complicated, lack relevancy, and become over-whelming. It's possible to know a company's strengths and weaknesses in so much detail that it becomes difficult to decide on a course of action. Indecision can be costly. It becomes imperative for the investor to find a way to quickly sift through the available information, draw conclusions, and arrive at a decision.

Use Clear, Concise Objectives

Clear, concise objectives will enable you to quickly analyze business information and reach a conclusion as to the success potential of a stock. This is true for selecting new stock, or for analyzing unexpected developments with currently held stock. Arriving at a conclusion based on facts provides you with the background on which to make a decision. Reaching a decision makes it easier to take action.

Simplify Analyses with the Objective

Stockbrokers, investment advisors, investment authors, and stock market commentators frequently and repeatedly stress the

importance of having good investment objectives, but few ever
describe a realistic method for constructing them. In Part One,
we simplify analyses by defining parameters for any objective.
For stock investing, we then divide objectives into four different
categories. The four objective categories for investing in common stock are:

1. Income.
2. Growth.
3. Total Return.
4. Speculation.

Part One will examine the advantages of each category individually and in combination.

Setting clear, realistic objectives is the strongest and most
important part of this book. The same is true of investing. A solid
understanding of what you expect from a stock will help prevent
losing money and can greatly improve your stock portfolio performance in terms of real dollar growth.

CHAPTER 1

Setting Objectives

What Do You Really Want?

"I want to make a lot of money in the stock market." That is what many stockbrokers hear when they ask an individual investor for an investment objective. Setting investment objectives is so important that the NASD (National Association of Securities Dealers) requires the stockbroker to ask for an investment objective when opening an account. The definition and the content of these objectives frequently provide important information in NASD arbitration hearings to investigate possible misconduct by a broker or firm.

A well-defined investment objective can protect the investor in such situations, but more importantly may be instrumental in preventing the need for an arbitration hearing in the first place. These are among the defensive reasons for setting objectives.

You also need to establish tight, specific objectives to avoid losing money. No one wants to lose money, but many investors do, often because they lack a clear objective. And from the offensive, positive view, well-defined objectives can help you make more money in the stock market.

The objective ". . . to make a lot of money . . . " is much too general. It is not measurable, does not consider risk, and has no time frame for achievement. Five people defining this objective could easily describe it in five totally different ways. They would almost certainly disagree as to how much money represents "a lot." Although they all might be able to tell you which stocks would fit this objective, they probably couldn't tell you which stocks to choose prior to the price actually going up.

Quantifying and Clarifying Your Objective

Defining an objective by quantifying investments and clarifying actions will make it more understandable and more easily attainable. Exactly how much is "a lot" to you? Do you expect a 10 percent annual return on your investment or do you want 20 percent? How much risk are you willing to take? Do you need regular income from your investment or can you lock the money up for five years? How often will you evaluate the progress of your investments—monthly, quarterly, or semiannually?

When you quantify and clarify your objectives with precise information, you can select, evaluate, and adjust your portfolio quickly and effectively. This ability will save you time and money, and can greatly increase your investment success.

Income Is the Name of the Game

Investment income[1] is the name of the game. It is what all investors are looking for and expect to receive. Their timing may differ: Some may want income now, through cash dividends paid quarterly; others hope to realize income later, through price growth. Some investors prefer to have both: a combination of dividends and price appreciation. The speculative investor usually seeks a higher rate of return and is willing to accept a higher risk factor to get it. All stock investors are looking for income from the different degrees of risk they are willing to take in the market.

Set a precise, specific objective and make the stocks come to you rather than attempting a mammoth, unreliable search for the best stocks in the market. If your objective is a 15 percent gain per year for the next five years and you look for stocks that have shown a 15 percent gain in sales, earnings, and price over the past five years and you have some idea where the increases will be coming from over the next five years, you stand a reasonable chance of earning 15 percent on that stock.

Making a Good Objective

Let's look now at one of the things you can control: setting objectives. Logically, an objective should meet the following criteria:

- *Be Specific.* Stated to be understood.
- *Be Reasonable in Expectations.* Base them on observable performance.
- *Consider Risk.* Modify it to your comfort level.
- *Have a Time Frame for Achievement.* Choose one year, two years, five years, and so on.
- *Be Measurable.* If it can't be measured, how can it be evaluated?

The Four Classifications of Objective

The primary requirement is to be specific. Tightening the focus to four general categories of stock quickly enables an objective to be stated in more specific terms. All stock investment objectives can be separated into these four categories:

1. Income.
2. Growth.
3. Total Return.
4. Speculation.

These categories are easy to use and align with our stock selection. In fact, they are the same categories that stockbrokers use to classify stocks according to their different characteristics.

Although there can certainly be other styles of defining objectives, some more general and others more specific, chances are any other objective statement will still work within these four categories. The wording might change, but the basic idea is the same.

Which Objective Category Fits Your Need?

You—the individual investor—are the only one who can decide what you want from your investments and what you are willing to do to achieve that objective. Your financial condition might indicate you can reasonably afford to take some risk, but if higher risk is something you don't want, stay away from speculation.

Income Stocks

These stocks provide current income (short term) for the investor looking for a reliable, regular income at a rate somewhat higher than current guaranteed rates, with the added possibility of higher future dividends. Such stocks are often the choice of risk-aversive investors who value safety as well as income.

Growth Stocks

Long-term growth stocks are suitable for the investor willing to pass on the current income of dividends in favor of price growth. Growth is for the investor who is willing to take some risk but moderates that risk whenever possible.

Total Return Stocks

Total return (long term) appeals to the investor who wants some of both—income and growth—from the same stock investment. Some income is sacrificed or put at risk in favor of moderate growth, while risk is lowered by the amount of the dividends paid out. In general, these stocks will have slightly more risk than income stocks but less than growth stocks.

Speculation Stocks

Speculation (short term) works for the investor willing and able to do the research and analysis—and accept considerably greater risk—to achieve superior returns. Such investors want to reach out and grab a piece of a growing market and aren't afraid to put money at risk. The rewards can be great and the risk can be high, but speculative investors buy and sell stock on a short-term basis. Risk can further be moderated by analysis and understanding of historical data, but speculation investors often buy a stock in anticipation of growth, so past history may contain no answers.

Risk Moderation—Determining a Threshold

Although it is possible to have all four objectives working in combination, tightening the focus to a single category clarifies as well as simplifies stock selection and evaluation.

If, for example, your main objective is current income (from dividends), any stock that pays no dividend is obviously not an appropriate selection. If you have set an objective of annual growth of 15 percent and a stock you've selected has earned only 8 percent after one year, it's time to consider changes.

In setting your own objectives, you must be specific about the kinds of stocks to purchase and the level of performance you expect. Select your primary goal from the list of four objectives: current income, total return, growth, or speculation. Then determine your risk threshold: low, moderate, high.

Make a Specific Objective Statement

Once you've selected a general objective category, make a more specific statement of objective. The procedure described in Table 1.1

Table 1.1 *Objective Selector*

Objective Selector
Objective Classification: *Income, Growth, Total Return, Speculation*
Clarify your objective parameters.
Specific: *This is a worksheet for planning your stock-investing objective. Write down precisely how much money you have to invest and how much you want to earn, actual dollar amount or percentage, and with what kinds of stock.*
How much money will be invested in what kind of stock?
Reasonable: *Calculate whether your expected return is reasonable by comparing it with returns from the current market. What are T-bills currently paying? What percentage gain is the stock market showing for the year? Using benchmarks like these can help determine a reasonable return.*
What return is currently reasonable? How do we compare?
Risk Moderation: *Here list specific things you will do to moderate risk; e.g., select stocks with an investment rating of "B" or higher.*
What steps will we take to moderate risk?
Time Frame: *How long do you intend to pursue the strategy? Three to five years should be a minimum, unless your objective is speculation, which can require a shorter time frame.*
How much time do we allow for objective achievement?
Measurable: *Obviously, if there is no way to measure the success, it is impossible to tell how successful your investing has been. Here you state precisely how the performance can and will be measured.*
What do we expect to earn? What annual return?

will help you establish your expected return, identify how you will modify risk and when you will evaluate results, and set the time frame for achieving results.

In setting the objective, it's not your choice of form that is so important, but rather that you establish the parameters of your objective clearly in writing. Planning, analyzing, and setting strategy do little good if you cannot remember and implement your ideas. Table 1.1 merely provides you with an easy format to follow.

Sample completed forms appear throughout the following chapters to help you define and work with your own objectives.

In Table 1.1, the Objective Selector sets and organizes the information in the parameters. Each parameter is listed separately, with a descriptive question. If you have difficulty thinking of specific statements, merely answer the questions provided (e.g., "How much money will be invested in what kind of stock?").

Filling out an Objective Selector before selecting stock will simplify the decision process. The idea is to set down specifically what you want and how you expect to get the results. Any stock that does not match the objective is then rejected.

Profiles Will Help You Select the Better Stocks

Completing the Objective Selector has created a profile for the kinds of stock you want to buy. A detailed profile will enable you to eliminate stocks not matching your minimum requirements. The early elimination process can save you several hours of time. Now you will analyze only those stocks with a track record similar to your stated objective. There is no point looking at stocks that early on are unlikely to meet your objective.

Key Ideas

Quantify and clarify your objective.
Income is the name of the game.

Make a good objective:
- —Be specific.
- —Be reasonable in expectations.
- —Consider risk.
- —Have a time frame for achievement.
- —Be measurable.

There are four objective classifications:
- —Income.
- —Growth.
- —Total return.
- —Speculation.

Notes

1. The Internal Revenue Service includes four categories of investment income: dividends, interest income, capital gains, and premium income from options.

CHAPTER 2

Current Income

The first main category of objective—income—is more correctly known as "current income." This means that cash income is to be received from a stock through dividends paid, usually on a quarterly basis. The fact that a stock pays dividends does not necessarily make it a good pick in the current income objective category. This chapter takes a look at some additional qualifiers.

High Safety Is Imperative

Safety of principal and income is an important feature of this category of investment objective. Dividend growth is also important. Without it, the investor would be better off buying fixed-income bonds or preferred stock. Income stocks long ago were dubbed "widow and orphan" stocks. Their reputation for safety of principal and regular income made them ideal for this low-risk investor group.

Widows and orphans aside, however, income stocks are found in many well-balanced portfolios because they offset the risks associated with more speculative investments. Some investors buy income stocks for their self-managed retirement plans, where high safety is crucial. Others use the income from these stocks for extra spending money. Whatever the reason, selecting the right income stock requires some analysis and understanding.

Moderate Returns Are Related to Safety

The high safety of current-income stocks mitigates the amount of income received. Don't expect, for example, an 18 percent annual dividend when the current rate on certificates of deposit (CDs)

10

or U.S. Treasury Bills (T-bills) is between 6 and 7 percent. Nor is it typical to buy an income stock with a price of $1.50 a share and receive a 50-cents-per-share dividend. Such a dividend will likely be discontinued and the stock price will drop accordingly. As a rule of thumb, the average dividend yield on the S&P (Standard & Poor's) 500 seldom goes below 3 percent or above 4 percent.

The exceptions are integrated international oils and banks, which usually pay between 4 and 5 percent; and telephone and electric utilities, which often pay between 5 and 7 percent.

Utility Income Stocks

We shall select utility stocks for our example portfolio. Utilities have a long reputation of being safer and less volatile than other stocks and they pay relatively high dividends compared with growth-oriented stocks. Since both these qualities are what we are looking for with our income stock, utility stocks are a logical selection.

The typical utility income stock costs around $20 a share and pays dividends near (or slightly higher than) the prevailing rates on CDs and T-bills. Utility stocks are easy to find, easy to follow, and usually reasonably safe.

Income Safety Checklist

The safety of any income stock can be determined by answering the following questions:

1. Is the dividend in line with comparable safe investments (such as CDs and T-bills)? The current yield on an income stock should be a percent or two higher, at most, than what CDs and T-bills are paying. Risk increases as the yield rises. A stock with a current yield lower than that of other safe investments may still be a good buy; the dividends on many income stocks rise every year. Check the stock's track record to see such a trend.

2. What is the investment rating on the income stock? An investment rating of B+ or better is considered "average

dividend and earnings stability" or "investment grade." A
low-risk investor may want an even higher rating.[1]

3. What is the dividend payment history? For how many
   years has a dividend been paid? Has it been lowered in
   the past five years; and, if so, why? More importantly, is
   the dividend growing each year? What is the average annual increase in dividends over the past five years?

4. What are the growth and development characteristics of
   the company? Is it expanding or buying up supplies of
   coal or other raw materials? Is the earnings growth consistent? How does earnings growth compare with similar
   stocks? Earnings growth is an important measure because
   it contributes to current dividend stability and the possibility of future dividend increases.

5. Do any situations make this company special? Is it, for example, an electric utility that has its own source of low-
   sulfur coal or that has no high-risk characteristics such as
   costly new plant construction or nuclear safety violations?

When put through the preceding screening questions, gas and
electric utility stocks tend to look better than most other potential income stocks. Others can certainly be selected for income,
but will probably bring additional risk and most income investors
should be risk aversive.

How Much Do You Expect?

Equal in importance to safety of principal in this investment classification is return on investment (ROI), which is the dollar
amount of the dividend divided by the dollar amount of the stock
purchase price.

Return on Investment (ROI)

Annual dividend (per share)	$ 1.50
Divided by stock purchase price	$25.00
Equals a return on investment of	6.0%

If the amount of dividend increases while the stock price stays the same, the return on investment goes up. You then receive more money.

Caution: Falling Dividends

If the dividend goes down, however, then it's time to take a close look at what is happening. If lowered dividends in turn cause the stock price to drop, this downward spiral could jeopardize the company's ability to pay the remaining dividend. Then the dividend could be lowered again, or canceled. Now the investor's income objective is not being met, and a loss of principal has occurred as well.

Hang on or Sell

If the price of any stock is dropping because of apparent internal problems in the company, then sell. This is in line with the time-honored and effective "sell the losers" strategy. If, however, the price of a stock is dropping because of external events such as rising interest rates or a weak stock market, it's usually best to hang on.

The Exception

The only exception is if you can sell early enough in the price slide to then be able to buy it back later at a much lower cost. Although this "sell high-buy low" strategy sounds easy, the implementation is often difficult due to the speed of many market drops. Now you've become a speculator in your income stock category because success is dependent on pinpoint accuracy in market timing.

Dividend Growth Is the Best-Case Scenario

Conversely, dividend growth has a positive impact on safety of principal. If the income increases enough, it helps counter inflation, even performs better than other safe investments. Also, although price growth is not the investor's primary goal when purchasing income stocks, growing dividends often nudge the stock price up. In this best-case scenario, twin goals of current

Table 2.1   *Objective Selector: Income*

Objective Selector
Objective Classification: *Income*
Clarify your objective parameters.

Specific: *$50,000 invested in income stocks paying current dividends.*
How much money will be invested in what kind of stock?

Reasonable: *7%, 1% higher than current T-bill rates (currently 6% annual).*
What return is currently reasonable? How do we compare?

Risk Moderation: *Avoid risk by selecting two or three (diversification) high-quality utility stocks.*
What will we do to moderate risk?

Time Frame: *Annual.*
What is the time for our objective achievement?

Measurable: *7% or better annually.*
What is our measure of success?

---

income stock and safety of principal are met. The following objective applies to the category of current income investment.

Income Objective Specific Statement

I will invest $50,000 in two or three high-quality (B+ or better) gas or electric utility common stocks that pay annual dividends of 7 percent or more. This rate is presently 1 percent or more higher than current fixed income Treasury bill rates.

The objective is clear and specific, allowing elimination of any prospects that do not meet the benchmark ROI of 7 percent. It meets all other parameters of objective selection, as shown in the completed Objective Selector form (see Table 2.1).

Lock in the Return

When you buy a stock, you effectively lock in the percent yield (ROI) at the time of purchase. The percentage received does not change when the stock price changes if you have already purchased the stock. As discussed earlier in this chapter, the percent yield, or ROI, will only change if the dividend amount changes.

For example: Union Electric (NYSE:UEP)

Current price   = $30.25 per share
Current dividend   = $ 2.16 annually
Return on investment =   7.10 percent annually

The return will remain 7.10 percent as long as you own the stock and the dividend remains at $2.16 a share. Even if the stock price drops, you still have $30.25 per share invested, so your income is constant at 7.10 percent unless the dividend changes. If the dollar amount of the dividend is increased, your percent return will increase.

Although future price fluctuations may affect the principal amount of your portfolio if you decide to sell, they will not affect the return on the shares you continue to hold.

What Is the Time Frame?

Time frame is not as important in the current-income category as it is with other investments. Whether you own an income stock one year or five years, the income percentage remains the same as long as the dividend amount is constant. Still, every income stock purchase should be evaluated on schedule (every six months and year end) to check for problems. In most cases, income stock purchases will be "buy and hold" decisions. For our purposes here, I've designated a time frame of one year.

Income Means a Regular Payday

To spread income out over the year, income investors often pick the stocks of companies based on their scheduled months for paying dividends (most companies pay dividends every quarter). The effect of a monthly paycheck can be accomplished with as few as three companies:

Stock A pays in January, April, July, and October.
Stock B pays in February, May, August, and November.
Stock C pays in March, June, September, and December.

A Sample "Current-Income" Portfolio

Table 2.2 shows how an income portfolio might be constructed. Note that any one current yield might be lower than the target, while another can be higher. The average of the three is what is important. This example is based on current yield alone and does not take into account analysis of safety, volatility, or growth. In Chapter 7, we'll select income stocks by taking these equally important factors into consideration.

Use Information from the Daily Papers

The sample portfolio in Table 2.2 was constructed by reviewing stock quotations in a major daily newspaper and selecting on the basis of data aligned with our major objective, in this case current

Table 2.2   *Sample Income Portfolio*[a]

	Sample Income Portfolio		
Stock	*AYP*	*CWE*	*DEW*[b]
Current price	$ 39.00	$ 38.50	$ 18.50
Number of shares	300	500	1000
Total cost	$11,700	$29,250	$18,500
Annual dividend	$ 3.16	$ 3.00	$ 1.54
Current yield	8.1%	7.9%	8.3%
Annual income	$ 948	$ 1,500	$ 1,540
Total annual income	= $ 3,988		
Portfolio return			
(Income) (ROI)	= 8.1%		

Yield equals:
  Total dividend income: $ 3,988
  Divided by
  Total amount invested: $49,450
  Yield (ROI) = 8.06571%

[a] All companies listed in this book are examples only. They are not intended to be current buy-or-sell recommendations.

[b] AYP = Allegheny Power Systems (rating A); CWE = Commonwealth Edison (rating A−); DEW = Delmarva Power & Light (rating A−). Ratings from *Standard & Poors Stock Guide*, January 1991.

yield. Stocks were selected merely as an example of an income portfolio.

Our actual selection process will also include close examination of safety and dividend growth. We can select a dividend yield lower than our objective if we feel the dividend growth will justify the selection in the next couple of years.

Now we will create a Prospect Selector (Table 2.3) that also takes into account the factors of price and volatility, some early safety indicators. Lower volatility with income stocks usually means lower risk. Risk tends to increase with higher volatility.

The Income Prospect Selector contains information found in the daily financial news, such as *The Wall Street Journal*. The top portion spells out our objective and tells where the information came from and on what date.

The lower section has detail on several different stocks. There is no magical quantity of stocks to choose from, although there should be enough for a selection based on comparison. We list the name (abbreviated), trading symbol, and place an "X" beside the stocks we select for further analysis.

Table 2.3 *Prospect Selector: Income*

Prospect Selector: Income									
Objective: 7%			*Financial News Information*				*Date: 2/28/91*		
Income from Dividends			*Annual Dividend*				*Price History*		
								12 Months	
Prospect Stock Name	*Symbol*	*X*	*$ Paid*	*% Yield*	*Rank*	*Today Price $*	*$ High*	*$ Low*	*% Chg*
Alleg Powr	AYP		3.16	8.1	8	39	41	34	21
Atlantic En	ATE	X	2.96	8.3	9	35¾	38	32	19
Con Edison	ED		1.86	7.8	6	24	26	20	30
Cmnwlth Ed	CWE		3.00	7.9	7	38½	39	27	44
Delmarva Pwr	DEW		1.54	8.3	10	18½	20	17	18
Detroit Ed	DTE	X	1.88	6.4	2	29⅜	31	25	24
MDU Resource	MDU	X	1.42	6.8	4	20⅞	22	18	22
OtterTailPwr	OTTR	X	1.60	6.0	1	26½	27	22	23
Union Elec.	UEP	X	2.16	7.2	5	30¼	31	25	24
Utilicorp	UCU		1.52	6.8	3	22¼	23	17	35

(X means selected for further analysis.)

Next we look at the current dividend dollar amount and calculate the annual yield (the current dividend divided by the current price, times 100 to state it as a percentage). We then rank the income from the lowest to the highest. High yields are very attractive, but we have to find out why the yields are high. They are frequently high because the dividend is not secure and is about to be reduced.

On the far right side of the form, we list the 52-week price history and calculate the percentage change, giving us a quick look at the volatility of the stock.

In measuring volatility, many investors prefer to use the beta factor, which is defined as a "coefficient measuring a stock's relative volatility." The beta is the covariance of a stock in relation to the rest of the stock market. The *Standard & Poor's 500 Stock Index* has a beta coefficient of one. Any stock with a higher beta is more volatile than the market, and any with a lower beta can be expected to rise and fall more slowly than the market.

A conservative investor whose concern is preservation of capital should focus on stocks with low betas (lower price volatility), whereas one willing to take high risks in an effort to earn high rewards should look for high-beta stocks.

Unlike the price high-to-low differential (Table 2.3, under "Price History 12 Months"), however, the beta factor is not generally published in newspapers. A stock's beta factor can only be found with some searching. One location of beta is the research information published by brokerage firms. It can also be found in the *Standard & Poor's* and *Value Line Investment Survey*.

Here we are beginning our analysis using information that is more readily available.[2]

What Are the Income Stock Selections?

The prospect list stocks indicated with an "X" are selected for further analysis because of *moderate dividends* in combination with *lower volatility*. Choosing more moderate selections is a risk-limiting measure. Atlantic Energy is included to have an example of a higher dividend stock (yield 8.3%).

One stock, Otter Tail Power, was selected partly on a whim, to see how a heartland utility compares with a heavy industry utility such as Detroit Edison. Understanding such differences can also be useful in modifying risk. Heavy industrial customers can make earnings more vulnerable to economic cycles.

If you have the time and desire, you can certainly analyze in detail all the stocks on your prospect list. We are not making a buy decision at this point, just refining the list. For our income objective, current yield, dividend growth, and safety of principal are our main concerns. Safety comes from the selection of stocks that have a yield at or slightly higher than the current yield on T-bills and CDs. We will enhance our safety by selecting stocks that have lower volatility and investment ratings of A− or higher as well as a history of growth in revenues, earnings, and dividends.

Diversification Helps Portfolio Safety

Diversification improves safety and requires special consideration when it comes to income stocks. Because we are dealing with utility stocks, we need to look at the utility's customer base and diversify based on the type of business serviced by the utility.

In Michigan, utility companies are affected by the health of the auto industry. In California, the fortunes of computer manufacturers can play an important role in a utility's profits. A deep regional recession can affect utilities servicing that particular region. All these factors can come into play when considering the safety of an income stock.

Recognize the Risk Factors—An Interest Rate Correlation

All stocks carry market risk and individual risk. (Individual risk is also known as "business risk.") In the income objective classification, market risk is seldom the main concern. Because it is the income that is important, not short-term price changes, short-term market corrections and secondary trends are generally best ignored.

In an extended bear market, theoretically you can sell the stock and buy at a lower price down the road, but you run the risk of not being able to buy back soon enough. As a bear market recovers, reentry can be difficult because rallies and corrections cause confusion. Therefore, income investors tend to choose stock carefully and ride out bear markets and other price fluctuations.

The fluctuation in interest rates is a market-related concern for income stocks. Because these companies depend heavily on borrowed capital, interest rate increases can affect their stocks long before they affect others. Not only do earnings drop as interest rates rise, threatening dividends, but an interest-rate increase also can cause many income investors to bail out and put their money into T-bills. Stock prices go down along with dividends. Accordingly, income stocks perform better when interest rates are low or declining.

Know When to Watch and Wait

Individual stock risk is a different story. Because safety is a high priority, investors buy these stocks based on perceived lower risk. Heightened investor nervousness makes these stocks sensitive to any threatening events. Business difficulties such as trouble with construction or inability to obtain rate increases can have a negative effect on the individual prices of utility income stocks.

When you're heavily invested in an income stock, you should also tap into a source of information (e.g., clipping service, daily newspaper) to keep you abreast of events in that company's region that could affect its profitability. Just because we call them "safe" doesn't mean they're guaranteed. There are no guarantees, only successful track records created by informed, disciplined investors who respond quickly to the right information. And if growth is your objective, Chapter 3 provides the information you'll need to set a good growth objective.

Key Ideas

High safety is imperative.

    —Moderate returns are related to safety.

    —Utility income stocks.

Income safety checklist:
> Is the dividend in line with comparable safe invest-ments (such as CDs and T-bills)?
>
> What is the investment rating on the income stock?
>
> What is the dividend payment history?
>
> What are the growth and development characteristics of the company?
>
> Do any situations make this company special?

How much do you expect?
> —Return on investment (ROI).
>
> —Caution: Falling dividends.
>
> —Hang on or sell.
>
> —The exception.

Dividend growth is the best-case scenario.

Lock in the return.

What is the time frame?

Income means a regular payday.

Use information from the daily papers.

Diversification helps portfolio safety.

Recognize the risk factors—An interest rate correlation.

Know when to watch and wait.

Notes

1. Investment ratings can be found in the *Standard & Poor's Stock Guide* or *Value Line Investment Survey.*
2. Downes, John and Jordan Elliot Goodman, *Finance & Investment Hand-book,* Barron's Educational Series, Inc., 1990.

CHAPTER 3

Growth Stocks: Steady as She Goes

A good growth-stock portfolio will show consistent gains in value and price over a period of several years for the careful and patient investor. The key is to find stocks that will perform at a rate better than their history, to diversify the portfolio, and to adopt buy-and-sell strategies that moderate risk and give the stocks room to grow.

Look for Consistent Growth

The objective for growth stocks similarly centers on consistency, starting with price growth and including gains in revenues, earnings, and market position (Table 3.1). Price growth—increase in cost per share from the purchase price—is vital because it contains the bulk of the profit. Dividends will add to the return but are of secondary importance in a growth stock.

Growth Objective Specific Statement

By investing $50,000 in common stock with an investment grade rating of B or better, I expect to achieve a 20 percent rate of return annually for the next five years. This return will be based on the total amount of price growth in the stock selected, including any dividend payments. I will enhance safety by investing in at least three to five companies in three different industries. Any losses will be subtracted from profits to arrive at a calculation of the net gain.

Table 3.1   *Objective Selector: Growth*

Objective Selector Objective Classification: *Growth* **Clarify your objective parameters.**
Specific: *$50,000 invested in growth stocks.* **How much money will be invested in what kind of stock?**
Reasonable: *20%, similar to current return. In the past five years the Dow has risen an average of 17% annually and S&P 500 has risen about 14% each year. Expected lower interest rates can increase this trend.* **What is currently reasonable? How do we compare?**
Risk Moderation: *Stocks with investment grade "B" or better with diversification in five different stocks from three different industries.* **What will we do to moderate risk?**
Time Frame: *Five years, evaluated annually.* **What is the time for our objective achievement?**
Measurable: *20% or better annually.* **What is our measure of success?**

Analysis Will Help Find the Right Mix

Now, we will use some basic analysis to find the mix of stocks to fit our objective.

Growth stocks tend to carry more risk than income stocks, but this has more to do with the financial condition of the company issuing the stock than with the particulars of the stock itself. The bottom line is that some fundamental and relatively simple research will help identify stocks with steady growth potential.

Standards Used to Analyze a Growth Stock

- Price History. Is the growth erratic or steady, or has most of the growth occurred in the past year and therefore is possibly unstable?
- Earnings Growth. How does the earnings growth compare to the price growth? If it is considerably slower, what are investors anticipating?

- Sales Growth. Are sales increasing but earnings decreasing, showing inefficiency, or does there appear to be a close relationship between the two (efficiency)?

- Current Price/Earnings Ratio. Is it lower than the five-year average, showing the stock to be undervalued, or is it higher (overvalued)? Overvalued stocks trade on strong anticipation and have greater risk.

- Financial Strength. What is the *Value Line* or S&P investment rating on the stock? A lower rating can mean higher risk.

- Product Spread. Is it a one-product or multiple-product company? Single-product companies can suddenly have problems directly affecting the price.

- Company Standing in the Industry. Is it a leader or a challenger? Leaders tend to be slower but stable. Challengers are often faster and riskier.

- The Source of Growth. Current trend or new developments? Current trend is wonderful; new developments are always subject to change, therefore have higher risk.

- Potential Problems. Areas that could affect earnings: What are they?

- New Developments. Are there new developments (new product, recent acquisition) and how will they contribute to the company's growth?

Graphs Provide Quick Information

A good way to begin a stock analysis is to look at a graph charting growth. The key is to find a stock that shows a consistent upward price trend for five, and possibly 10, years. Take a look at a five-year price history on Albertson's Inc. (NYSE: ABS), a specialty retail store, as shown in Figure 3.1.

This could be an ideal growth stock. Note the relatively steady price gains, with a 2-for-1 stock split in 1987, another in 1990, and accelerated growth in 1991. The growth is not spectacular, but the risk is low and returns appear reliable. With that

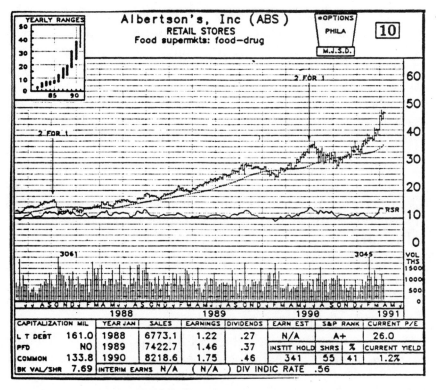

FIGURE 3.1 **Albertson's, Inc.** (Chart courtesy of Trendline, a division of Standard & Poor's Corporation. *Current Market Perspectives,* April 1991, p. 24.)

example in mind, let's start the search for components to a strong growth-oriented portfolio.

Simplify the Analysis Process

Since we have several thousand prospects to choose from, let's simplify the process by limiting the initial selection to familiar companies. For instance, we could choose a well-known company, such as Apple Computer, or investigate highly specialized companies, such as Novell or Amgen. At this point, we don't have to know much about the companies; we just need to be familiar with their products and reputation.

There are many avenues for researching prospect stocks. For a fee, several market-watch agencies will provide lists of stocks showing specific historical growth traits. The *Value Line Investment Survey* publishes lists of "Timely Stocks," from which you can select any number of useful qualities.

There are only two problems in depending on outside research. First is the age of the information—it may not be relevant anymore. Second is that the market still might not like a stock even though someone thinks it is a "timely pick."

While such information is helpful, our initial selection actually requires little in the way of sophisticated analysis. For example, using our growth stock objective as a guide, we gleaned the information in Table 3.2 from a daily newspaper. The percentage differential between low and high price took less than five minutes to calculate.

Remember the Basics

Here again, we state the basics of our investment objective. We are prospecting for growth stock with the potential to provide a 20 percent return annually for the next five years. The 20 percent

Table 3.2 *Prospect Selector: Growth*

Prospect Selector: Growth								
Objective: 20%			*Financial News Information*			*Date: 2/28/91*		
							Price History	
							12 Months	
Prospect *Stock* *Name*	*Symbol*	*Type* *of* *Business*	*X*	*Today* *Price* *$*	*Rank*	*$* *High*	*$* *Low*	*%* *Chg*
Albertson's	ABS	Ret Groc	X	38½	3	41	25	63
Apple Cptr	AAPL	Computer	X	57¼	7	62	24	57
Coke	KO	Soft Drink		52⅜	6	54	34	61
Conagra	CAG	Food Sup	X	41⅞	4	43	25	72
Dayton Hudson	DH	Ret Cloth		68¼	8	80	46	72
Disney	DIS	Entertain		123⅜	10	137	86	59
McDonald's	MCD	Fast Food		31⅝	1	59	25	54
Novell	NOVL	Cptr Netwrk	X	48⅞	5	31	17	197
Pepsico	PEP	Soft Drink		32¾	2	35	19	87
Syntex	SYN	Drugs	X	75½	9	78	47	65

is a reach for growth stock and that means we will have to select some stocks that range toward the speculative side of the spectrum. The fact that interest rates are dropping and we have come off a difficult year (1990) means that we can expect some extra stretch in a growth objective.

What Kind of Business Is It?

Next, we list the name of the company, its trading symbol, and the type of business it does. This simple information will help us plan diversification for the portfolio. Then, we list the current price and a ranking of low to high. Finally, list the high and low price as well as the percentage of change for the past 52 weeks.

What Is the Price Volatility?

All our initial selections show a price difference of at least 50 percent from the highest to lowest price over a 12-month period (Table 3.2, far right column). The differential certainly is not entirely growth; some of it is obviously price volatility.

Because it is difficult to calculate what portion of that price differential is growth and what amount is fluctuation, we will instead refer to our preset standards (consistent sales gains, earnings growth, etc.) in selecting those stocks with a potential for annual growth of 20 percent for the next five years. If a stock shows price fluctuation of less than 20 percent for the past 52 weeks, we want to look at others.

Narrow the List

To make the portfolio manageable—in keeping with our stated objective—let's narrow our initial list to five stocks, representing at least three industries. The initial selection is of two food stocks, two computer stocks, and one pharmaceutical stock (the selections are marked with an X).

The food stocks represent different aspects of the industry (retail and wholesale supplier), while one computer stock is in personal systems and the other is in network systems. The idea is to avoid selecting stocks in companies that are in direct competition with one another, and to spread our investment across several industries as a buffer against industry-specific downturns.

Deal with Risk

Our goal with growth stocks is not to eliminate risk; indeed, with no risk there is no profit. Rather, we must ask ourselves how much risk we are willing to accept, for that will help determine the amount of gain we can expect. While risk assessment is a far more intricate process, establishing expected gain is an important starting point.

What Is the Objective?

Our objective states an expected gain of 20 percent annually, which is reasonable when weighed against current returns on investment in growth stocks, and that standard should be applied to the multiple-year price performance of suspect stocks. Our objective also limits risk by specifying that stock purchases be spread over three industries.

The potential of each stock must be weighed separately. Our initial analysis, using preset standards, will have modified the risk, but there are further standards to apply. For example, is the stock trading at an all-time high price, or is it off slightly? If it is at a high, it is appropriate to wait for a correction before buying. Does the stock pay a dividend? Any dividend, no matter how small, lowers the risk factor.

What Is the Market Doing?

Market conditions must also be assessed. If the market is up, we should try to buy our stocks on a day when the market is correcting; if it is down, we should wait for a sign—a cut in interest rates, positive economic indicators, or a new upward trend—something that indicates encouragement for investors.

Deciding When to Buy and When to Sell

We've prepared ourselves for investing in growth stocks through careful research and selection; now we need a game plan for buying and selling to maximize the value of the portfolio. There are a number of commonly used strategies.

Market Order

Market orders are favored by most buyers. The strategy simply is to agree to purchase stock at the "best available price." The order is normally entered and filled in a matter of minutes.

Limit Order

Limit orders set buy orders at a predetermined level under the current trading price; when the price drops to the preset level, the purchase order is automatically filled. It is important to remember that an order of multiple lots (200, 300, 500 shares, etc.) can be partially executed over a number of days. As each day's order execution is considered a separate trade, commissions can quickly mount.

Target Pricing

To unload stock, some investors set a sell target price when they buy the stock. When the price of the stock reaches the target price, the sell order takes effect and the investor earns a profit. While this method is expedient, it should be carefully weighed for use in a growth-stock portfolio. You could be selling the stock just as the growth is getting started.

Sell Stop Order

A sell stop order guarantees that you will sell a stock at a loss, since the stop must be entered below the current price. While the approach cuts a loss short, it can do more harm than good to a long-term portfolio. If you do use a sell stop order as part of a growth plan, consider placing it far enough below the stock's current price trading range that it will not be triggered by day-to-day price fluctuations.

Achieving Long-Term Satisfaction

Remember, with the growth stock approach we're looking for measured gain in the market over several years. The goal is to find performers with a solid track record, to modify risk, and to exercise patience and restraint in buying and selling. If a portfolio of growth stocks is selected and managed properly, it probably won't generate much excitement, but will ultimately reward the investor with a sizable increase in value.

Key Ideas

Look for consistent growth.
Analysis will help find the right mix.
Greater risk can mean higher potential.
These standards are used in analyzing a growth stock:
　—Price history.
　—Earnings growth.
　—Sales growth.
　—Current price/earnings ratio.
　—Financial strength.
　—Product spread.
　—Company standing in the industry.
　—The source of growth.
　—Potential problems.
　—New developments.
Graphs provide quick information.
Simplify the analysis process:
　—Remember the basics.
　—What kind of business is it?
　—What is the price volatility?
　—Narrow the list.
　—Deal with risk.
　—What is the objective?
　—What is the market doing?
We must decide when to buy and when to sell:
　—Market order.
　—Target pricing.
　—Sell stop order.
We want long-term satisfaction.

CHAPTER 4

Total Return Stocks: Growth with a Twist

An investor might start with a growth objective, but later find greater safety and comfort in stocks that pay a regular dividend and appreciate at a rate greater than more conservative income stocks. If that sounds like you, a portfolio of total return stocks may be ideal.

Benefits of Income and Growth from Bigger Companies

Total return stocks are, in effect, growth stocks. They represent investments in large, established companies that grow slowly but steadily. These companies—American Home Products, IBM, and General Electric are examples—share another important characteristic: They pay dividends. When factoring the total annual return in such a portfolio, dividends are added to the growth in value of the stock to determine overall gain.

The obvious benefit of a total return stock is that it provides regular income to the investor, in the form of dividends. An obvious drawback is slower growth for these companies because the money is being paid in dividends instead of being put back into research, development, or other activities that might increase the long-term value of the stock. Because dividend payments and price growth are important factors, calculations must include all dividends and stock value increases.

Total Return Objective Specific Statement

By investing $100,000 in common stock, I expect to achieve a 12 percent rate of return annually for the next five years. Risk will be moderated by the stock dividends, diversification into at least three different stocks in three different industries, and a minimum investment rating of B. The rate of return will be calculated by adding the annual price increase of the stock to its annual dividend payout.

Our objective is specific—looking for a 12 percent return, as opposed to the goal of 20 percent with growth stocks. Setting the return objective higher would require seeking out depressed stocks in a turnaround situation, and that's too risky for a total return plan.

And, because total return stocks tend to be more conservative, we are setting the grade level at B. In reality, the level will likely be higher as we begin to examine growth records.

List the Prospects

Now, we will create a list of 10 prospects that meet the criteria for a total return portfolio. A few minutes with the stock quotation page of the newspaper yielded the following stocks shown in Table 4.1.

Current dividend yields are listed as a percentage of the stock's market price. The list does not include utility stocks or preferred stocks; utility stocks better fit an income objective, and preferred stocks are more like bonds than stocks.

Look at Both Growth and Income

Our data collection from the daily newspaper is similar to that of income and growth, but now we are also concerned with the dividend amount and yield (columns 4 and 5). In Table 4.2, the dividend yield is the focus of the ranking.

Higher dividend yields are possible, but as with income stocks, a higher yield among total return stocks usually means

Table 4.1   *Objective Selector: Total Return*

Objective Selector   Objective Classification: *Total Return*   **Clarify your objective parameters.**
Specific: *Invest $100,000 in total return stocks paying current dividends.*   **How much money will be invested in what kind of stock?**
Reasonable: *12%, similar to current growth.* [a] *In the past five years, the Dow has risen an average of 17% annually and S&P 500 has risen about 14% each year. Expected lower interest rates can increase this trend.*   **What return is currently reasonable? How do we compare?**
Risk Moderation: *Stocks with investment grade "B" or better; diversification in three unlike companies (three different industries).*   **What will we do to moderate risk?**
Time Frame: *Five year/evaluated annually.*   **What is the time for our objective achievement?**
Measurable: *12% or better, annual return.*   **What is our measure of success?**

[a] This can be verified when evaluating stocks in the Stock Selector.

Table 4.2   *Prospect Selector: Total Return*

Prospect Selector: Total Return									
Objective: 12%			*Financial News Information*				*Date: 2/28/91*		
			Annual Dividend				*Price History*		
							12 Months		
Prospect Stock Name	*Symbol*	*X*	*$ Paid*	*% Yield*	*Rank*	*Today Price $*	*$ High*	*$ Low*	*% Chg*
Aetna Life	AET		2.76	6.1	10	45⅛	54	29	86
Am Home Prod	AHP	X	2.30	4.0	7	57	60	43	40
AT&T	T	X	1.32	4.0	6	33⅜	44	29	52
Emerson Elec	EMR		1.32	3.0	4	43½	45	31	45
Exxon	XON	X	2.68	4.9	9	55⅛	56	45	24
Gen Elec	GE	X	2.04	3.0	2	68	76	50	52
IBM	IBM	X	4.84	3.8	5	128¾	140	96	46
KMart	KM		1.74	4.9	8	35	37	23	61
Sara Lee	SLE		.94	2.7	3	34⅜	36	24	50
Woolworth	Z		1.04	3.2	1	32¾	37	24	54

that the stock price is depressed due to selling activity. Also, the stocks we've chosen all have a current yield of roughly 3 percent to 5 percent; the assumption is that current short-term interest rates are at 6 percent.

Look at the Prospect List

Our list of prospects contains stocks priced between $32 and $130 per share, with dividend yields ranging from 2.7 percent to 6.1 percent. That top yield belongs to Aetna Life, but the wide fluctuation in the stock's 12-month high-to-low price differential puts this stock in a speculative standing, at least until stability returns. So, Aetna is out, and instead we will prefer stocks tending to rank between the highs and lows in the various categories. That strategy will moderate risk as we attempt to satisfy our total return objective.

Think about Buying and Selling

The ideal time to buy total return stocks is either at the apparent end of a bear market or during a correction that shows signs of rapid stabilization. The second-best time to buy is during a flat market, while the market is fluctuating in a narrow range. The only certain time not to buy total return stocks is when interest rates are rising.

The market reacts bearishly to such increases; but perhaps more importantly, most large companies are heavy borrowers, and higher interest rates dramatically boost their operating costs. That in turn negatively affects both price growth and dividends, the two key ingredients in a strong total return portfolio.

Determining when to sell can be more difficult. Sells are generally most ideal as a defensive move after an unusual surge, or when the market is showing signs of weakness. In other words, sell total return stocks if you believe their price will drop; this is almost always better than selling a stock because you made some money. Profit taking is more of a speculative trading technique than an investment action.

Watch the Dow Averages

You need not keep a constant watch on all your total return stocks. Many of them likely will be part of the Dow Averages or other indexes, or they will track a parallel course. If you are aware of market swings, you will have a good idea of how your portfolio is performing.

Key Ideas

Bigger companies provide the benefits of income and growth.
List the prospects:

    —Look at both growth and income.

    —Look at the prospect list.

Think about buying and selling.

Watch the Dow Averages.

CHAPTER 5

Speculative Stocks: Big Returns, Big Risk

There are two established ways to win big at the racetrack: (1) Put a large bet on the favorite, or (2) win with a modest wager on a long shot. While the science of the stock market is a little more precise than that of a horse race, some elements are similar: One tactic is to bet on the favorite, with a conservative return, and the other is to take a chance on a long shot that might have a considerable payoff.

The factor at work is risk. If you are adventurous, you may prefer a portfolio of speculative stocks. A speculative situation can exist when income stocks pay unusually high dividends, when growth stocks have a bad year, or when total return stocks fall on hard times. The hope is that a change in conditions will prompt a turnaround in a low or depressed stock and will in turn reward the speculative investor with great returns in dividends and price growth.

The key is for the investor to avoid being a captive to risk, but rather to understand it and, when possible, to moderate it through analysis and an understanding of growth fundamentals. Risk in speculative situations also is tempered by constant vigilance; an awareness of economic and market conditions can do more to mitigate risk than any other defensive action.

Most Speculative Stocks Are Volatile

- *The prices of speculative stock are volatile,* often showing wide swings between annual highs and lows, because growth is based more on anticipation than the actual earnings growth.

- *The earnings are volatile;* they may show losses in previous years, followed by increases of several hundred percent in recent years.
- *The annual sales growth will have volatility,* similar to that of the earnings.
- *Price/earnings ratios seem high,* but sometimes they can be deceptively low when averaged over a period of time. That volatility both feeds off and contributes to the risk.

Risk in speculative stocks is the highest among companies with earnings losses and is also considerable among companies heavily in debt. In fact, it is often the borrowing that causes the stock to show weaker earnings and lower prices. This can be especially true when a company has gone deeply into debt to acquire another company. (See Table 5.1.)

In short, long shots are a part of the speculative stock game, but blind betting should not be the strategy. Information is available that will contribute to an educated forecast, and the key is to find and weigh as much of that information as possible in advance.

Speculation Objective Specific Statement

I will invest $30,000 in stocks that are expected to increase in price more than 30 percent annually, over the next three years. Risk will be moderated by the amount of money invested, diversification into a minimum of three companies, and also by analysis and daily monitoring.

A 30 percent return may seem high, but when compared with the 20 percent return planned for growth stocks, it is reasonable for the risk we plan to accept. Also, we're going to work a bit harder for the return, doing more homework in advance of our choices, monitoring market conditions constantly, and being prepared to change our strategies frequently for individual stocks.

Know the Speculative Situation

Before we choose our stock prospects, however, let's look at some different types of speculation.

Table 5.1   *Objective Selector: Speculation*

Objective Selector
Objective Classification: *Speculation*
Clarify your objective parameters.

Specific: *$30,000 invested in speculative stocks for price growth for the short term.*
How much money will be invested in what kind of stock?

Reasonable: *30% annual return, similar to current growth, to be verified in the stock selection.*
What return is currently reasonable? How do we compare?

Risk Moderation: *Risk will be modified through diversification, analysis, and monitoring.*
What will we do to moderate risk?

Time Frame: *Three years' portfolio growth. Actual stock ownership may be for less time.*
What is the time for our objective achievement?

Measurable: *30% or better annual return on investment.*
What is our measure of success?

Market Damage

These stocks can be any stock that has declined in price due to a severe market correction or bear market; in effect, the market, not the stock, is in a speculative condition. The speculation in this situation is when the market will bottom out. Probably the most frequent form, this bargain hunting actually becomes part of the market recovery and is often responsible for frequent false starts in the process.

New Companies

Such companies have traded stocks for a short period, or might be a recent initial public offering (IPO). Financial histories are available, but many times are limited to the information in the prospectus. The biggest disadvantage is the lack of trading history.

New Growth

These situations can be exciting forms of investment speculation. For example, Amgen, a pharmaceutical company, showed price growth of more than 500 percent, rising from about $25 per share in early 1990 to more than $130 per share in March 1991. The company's IPO was in June 1983, with 2.3 million shares issued, and the per share value hovered in the $20 range for many years.

The sudden growth was largely due to the company's development of a red blood cell stimulator; the more recent development of a white blood cell stimulator created additional interest. The latter showed that anticipation alone can cause an attractive speculative stock situation.

Takeover

Acquisition speculation was popular in the late 1980s and always will appeal to many investors. It is important to recognize that takeovers quickly become highly speculative situations and that there is no guarantee of a large payoff based on price growth as part of the acquisition. Holding stock for a buyout to be completed can place the investor at great risk.

Echo investing is a hedge in a takeover situation. It involves buying the stock of a company that is similar in product or industry to a company in which stock is already held. The reasoning is that the echo company also may become an acquisition target, either by itself or as a secondary selection if the first choice falls through.

Turnarounds

While turnarounds can be profitable they also can be difficult to time. Turnaround investing should focus on well-established companies because there is likely to be more media attention—hence, more current information available—on developments that can affect the price of stock.

A regular form of turnaround stock is among so-called cyclical companies, such as those in the automotive industry. Sales, earnings, and stock prices will tend to follow a cyclical pattern, and the strategy is to purchase stocks as they cycle down and sell them as the cycle approaches its perceived peak. Other cyclically traded stocks are airlines, tire companies, steel companies, chemical companies, and defense companies. While such stocks offer regular profit opportunities, heed this warning from Peter Lynch:

Cyclicals are the most misunderstood of all the types of stocks. It is here that the unwary stock picker is most easily parted from his money, and in stocks he considers safe. Because the major cyclicals are large and well known companies, they are naturally lumped together with the trusty stalwarts.[1]

High Dividends

These stocks pay a considerably greater yield than current safer, fixed income investments. If the current safer yield is 6 percent, speculative yields would be 9, 10, 20 percent or even higher. The yield goes up as investors sell the stock and drive the price lower. The risk is twofold: First, the dividend may be discontinued; second, the price could drop even lower. In most cases the price drops as soon as the dividend is discontinued.

Other Forms of Speculation

Of the plentiful strategies for speculation, one of the more common is the "gut feeling," a seduction that we instinctively know should be resisted but that is so satisfying to indulge. Emotions come into play, and we often begin to look for reasons to justify purchasing a stock. Investors with the benefit of wisdom gained from bad experiences simply force themselves not to react to a gut feeling, but instead to buttress the instinct with good old-fashioned research and analysis.

Avoid the Sucker Bait

A form of speculation that can serve as sucker bait for many individual investors is the company with some quality assets and a low-priced stock. Pan Am traded at less than $4 a share for several years. It would occasionally run up to $4.50, only to drop back to $2. It was not uncommon for the stock to trade several million shares in a day, with much of the trading coming among large, institutional investors who could turn a viable profit on a small price move.

Individual investors often were pulled into the wake of an upward move, believing the stock to be an attractive turnaround.

The flaw in their strategy was that they bought on price move-ment, rather than on an improvement in fundamental conditions. As institutions gained 50 cents or $1 on the stock, they would sell their holdings for the profit. Consequently, the price would plummet, and the individual investors were left with a devalued stock and a lot of regrets.

Speculative conditions such as these can be traded success-fully by the individual investor, but it is critical to be aware of the pattern while realizing that it can change with little warning. To easily find these speculative opportunities, look at the stocks showing the highest share volumes in daily trading.

We'll place no such sucker bets in our selection of specula-tive stock prospects although we will choose some that are in a turnaround posture. The picks are again taken from the financial pages of the daily newspaper (see Table 5.2).

Table 5.2 Prospect Selector: Speculation

Prospect Selector: Speculation								
Objective: 30%		Financial News Information				Date: 2/28/91		
						Price History		
Prospect Stock Name	Symbol	Type of Speculation	X	Today Price $	Rank	$ High	$ Low	% Chg
Amgen	AMGN	New Growth	X	91¼	7	105	27	289
Cray Resch	CYR	Turnaround	X	41¼	6	51	20	155
Dekalb Gen	SEEDB	New Company		38½	4	45	30	50
Ford Motor	F	TA—Cyclical		32⅝	3	49	25	96
Gen Motors	GM	TA—Cyclical		39½	5	51	30	70
Quantum Co	QNTM	New Growth	X	23⅜	2	26	11	136
UAL Corp	UAL	Takeover		114½	8	170	84	102
Unisys Co	UIS	Turnaround	X	4⅜	1	17	2	850

- Types of Speculation -

Market Damaged	New Company
New Growth	Takeover
Turnaround (& Cyclical)	High Dividend
High Risk	Other

Understand the Type of Speculation

When you buy speculative stocks, understanding the type of speculation will help you know what type of recovery to look for as
the market and the individual stock prices fluctuate. If you buy a
market-damaged stock and the market is recovering but the stock is
lagging, there might be deeper problems. If you buy a cyclical stock,
say an automobile company at the bottom of the cycle, your selection should be recovering in line with similar auto stocks.

From the 10 prospects, we have chosen for further analysis a
new growth pharmaceutical company (Amgen), a new growth computer supply company (Quantum Corp.), and two computer companies (Cray Research and Unisys) that are in classic turnaround
situations. This is an initial screening, and we can consider any of the
other candidates should analysis eliminate one of our four choices.

Meeting the Objective Takes Time

Many brokerage firms recommend holding rapid growth stocks
for a three- to five-year period, and they select and recommend
stocks based on anticipation of growth. For the purposes of our
objective, a three-year time period is considered long enough to
observe growth, yet short enough to allow for adjustments.

Evaluate Speculation Stocks Often

Evaluations should be performed frequently on the progress of
the portfolio, as well as on the condition of the market and of the
individual stocks. The investor must change the mix quickly if
speculative investments are not performing properly or if they en-
counter unforeseen difficulties. Buy-and-sell decisions must be
promptly made and carried out if the investor expects to protect
gains and prevent losses.

Watch the Market Carefully

Investors who choose speculation as a part of an investment objective must be aware that speculation is not only investing in risky
stocks—the activity of the market or timing of the purchase can
also be speculative.

Which brings us back to careful planning. Speculative investing requires paying time and attention to details of what is likely to happen, why it is expected to happen, and then what actually happens. There are not many defensive strategies for speculative stock trading; rather than avoiding volatile conditions, you now may be courting them for opportunities. The process can become less of a horse race, however, if you understand the situations at hand, set realistic expectations, diversify your approach, and react quickly to changes.

Key Ideas

Most speculative stocks are volatile:
—The prices are volatile.
—The earnings are volatile.
—The annual sales growth will have volatility.
—Price/earnings ratios seem high.
Know the speculative situation:
—Market damage.
—New companies.
—New growth.
—Takeover.
—Turnarounds (and cyclicals).
—High dividends.
—Other forms of speculation.
Avoid the sucker bait.
Understand the type of speculation.
Meeting the objective takes time:
—Evaluate speculation stocks often.
—Watch the market carefully.

Notes

1. Lynch, Peter, *One Up on Wall Street* (New York: Simon & Schuster, 1989), p. 112.

CHAPTER 6

The Combination
Approach: The Best
of the Rest

Income, growth, and speculative objectives all have their strengths and weaknesses. But what if we could create a portfolio that would draw on the strengths of each approach while reducing their risks?

A Combination with Focus

With a little extra homework, we can do just that, using a combination approach. While such an approach can produce some extra rewards, its viability depends on the investor's comfort level with the time necessary for analysis, evaluation, and decision making, and it hinges on the amount of money available for investment.

A person with investable assets of $250,000 or more may wish to have secure income-producing stocks and another portion of the portfolio in growth or total return stocks. A combination approach with the main focus on one objective classification will give the investor additional advantages of diversification and risk modification.

The Problems of Diversification

A key to combination is diversification, which is necessary and virtually endless in its possibilities. But there is such a thing as too much diversification, and it can become impossible to follow large numbers of stocks.

It Takes a Lot of Time

Someone once said that a good rule of thumb for analysis is to plan on spending a minimum of one hour per week analyzing developments with each stock. An additional one hour per week should be spent analyzing the progress of the economy and the market indicators or trends. Few people would have the time or the patience to spend an average of four or more hours each day analyzing the stock market. Yet that's about what is required if you own a portfolio of 20 stocks.

It Takes a Lot of Money

The fact is that time probably would be better spent studying the progress of 5 or 10 stocks and the positive effect of diversification will be nearly the same. Also take a look at the numbers. The assumption in Table 6.1 is that you will purchase the same number of shares in each company.

Table 6.1   Diversification of Investments with $100,000

If You Invest $100,000 in Stock	When You Pay a Share Price of	And Buy This Total Number of Shares	You Will Be Able to Buy Stock in This Many Companies
Buy:	$100	1000	1
1000 Shares	50	2000	2
per Company	25	4000	4
Buy:	$100	1000	2
500 Shares	50	2000	4
per Company	25	4000	8
Buy:	$100	1000	5
200 Shares	50	2000	10
per Company	25	4000	20
Buy:	$100	1000	10
100 Shares	50	2000	20
per Company	25	4000	40

Many authors and investment advisers suggest a great number of stocks in a combination portfolio—sometimes as many as 20 stocks—without actually calculating the numbers such volume creates. Too much diversification can create a portfolio of stocks with thin positions of one or two hundred shares.

Diversification Can Water Down Results

While the results of overdiversification can moderate risk, they can water down the performance of the portfolio plus make it a nightmare to manage. It's best to heed the words of A. I. Nelson: "It is better to follow a few stocks well than it is to follow a well full of stocks."

With that in mind, let's set our objective for a combination approach.

Specific Combination Objective Statement

By investing $250,000 in stocks that provide income (20 percent of invested funds), growth (30 percent of funds), and total return (50 percent of funds), the portfolio will earn an annual total

Table 6.2   *Objective Selector: Combination*

Objective Selector Objective Classification: *Combination* **Clarify your objective parameters.**
Specific: *Invest $250,000: 20% into income stock, 30% into growth stock, and 50% into total return stock.* **How much money will be invested in what kind of stock?**
Reasonable: *Expected returns: Income 7%; growth 25%; total return 12%; grand total = 15% annual return.* **What return is currently reasonable? How do we compare?**
Risk Moderation: *Risk is moderated by dividends received, with diversification, in the combination of three to five different stocks in each category.* **What will we do to moderate risk?**
Time Frame: *Five years.* **What is the time for our objective achievement?**
Measurable: *15% or better, annually.* **What is our measure of success?**

return of 15 percent or better during the next five years. The expected return from income stocks will be 7 percent, expected return from growth stocks will be 25 percent, and expected return from total return stocks will be 12 percent. Risk will be moderated by the dividends received and diversification into different categories, as well as by holding three to five significantly different stocks in each category. The portfolio will be evaluated on a monthly basis.

In addition to our Objective Selector matrix, let's set up a table that breaks down our strategy by the component objectives (see Table 6.3).

Once the general combination objective has been established, the investor should develop specific objective statements for each of the selected classifications. Eventually, the investments no longer will reflect the original portfolio symmetry.

In a strong market, the growth and total return portions may become significantly larger. Income might only be 7 percent, with growth at 60 percent and total return at 30 percent of the portfolio. The investor then will have to decide whether to reorganize the assets. Remember, while reducing the growth portion of the portfolio will reduce the risk, it can also lower the return.

Consider the Balanced Approach

Investors with a great deal of investable assets—for example, $1 million—could find greater success by evenly dividing their

Table 6.3   *Total Return Analysis*

Main Focus Objective: $250,000 for Total Return

Objective	Invested Percent	Invested Dollars	Annual Return	Dollar Return
Income	20%	$ 50,000	7%	$ 3,500
Growth	30	75,000	25%	18,750
Total Return	50	125,000	12%	15,000
	100%	$250,000		$37,250
Return	Dollar return	$ 37,250		
Calculation	Invested dollars	$250,000		
	Equals: 15% Annual return			

investment among the combination classifications. Putting 25 percent of assets into each of the four objective categories still would
allow for diversification by company and industry, would spread
risk, and would produce a return somewhat similar to a mutual
fund. An evaluation can be established to make comparisons
among the four classifications. And, to moderate risk, the investor
will need to make periodic adjustments to balance the portfolio.

It Takes Capital to Make It Work

Small investors are not encouraged to embark on a combination
approach because it depends on diversification and can only work
well when the investor holds sizable numbers of shares in each selected classification.

Even $50,000, divided among the four classifications, leaves
only an average $12,500 for each category. That in turn will limit
the investor to a hundred shares of a few low-priced stocks in each
category. And because low-priced stocks tend to have higher risk,
the strategy can become counterproductive. Further, a combination approach significantly increases the time necessary for analysis and evaluation; holding a few shares of a company in each
objective probably would not be worth the extra work. Thus, an
investor with $50,000 will find it easier, and probably more effec-
tive, to buy three or four different stocks and employ one objective classification.

Key Ideas

Develop a combination approach with focus.
Understand the problems of diversification:
    —It takes a lot of time.
    —It takes a lot of money.
    —Diversification can water down results.
Consider the balanced approach—it takes capital to make it work.

PART TWO

Selection

An old Wall Street axiom says an investor should "be either a good stock timer or a good stock picker." The timer is a "technical" analyst, trading in or out of stocks according to how the market moves their individual prices.

The stock picker is the "fundamental" analyst looking for good companies whose outlook for business growth will be positively reflected in price increases. Although it helps to be a little of both, it is usually easier to be a good stock picker.

Using the Stock Selector to Organize for Focus

Each selector will look at a group of stocks using dividend income and/or price growth information, our main concerns. Additionally, the selector will look at other information showing stability and company growth in support of the dividend and price growth. The selector will also list news or analysis information about the individual stocks, such as new acquisitions or other developments. All these facts will help us decide which stocks are most likely to achieve our objective.

Classifying Stock in Terms of Objectives

Classifying stocks by similarities makes it easy to compare the progress of one company with another. Looking at, analyzing, and classifying different stocks through the viewpoint of objectives has advantages of simplicity and a direct line of thought. Objectives have been established; stock is now selected and the performance will be evaluated using the same objective throughout the process.

The category objectives established in Chapter 1 were *income, growth, total return,* and *speculation.* What kinds of stock fit into these categories? What qualities does the investor look for in a good growth stock or a high potential speculative stock? Part Two will examine these questions as well as other qualities of specific stocks in each category.

What Are the Basics of Fundamental Analysis?

Fundamental analysis looks at the business numbers of a company. Sales, earnings, amount of debt, balance sheet, and ability to handle debt are among the fundamentals that investors use to evaluate the company's past growth and ability to continue growing. The growth in fundamentals leads to a growth in value and ultimately to a growth in price.

Even More Basic Analysis

The analysis outlined in Part Two is a brief form of full fundamental analysis, which is more time-consuming. Rather than using all the financial numbers, our system of basic analysis looks strictly at the most important data. In-depth fundamental analysis can tell you a lot about the financial growth of a company, but the information does not always relate to the price growth of the stock.

Price Growth Shows Anticipation

Price growth is based on the market's anticipation of the future. Investor expectations tend to focus on financial data that are the slowest and most difficult to change: revenues (including sales), earnings, and debt management.

The shortened basic analysis, presented here, gives the investor the most important information on which to reach a selection decision. It offers a higher chance of success than merely choosing a stock by yield alone or selecting companies currently in the news.

Many books are available on the subject of fundamental analysis of stocks. If the investor has the time and resources to spend on complete analysis, the selection process can be fine-tuned to minimize risk and increase the potential gains.

The Stock Market Has to Like It

The most important rule for fundamental analysis is to avoid stocks that the stock market doesn't favor.[1] It is possible to find a company with great-looking fundamentals that never does well in terms of price growth. This phenomenon occurs because many analysts simply do not see significant future growth for the stock or its industry.

Sometimes, the analysts are wrong and the stock becomes "discovered." Other times, the stock just continues to be thinly traded in a repetitive, narrow price range. It is extremely difficult to tell which of these good companies will do well and which ones will continue to be lethargic.

Notes

1. Not to be confused with out-of-favor stocks—stocks that the market doesn't like at the current time, but probably will in the future. Cyclical stocks are out of favor at times.

CHAPTER 7

Pay Me Now

Selecting Safe Income Stock

As discussed in Chapter 2, a good income stock has a current yield (which will be our return on investment) in line with other safe investments. It has an investment rating of at least a "B+" and shows consistent growth in revenues, earnings, and dividend payout.

Return on investment (ROI) is important because it becomes the actual income received from the stock (the dollar amount of the dividend divided by the dollar amount of the purchase price). A yield more than 1 or 2 points higher than current, safe-money investments is a stock with high risk. Consistent dividend growth is important as it illustrates the stability of the dividend as well as future income. Selecting a stock with a higher investment rating will help to moderate the risk.

In Chapter 2, we established a concise, specific income objective:

Income Objective Specific Statement

I will invest $50,000 in two or three high-quality (B+ or better) gas or electric utility common stocks that annually pay dividends of 7 percent or more. This rate is presently 1 percent or more higher than current fixed income U.S. Treasury bill rates.

Three Important Criteria

Within the parameters of the objective, three criteria are most important:

1. Current yield.
2. Safety.
3. Dividend growth.

The importance of current yield is obvious. It is the value of the income, an integral part of the objective. A high degree of safety provides the assurance that the income will be paid in a timely manner. The dividend growth is your hedge against inflation. If the dividend is not increasing, the real value of the income is declining. Also the growth of the dividend increases the degree of safety by paying out more dollars.

Check the Prospects

Our prospect list for income stocks (Table 7.1) selected five utilities for further analysis.

Use Stock Selector Analysis to Simplify the Process

The Stock Selector provides the format for comparing basic analysis fundamentals of one stock with another. We look only at the

Table 7.1 *Prospect Selector: Income*

Prospect Selector: Income										
Objective: 7%			*Financial News Information*					*Date: 2/28/91*		
Income from Dividends				*Annual Dividend*				*Price History*		
Prospect Stock Name	*Symbol*	*X*	*$ Paid*	*% Yield*	*Rank*	*Today Price $*	*12 Months*		
							$ High	*$ Low*	*% Chg*
Atlantic En	ATE	X	2.96	8.3	1	35¾	38	32	19
Detroit Ed	DTE	X	1.88	6.4	4	29⅜	31	25	24
MDU Resource	MDU	X	1.42	6.8	3	21	22	18	22
OtterTail Pw	OTTR	X	1.60	6.0	5	26	27	22	23
Union Elec	UEP	X	2.16	7.1	2	30¼	31	25	24

most important information. When you want to know what time it is, you don't want to learn how to build a clock. If you are investing in stock, you want to be able—in as brief a time as possible—to analyze, evaluate, and compare, the select those stocks that best fit the stated objective.

You don't necessarily want to become a full-time stock analyst. The selector helps you to stay in control of the most important information and simplifies the selecting process. When you are selecting stocks for income, the selector will help locate a combination of the highest current income, safety, and dividend growth.

Focus Analysis on Main Concerns

Now consider all five stocks in light of our main concerns: safety, current yield, and dividend growth. Three of the stocks have about the same risk (based on the current investment rating), only Detroit Edison has slightly greater possible risk, based on an investment rating between A− and B (a minimal difference).[1]

The Stock Selector provides a shorthand view of the most important information, making comparisons easier.[2] Any one of these stocks can become a good investment. While each one has certain advantages and disadvantages, we want to select the stock that currently offers the greatest advantages.

Compare the Facts on Dividends

Atlantic Energy has the highest dividend at $2.96 per share and, at 8.3 percent, has the largest yield. Union Electric currently pays the second largest dividend, has the highest average annual dividend increase at 3.4 percent ($.07 average per year) and has the second highest current yield of 7.1 percent. MDU Resources comes in third with current yield of 6.8 percent, but has the lowest five-year average dividend growth rate at 1.6 percent ($.02). Lack of dividend growth could be one of the factors holding down the price, which is increasing the current yield. Otter Tail Power has a low dividend but good growth at an annual average of 2.6 percent.

The dollar payout on Detroit Edison is high at $1.88 per share, but its current yield pulls fourth place. Detroit Edison did not raise the dividend from 1986 through 1989. It was then raised

$.10 in 1990, with plans for an identical increase in 1991. The stock lacks consistent dividend growth from year to year but may be on its way to recovery.

Analysis Stocks Individually

Table 7.2 provides the necessary information to analyze our prospective stocks. For clarity, we will break down the selector into its separate segments, which give the complete description and definition for each stock. Then we'll compare each stock with the others. Let's begin with Table 7.3, the Stock Selector for Atlantic Energy.

Table 7.2 Dividends, Growth Rating

Stock	Price	Dividend	5-Yr Average Div. Growth		Current % Yield	S&P Rating
ATE	$35¾	$2.96	2.36%	$.07	8.3%	A−
UEP	30¼	2.16	3.4	.06	7.1	A−
OTTR	26½	1.60	2.6	.04	6.0	A−
MDU	21	1.42	1.6	.02	6.8	A
DTE	29⅜	1.88	2.4	.04	6.4	A−

Atlantic Energy

Table 7.3 Stock Selector: Income, Atlantic Energy

Stock Selector Date: 2/28/91	Objective: Income 7%				Research from Value Line		
Stock	Current Price $	S&P Rating	Annual $ Paid	Dividend % Yield	Current T-Bill % Yield	5-Yr Average Annual Dividend Increase $ %	Dividend Paid Since
ATE	35.750	A−	2.96	8.0	6.01	.07 2.36	1919

Notes: Electricity to ⅓ of S. New Jersey/sales decline final quarter of 1990/profits hurt by purchased power/earnings may be lackluster for awhile/Financial Strength A.

Source: *Value Line Investment Survey*, March 22, 1991, Analyst Milton Schlein.

Know Where to Find Information

The numerical data and other information here is from either *Value Line Investment Survey,* the *Standard & Poor's Stock Guide,* or *The Wall Street Journal* stock quotation pages, all of which are readily available by subscription, through many stockbrokers, or at a public library.

The first selector line in Table 7.4 contains the name of the selector (in this case Income), the date on which we did the research and where the information originated (*Value Line Investment Survey*). The objective is stated (Income) and the return we expect (7% annual interest income). Next is the stock trading symbol (ATE).

Our selection is Atlantic Energy, a utility stock supplying electricity to the areas of southern New Jersey.

From the information collected at the end of February, 1991, we see a current price of $35.75 per share. The current dividend yield on ATE is 8.3 percent (by using formulas in the Word-Perfect tables, you can round the percentage off to 8%, as shown here, or set decimal places to the specific number of digits in the tables format function: 2-2-4), which compares to the then current T-bill interest rate (3-month) of 6.01 percent. The stock yield is on the high side given the current short-term interest rate. The current annual dividend amount is $2.96 per share.

The investment rating on the stock is A−, which is currently acceptable but suggests there is something in the company's financial picture to examine for possible future difficulties. The dividend has been paid since 1919 and has had an average annual

Table 7.4   Stock Selector: Income, Atlantic Energy (detail)

Stock Selector Date: 2/28/91		Objective: Income 7%			Research from Value Line		
Stock	Current Price $	S&P Rating	Annual $ Paid	Dividend % Yield	Current T-Bill % Yield	5-Yr Average Annual Dividend Increase $ %	Dividend Paid Since
ATE	35.750	A−	2.96	8.0	6.01	.07 2.36	1919

increase of 2.6 ($.07) over the past five years. So far, this stock looks like a good candidate for meeting our income objective.

Check the Information behind the Numbers

The Notes section (see Table 7.3) gives a summary of information behind the numbers, basic business development information, and a caution.

The notes indicate that much of the electrical power is purchased; therefore it is more expensive. Producing more power will require expensive capital outlay, since it cannot be generated from the company's own plants. Although the company is currently financially strong, this places the future growth of the dividend in question. Now study the graphs in Figure 7.1.

Look at the Price History

The price history graph for Atlantic Energy (Figure 7.1(a)), illustrating the high and low prices as well as last price for the year, shows that although the current price is above the closing price in 1990 (represented by the solid line between the high and low prices), price performance has been weak since the end of 1989. The drop in 1987 is not unusual as that was the year of the market crash. Nearly every stock will show a decline for the year 1987, but the weakness since 1989 is a concern. There appears to be a growing doubt among investors, who are selling and causing the price to drop.

What about Sales and Earnings?

The sales and earnings picture (see Figure 7.1(b)) should be the investor's main concern. Since 1987, both sales and earnings have been on a decline, which brings into question the company's ability to keep raising the dividend. Even the projected earnings increase for 1991 is difficult to get excited about. The sales and earnings trend is what income investors should seriously consider before buying the higher yield from the dividend. To pay dividends and keep increasing them, it is necessary to bring in more income. The trend shown here suggests that income will likely decline, rather than increase.

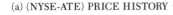

(a) (NYSE-ATE) PRICE HISTORY

(b) ANNUAL SALES & EARNINGS

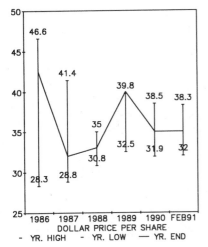

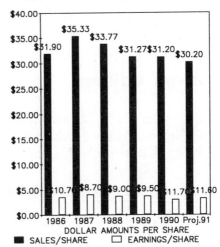

(c) ANNUAL DIVIDENDS

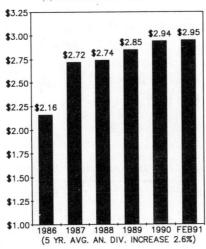

FIGURE 7.1   **Atlantic Energy**

Look for Consistent Dividend Growth

The dividend increase trend for ATE is consistent, though somewhat sporadic: up 11 cents in 1987 and 2 cents the following year; another 9-cent bump in 1990 and a projected 1 cent increase for 1991 (see Figure 7.1(c)). The company knows it will lose investor

confidence if the dividend is not increased, but the raises have
been given with difficulty. Unless the decline in sales and earnings
reverses, further dividend growth could be even more sporadic.

Detroit Edison

Now look at Table 7.5, which displays the information about Detroit Edison. Although this stock has a lower yield, analysis may
indicate that it is a better choice.

More about Price and Dividends

Figure 7.2(a) shows that Detroit Edison, with a current yield of
6.4 percent and dividend growth of 2.4 percent ($.04), had its
price move from a high of $19 in 1987 to a high of just over $30 a
share in 1990, a gain of 58 percent (12 percent annually).

As shown in Figure 7.2(c), the annual dividends were steady
at $1.68 per share from 1986 through 1989, with an increase in
1990 and a projected additional increase for 1991. Even though
current income is the main objective, price growth can help to
make the picture more complete. Price growth reflects investor
confidence in the company.

Table 7.5   *Stock Selector: Income, Detroit Edison*

Stock Selector Date: 2/28/91		Objective: Income 7%			Research from Value Line		
Stock	Current Price $	S&P Rating	Annual $ Paid	Dividend % Yield	Current T-Bill % Yield	5-Yr Average Annual Dividend Increase $ %	Dividend Paid Since
DTE	29.375	A−	1.88	6.4	6.01	.04 2.13	1909

Notes: Electricity to Detroit & 400 SE Michigan cities/nuclear concern auto sales concern/
plants good shape/dividend growth potential/1995/financial condition fair/Financial Strength B.

Source: *Value Line Investment Survey,* January 18, 1991, Analyst Paul E. Debbas.

(a) (NYSE-DTE) PRICE HISTORY   (b) ANNUAL SALES & EARNINGS

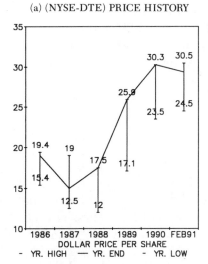 

(c) ANNUAL DIVIDENDS

FIGURE 7.2 **Detroit Edison**

Price Growth Is More Important than History

As Figure 7.2(b) shows, the most recent and therefore most significant price growth occurred from 1988 through 1990. Sales and earnings follow a similar upward trend. Earnings growth is coming out of a slump, and the company projects that in 1991 it will be slightly ahead of the good increase in 1990 (up an estimated 23%). The slight decline in 1988 and 1989 is also cause for moderate caution. The caution on earnings comes from the company's involvement with nuclear energy and the uncertainty of the auto industry.

MDU Resources

Table 7.6 highlights MDU Resources, an energy company serving some of the central mountain states. MDU Resources provides gas and electricity to Montana and the Dakotas. The company has traveled somewhat of a rocky road for the past five years. This can be seen in the price fluctuation, the sales and earnings, and the dividends paid out.

Prices for the year 1986 had both the top high and the top low. It was also a year with the highest sales and earnings. Sales and earnings weakness appeared through 1990, although higher earnings are projected for 1991.[3] The data show that it is difficult to maintain dividend increases without corresponding increases in sales and earnings. Other than the decline in 1990, dividends have remained relatively steady with a small increase.

Now look at the information shown on the graphs in Figure 7.3.

Table 7.6   *Stock Selector: Income, MDU Resources*

Stock Selector Date: 2/28/91		Objective: Income 7%			Research from Value Line		
Stock	Current Price $	S&P Rating	Annual $ Paid	Dividend % Yield	Current T-Bill % Yield	5-Yr Average Annual Dividend Increase $ %	Dividend Paid Since
MDU	21.000	A	1.42	6.8	6.01	.02 1.41	1937

Notes: Diversified Energy holding Co. main area Montana & Dakotas/legal concern with Koch, expect reasonable settlement/Clean air act may be heavy expense mid-decade/Financial Strength A.

Source: *Value Line Investment Survey,* January 18, 1991, Analyst Alan N. Hoffman.

Table 7.7   Stock Selector: Income—All

Stock Selector: Date: 2/28/91	Objective: Income 7%				Research from Value Line		
Stock	Current Price $	S&P Rating	Annual $ Paid	Dividend % Yield	Current T-Bill % Yield	5-Yr Average Annual Dividend Increase $ %	Dividend Paid Since
ATE	35.750	A−	2.96	8.0	6.01	.07 2.36	1919
DTE	29.375	A−	1.88	6.4	6.01	.04 2.13	1909
MDU	21.000	A	1.42	6.8	6.01	.02 1.41	1937
OTTR	26.500	A−	1.60	6.0	6.01	.04 2.50	1938
UEP	30.250	A−	2.16	7.1	6.01	.06 2.78	1906

Notes: **Atlantic Energy:** Electricity to ⅓ of S. New Jersey/sales decline final quarter of 1990/profits hurt by purchased power/earnings may be lackluster for awhile/Financial Strength A. Source: *Value Line Investment Survey,* January 18, 1991, Analyst Arthur H. Medalie.

Detriot Edison: Electricity to Detroit & 400 SE Michigan cities/nuclear concern auto sales concern/plants good shape/dividend growth potential/1995/financial condition fair/Financial Strength B. Source: *Value Line Investment Survey,* January 18, 1991, Analyst Stuart Novick.

MDU Resources: Diversified Energy holding Co. main area Montana & Dakotas legal concern with Koch, expect reasonable settlement/Clean air act may be heavy expense mid-decade/Financial Strength A. Source: *Value Line Investment Survey,* January 18, 1991, Analyst Stuart Novick.

Otter Tail Power: Electricity to West Minnesota, N&S Dakota/agricultural customers who are doing well/low debt/stock repurchase plan near done/finances in good shape/Financial Strength B++. Source: *Value Line Investment Survey,* January 18, 1991, Analyst Alan N. Hoffman.

Union Electric: Electrical & gas to St. Louis area/some nuc, 6 coal plants to finance construction with internal generated $/Clean air act may be heavy expense in mid-decade. Financial Strength A. Source: *Value Line Investment Survey,* January 18, 1991, Analyst Arthur H. Medalie.

Table 7.8   MDU Resources Growth Data

Year	Price High	Price Low	Per Share Annual Sales	Earnings	Dividends
1986	$27.90	$19.00	$20.41	$1.90	$1.39
1987	26.40	17.00	17.77	1.46	1.42
1988	20.10	17.25	18.11	1.81	1.42
1989	23.00	18.00	17.82	1.89	1.47
1990	22.90	18.50	17.10	1.75	1.42
1991	21.63	18.50	18.40	1.95	1.50

Check the Price Volatility

Figure 7.3(a) illustrates the price volatility of MDU Resources; examine the actual dollar difference between the high and low prices for each year. High-to-low price variation for MDU Resources is:

Year	Hi-Lo Price	
1986	$8.60	
1987	9.40	Volatility increase
1988	3.00	
1989	5.10	Volatility appears to be calming
1990	4.80	
Feb '91	3.50	

Price volatility can be a problem with an income stock, if it is unique to that company. Price volatility in utility stocks was common between 1986 and 1987 and is not as much of a concern as it might be in other years. The flat-to-down price characteristic from the end of 1989 to February 1991 is a concern with MDU Resources. The lack of price growth shows that other investors have continued to have reservations about the progress of the company.

The largest concern with this stock shows in the volatility of the other two graphs (Figures 7.3(b) and (c)). Sales, earnings, and dividend increases are showing distinct fluctuations since 1987. This clarifies the investor caution shown in the lack of price growth.

The question here is whether the company will be able to continue increasing the annual dividend or whether it might have to reduce that dividend sometime in the future. Investors are showing a definite lack of confidence, evidenced by the downward price action, which results in a higher current yield.

Otter Tail Power

Now we look at Otter Tail Power (Table 7.9), which has a good dividend growth rate at 2.5 percent ($.04) average per year, but has the lowest current yield, 6.0 percent annually.

(a) (NYSE-MDU) PRICE HISTORY   (b) ANNUAL SALES & EARNINGS

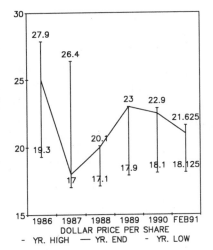

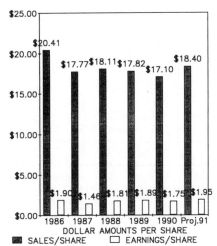

(c) ANNUAL DIVIDEND

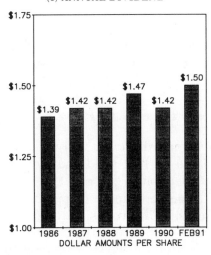

FIGURE 7.3   **MDU Resources**

Price Action

While the price showed a wider than normal swing ($8.10 high to low) in 1987, the current price of $26.50 has recovered from under $20.00. Figure 7.4(a) shows the growth to be steady since 1988 with a $5 to $6 swing between the annual high and low. This

Table 7.9   Stock Selector: Income, Otter Tail Power

Stock Selector Date: 2/28/91		Objective: Income 7%			Research from Value Line		
Stock	Current Price $	S&P Rating	Annual $ Paid	Dividend % Yield	Current T-Bill % Yield	5-Yr Average Annual Dividend Increase $ %	Dividend Paid Since
OTTR	26.500	A−	1.60	6.0	6.01	.04 2.50	1938

Notes: Electricity to West Minnesota, N&S Dakota/agricultural customers who are doing well/low debt/stock repurchase plan near done/finances in good shape/Financial Strength B++.

illustrates price stabilization, as well as annual price growth. The graph reflects 1991 prices through February. Earnings growth for Otter Tail Power (Figure 7.4(b)) has been steady for the past five years, even though sales declined in 1988. The dividend increases have been modest ($.04 per year average; Figure 7.4(c)) but consistent.

A Lower Price on Otter Tail Power

A lower price on Otter Tail Power will make it more attractive. This will increase the current yield and, with dividend growth, make it a stronger selection. A price of $23 a share increases the current yield to 7.3 percent, more comparable to that of Union Electric. As Figure 7.4(a) illustrates, Otter Tail Power has been as low as $22 a share in the 12 months preceding February 1991, with a lower price. Otter Tail Power is a good future target.

Union Electric

In Table 7.10, we look at Union Electric, which has some interesting fundamentals. Union Electric is a utility stock supplying electricity and natural gas to the areas of St. Louis, Missouri, southern Iowa, and western Illinois.

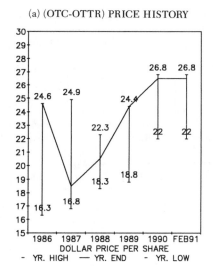

(a) (OTC-OTTR) PRICE HISTORY

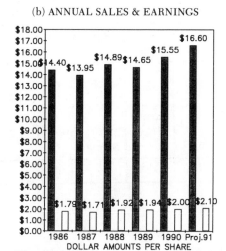

(b) ANNUAL SALES & EARNINGS

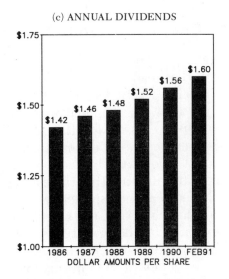

(c) ANNUAL DIVIDENDS

FIGURE 7.4   **Otter Tail Power**

What's the Current Information?

We see a current price of UEP at $30.25 per share as of February 28, 1991. The current dividend yield on UEP is 7.1 percent which compares to the then current T-bill interest rate (3-month) of 6.01 percent. The stock yield is reasonably in line with the

Table 7.10   *Stock Selection: Income, Union Electric*

Stock Selector Date: 2/28/91		Objective: Income 7%				Research from Value Line		
Stock	Current Price $	S&P Rating	Annual $ Paid	Dividend % Yield	Current T-Bill % Yield	5-Yr Average Annual Dividend Increase $ %		Dividend Paid Since
UEP	30.250	A−	2.16	7.1	6.01	.06 2.78		1906

current short-term interest rate. The current annual dividend cash amount is $2.16 per share.

The Investment Rating Can Help Moderate Risk

The investment rating on the stock is A−, which suggests that something minor in the financial data could lead to future difficulties; but it is currently acceptable. The dividend has been paid since 1906 and has an average annual increase of 9.8 percent ($.06) over the past five years. So far, this stock looks like an excellent candidate as an income-producing stock.

The notes provide good basic business development information and a warning. They indicate that the electrical generation is produced partly by nuclear and six active coal-burning plants. Some debt will have to be paid off, and the Clean Air Act is likely to cause extra expense in the mid-1990s. Modifying current equipment to clean emissions is important for the environment, but it is also costly. Now look at the information displayed in Figure 7.5.

Table 7.11   *Stock Selector: Income, Union Electric (detail)*

Notes: Electricity & gas to St. Louis area/some nuc, 6 coal plants to finance construction with internal generated $/Clean air act may be heavy expense in mid-decade/Financial Strength A.

Source: *Value Line Investment Survey,* January 18, 1991, Analyst Arthur H. Medalie.

(a) (NYSE-UEP) PRICE HISTORY

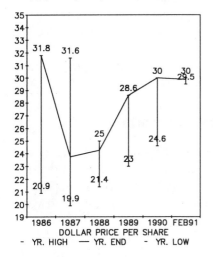

1986 1987 1988 1989 1990 FEB91
DOLLAR PRICE PER SHARE
- YR. HIGH — YR. END - YR. LOW

(b) ANNUAL SALES & EARNINGS

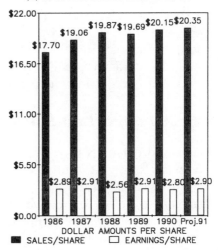

1986 1987 1988 1989 1990 Proj.91
DOLLAR AMOUNTS PER SHARE
■ SALES/SHARE ☐ EARNINGS/SHARE

(c) ANNUAL DIVIDENDS

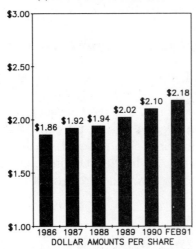

1986 1987 1988 1989 1990 FEB91
DOLLAR AMOUNTS PER SHARE

FIGURE 7.5 **Union Electric**

Price History for Union Electric

The price history graph (Figure 7.5(a)) shows us that the current price is below the 1986 high and closing price for that year. At the end of 1986, it closed at $31.87 and in February 1991 was trading at $30.25 a share, near the closing price for 1990.

The high-to-low volatility has become considerably less than in 1986 and 1987. In fact, this volatility has declined by nearly 50 percent. The price growth has been steady since 1988, with a modest increase in 1990 (just over $1.25). More price growth would be attractive, as it tends to give more stability to the dividend, but current income is really our main focus.

The All-Important Sales and Earnings

Sales and earnings growth are important to any stock. They are the basis for investor interest, hence price growth. Sales and earnings growth are also linked to dividend growth. For a company to have enough cash to increase the amount of a dividend each year, it also must show growth in sales and earnings.

Sales[4] are showing a slight decline in 1989 ($19.69 per share), with a recovery in 1990 ($20.15) and a projected increase for 1991 ($20.35). Earnings, on the other hand, are still expected to be down a small amount from the 1989 level (see Figure 7.5(b)).

How Strong Is the Dividend Growth?

A strong case for Union Electric can be seen in the annual dividend graph (Figure 7.5(c)). Dividends are showing a steady increase from 1987 through the 1991 projections. The dividend has been increased an average of 3.4 percent ($.06) each year illustrating Union Electric's commitment to dividend growth. It is questionable, however, whether Union Electric will be able to maintain this dividend growth through a future time of earnings weakness.

Making the Income Picks

The next stock selector (Table 7.12) selects some of the vital fundamental information for comparison. We can also go one step further and decide how many shares of each stock to buy.

You are ready to buy stock now, based on the information before you (see Table 7.12). It is easy to see that Union Electric has an acceptable rating on its debt and safety. The current yield falls into the number 2 spot, and the average annual dividend growth of 2.8 percent for the past five years ranks number 1. We know

Table 7.12 *Stock Picks: Income*

Stock Picks: Income						Objective: 7%			
Funds: $50,000			Actual Cost: $49,950				Leaves: $50		
Final Selection Based on Research Analysis.									
Stock Symbol	Current Price	$ Dividend	Rank	% Yield	S&P Rate	Yearly Dividend Average Growth $	%	Rank	X =Selected Today
ATE	$35.750	$2.96	1	8.3%	A−	$0.07	2.4%	5	X 3/1/91
Notes: Low sales & earnings growth					Buy: None at this time				
DTE	$29.375	$1.88	3	6.4%	A−	$0.04	2.1%	2	X 3/1/91
Notes: High dividend growth					Buy: 400 shares = $11,750				
MDU	$21.000	$1.42	5	6.8%	A	$0.02	1.4%	4	3/1/91
Notes: Low dividend growth					Buy: None at this time				
OTTR	$26.500	$1.60	4	6.0%	A−	$0.04	2.5%	3	X 3/1/91
Notes: High dividend low price					Buy: 300 shares = $7,950				
UEP	$30.250	$2.16	2	7.1%	A−	$0.06	2.8%	1	X 3/1/91
Notes: High dividend growth					Buy: 1000 shares = $30,250				

from the research that there could be an impact on future earnings with the additional expense of cleaning emissions. For now, we decide that this is a stock to buy as an income-producing stock with an acceptable amount of risk.

MDU resources ranks number 2 in current yield and has the slowest growing dividend, although this is expected to increase. The outcome of a pending legal situation could determine the attractiveness of this stock at a later time.

Otter Tail Power is also a good selection, although a slightly lower price could greatly improve the current yield of 6 percent annually. The consistent dividend growth of 2.5 percent makes the stock quite attractive.

Detroit Edison's dependence on the auto industry is a concern, but dividends are beginning to show growth and earnings are showing significant increases. Earnings were up 23 percent in 1990 and dividends were increased $.10 in 1990 (after being flat since 1986). The dividend is projected to increase another $.10 in 1991. The stock has some risk, but it shows signs of stability and a return of growth.

Detroit Edison, Otter Tail Power, and Union Electric are the income picks for this portfolio (see Table 7.12). At their current dividends, they will produce income of $3,392 annually, which is a 6.9 percent current yield. This is close enough to our objective of a 7 percent annual yield as the dividends will increase during 1991.

Summary

The most important criteria in selecting stocks for an income objective are safety, current yield, and dividend growth. Safety is observed in the consistency of sales and earnings growth and the investment rating given by Standard & Poor's, or the financial strength rating from *Value Line Investment Survey*. Price movement, which reflects investor confidence, is also a factor, but an increase in price is not the main focus.

The brief version of fundamental analysis presented here can assist the investor in selecting stocks that will provide a good source of income with an acceptable degree of safety.

Key Ideas

There are three important criteria for selecting safe income stock:
—Safety.
—Current yield.
—Dividend growth.
Check the prospects.
Use Stock Selector analysis to simplify the process:
—Focus analysis on main concerns.
—Compare the facts on the dividends.
Analyze stocks individually.
Atlantic Energy:
—Know where to find information.
—Check the information behind the numbers.

—Look at the price history.

—What about sales and earnings?

—Look for consistent dividend growth.

Detroit Edison:

—Learn more about price and dividends.

—Price growth is more important than history.

MDU Resources:

—Look at MDU Resources growth data.

—Check the price volatility.

Otter Tail Power:

—Watch Price action.

—There is a lower price on Otter Tail Power.

Union Electric:

—What's the current information?

· —The investment rating can help moderate risk.

—Study Price history for Union Electric.

—Look at The all-important sales and earnings.

—How strong is the dividend growth?

It's time to decide on our income picks.

Notes

1. The A— rating is Standard & Poor's and the B is from the *Value Line Investment Survey*.
2. See Appendix A for set up instructions.
3. Figures through February 1991 or projections.
4. Although the term "sales" is used, it refers to all revenues.

CHAPTER 8

Pay Me Later

Select Stock for Growth

The growth stock objective tells us specifically what to look for in the stocks to be reviewed. Many stocks will show growth higher than the 20 percent minimum set in the growth objective. They can still be acceptable candidates, as long as the fundamentals show an acceptable risk level, as also defined in the objective:

Growth Objective Specific Statement

By investing $50,000 in common stock with an investment grade rating of B or better, I expect to achieve a 20 percent rate of return annually for the next five years. This return will be based on the total amount of price growth in the stock selected, including any dividend payments. I will enhance safety by investing in at least three to five companies in three different industries. Any losses will be subtracted from profits to arrive at a calculation of the net gain.

Narrow the Prospect List

Our Prospect List from Part One is narrowed down to five stocks for further analysis (see Table 8.1).

Look for Ambitious Growth

We are looking for some ambitious growth, 20 percent annually for a five-year period, which can be difficult. It means that we

Table 8.1 *Prospect Selector: Growth*

Prospect Selector: Growth Objective: 20% Source: Financial News Information (*X means selected for further analysis*)								*Date: 2/28/91*
						Price History		
						12 Months		
Prospect *Stock* *Name*	*Symbol*	*Type* *of* *Business*	*X*	*Current* *Price* *$*	*Rank*	*$* *High*	*$* *Low*	*%* *Change*
Albertson's	ABS	Retail Groc	X	38.500	3	41	25	64
Apple Computer	AAPL	Computer	X	57.250	7	62	24	158
Coke	KO	Soft Drink		52.375	6	54	34	59
Conagra	CAG	Food Supply	X	41.875	4	43	25	72
Dayton Hudson	DH	Retail Cloth		68.250	8	80	46	74
Disney	DIS	Entertainment		123.375	10	137	86	59
McDonald's	MCD	Fast Food		31.625	1	59	25	136
Novell	NOVL	Comp Network	X	48.875	5	31	17	82
Pepsico	PEP	Soft Drink		32.750	2	35	19	84
Syntex	SYN	Drugs	X	75.250	9	78	47	66

will have to take some chances, but we will also do what we can to moderate and control some of the risk.

Since we are looking for a 20 percent annual gain, we first selected a few stocks that showed at least that much volatility between their 12-month high and low prices. The list was then narrowed to five stocks for further study, thus giving us diversification and some variety of volatility. The other stocks on the prospect list could be good future selections or may serve as alternate choices for further study.

To analyze the details of growth stocks, we again use the Stock Selector, which makes vital statistics and other information available at a glance. This is the most important information to monitor when reading the financial news reports.

Be Careful Using Average Numbers

Notice that many of these figures are averages. The difficulty with averages is their tendency to hide a developing problem or make a resolving crisis appear worse than it is. Here, we will deal with this difficulty by observing the trends on a graph that shows results for each year individually. Graphing statistics pinpoints any problem areas and identifies the long-term trends. The graphs help to clarify the average numbers used in the Stock Selector.

There Are Three Ways to Make Graphs

There are three ways to construct graphs. The least expensive is to get some graph paper and draw your own by hand. If you have a computer, many spreadsheet programs have excellent graphing abilities. Finally, you can purchase chart and graph services that will provide you with weekly reports, such as *Trendline's Daily Action Stock Charts* from Standard & Poor's.

Use Averages for Comparison

Average numbers are used as a summary for the performance comparison of one stock to another. A growth stock showing a 20 percent average annual gain for the past five years is usually preferable to another that shows only a 12 percent average gain for the same time period. Averages also help establish benchmarks for the investor's portfolio performance evaluation in the individual stocks. If a stock price has grown at a 16 percent average annual rate, it is reasonable to expect a similar growth. But, if for the past year (while the investor has owned the stock) it has only grown 9 percent, it is time to look for the problem. The investor must now examine the company to learn what has changed to cause below-average growth.

Be Wary of Undiscovered Gems

A common mistake of investors who get too carried away by fundamental analysis is to analyze the fundamentals of stocks they believe to be "undiscovered gems," only to be disappointed. Many of these stocks stay undiscovered because the main buyers in the market don't like them. A probable reason for the dislike is the market's perception of the company's lack of growth potential. The sad situation of undiscovered stocks is that they are usually not the leaders of their industry, nor are they in an industry that is showing a high growth potential.

With the Stock Selector, we are analyzing stocks that interest the market. We are looking for stocks with acceptable levels of growth that will likely continue for the next five years. We are also looking for stocks that appear to have low levels of risk. Although the analysis does not eliminate risk, it helps limit it by focusing our selection on the more financially sound companies.

Table 8.2 is a full Growth Stock Selector, showing all five candidates. The information presented is brief, but it gives a good picture of the progress of each stock over the past five years.

Compare the Growth Attributes

In comparing the five stocks, it is easy to see which stock has the highest rate of price growth over the past five years. The closing

Table 8.2 *Stock Selector: Growth—All*

Stock Selector Date: 2/28/91	Objective: Growth 20%				Research from Value Line			
		P/E Ratios				5-Yr Average Annual Growth		
	Current Price	5-Yr Curr/Avg	Annual Dividend	Price + Dividend	Sales	Earn's	Price & Divs	
Stock	$	$ %	$	$	%	%	$	%
CAG	41.875	21 14.8	.67	42.545	20.6	16.2	4.71	22.0
ABS	38.500	23 17.3	.58	39.080	11.2	22.0	5.72	46.2
AAPL	57.250	14 13.9	.50	57.750	30.0	34.6	· 6.38	49.2
NOVL	48.875	31 21.9	0	48.875	36.0	54.2	6.35	102.0
SYN	75.250	22 16.3	1.75	77.000	14.4	22.8	7.71	24.2

Notes: Base Price-CAG $21.40, ABS $6.50, AAPL $21.90, NOVL $6.25, SYN $32.00

CAG The nation's 2nd largest food processor, recently added Beatrice/expected to be market leader in '91/Financial Strength B++
Current debt is 52% of capitalization from 38%.

ABS The 6th largest retail grocery chain/Store opening program will help sustain rapid sales growth/Financial Strength A, debt 14%/significant insider buying and selling last half of 1990.

AAPL Price increase Nov-Jan, strong new product sales/Financial Strength A++
Long-term debt is none/recession concern/new low-cost Macintoshes are a big hit.

NOVL Designs and services local area networks for personal computers profitability increases since 1988/Financial Strength A
Long term debt 1% of capitalization.

SYN Prescription pharmaceutical/Financial Strength A+/earnings momentum is strong & building/50% sales depend on one drug, Naprosyn/new drugs recently introduced/Debt = 23% of capitalization.

price from 1986 is used as a base. Also, some of the low prices were created by stock splits rather than by the stock actually trading at the low price.

Novell, Inc., with average annual growth of more than 100 percent, also has the highest average price/earnings ratio (21.9). Apple Computer is second with an average increase of 49.2 percent each year. Albertson's comes in third with a 46.2 annual growth rate. Even though dividends are not a major concern with growth stock, they should be included in the growth calculations.

If we rank the stocks in terms of average annual price increase (including dividends) for a five-year period, it looks like this:

Stock Increase	5-Year Average Annual Price + Dividend
Novell, Inc.	102.0%
Apple Computer	49.2%
Albertson's	46.2%
Syntex Corp.	24.2%
Conagra	22.0%

Any one of these average annual returns would be acceptable to individual investors with a growth objective of 20 percent annually for the next five years. Remember, however, that these are historic returns. What happened in the past does not guarantee performance in the future, but the analysis of what has happened gives us some idea of the companies' performance capability.

Concentrate on Growth

The Stock Selector for growth stocks is slightly different from the one used with income stocks to reflect concerns related to growth in sales, earnings, and price. Table 8.3 presents a single segment from Table 8.2 so that we can study it in greater detail.

The Stock Selector provides enough information to choose one stock over another. Average numbers for sales, earnings, and dividends are somewhat overstated as they use current-year projections. The advantage of projected figures is that they will create a stronger standard for future performance evaluation of stocks.

Table 8.3 *Stock Selector: Growth, Conagra*

Stock Selector Date: 2/28/91		Objective: Growth 20%			Research from Value Line			
		P/E			*5-Yr Average Annual Growth*			
	Current Price	*Ratios 5-Yr*	*Annual Dividend*	*Price + Dividend*	*Sales*	*Earn's*	*Price & Divs*	
Stock	*$*	*Curr/Avg*	*$*	*$*	*%*	*%*	*$*	*%*
CAG	41.875	21 14.8	.67	42.545	20.6	16.2	4.71	22.0

Notes: Base Price $21.400
The nation's 2nd largest food processor, recently added
Beatrice/expected to be market leader in '91/Financial Strength B++
Current debt is 52% of capitalization from 38%.

Look at Prices and Dividends

The growth of price and dividends for Conagra starts with the price at the end of 1986 (base price: $21.40) (see Notes, Table 8.3). Establishing a base price in this manner shows what the return would be if the stock had been purchased at the end of the year in 1986 and held until the data were collected. Conagra trades under the trading symbol "CAG." The information was compiled February 28, 1991.

What Is the Five-Year Average Price/Earnings Ratio?

The five-year average price-to-earnings ratio (P/E ratio: price divided by earnings) is 14.8. The simple average is calculated by taking the annual average P/E ratio[7] for each of five years, adding them together and dividing by five. The average P/E ratio can be a useful benchmark for the determination of value.

Investment analysts will often state that a prudent investor should look for stocks with a low P/E ratio, but they seldom say exactly what constitutes such a ratio. An investor who knows the five-year average[8] ratio has established a benchmark.

More about Price/Earnings Ratios

If a stock's average P/E ratio is 14.8, and the stock is trading currently with a P/E ratio of 19 or 20, it can be considered high and the stock currently a bit overpriced. Conversely, if the P/E ratio is currently at 10 or 11, the stock could be undervalued.

Some cautions go with this line of thinking. The buying and selling in the stock market is in anticipation of future events. A stock trading with an above-average P/E ratio can be anticipating a higher earnings report, while a stock with a below-average ratio might be expecting the earnings to drop in the next few months. Although our earlier estimations that the stock is either undervalued or overvalued would still be correct, the earnings may adjust to the price before the price changes to more closely reflect the current earnings.

Occasionally, good stocks will have unusually high or low P/E ratios because of a unique one-time event. An important acquisition of another company might have caused earnings to be reported extraordinarily low. In another situation, a special windfall sale may have given earnings an unusual boost.

If a company's earnings seem unusually high or low, it is worthwhile digging deeper to learn the reason. Understanding whether the situation is a one-time occurrence or part of a regular business trend can help the investor avoid costly mistakes.

It is also possible that an earnings report issued yesterday has not been factored into the current news information or the quotation data. This is why it is so important to be certain that the information used in stock analysis is the most current.

How Do the Price/Earnings Ratios Compare?

Apple has an average P/E ratio of 13.9, the lowest average of the five stocks. The high P/E ratio of Novell at 21.9 suggests that the price has been driven by anticipation of even higher earnings. To find more relevance in the P/E ratios,[9] we must look at them by comparing the average with the current. Now look at a ranking (from the lowest to the highest) according to ratios and compare the average to a current P/E ratio:

Novell is trading at a significantly higher ratio than the other stocks, as well as considerably higher than its five-year average. There are obviously a lot of believers in the stock, and they are

Table 8.4   *Stock P/E Ratios 2/28/91*

	5-Year Average	Current P/E	Point Change
Conagra	14.8	21	+6.2
Albertson's	17.3	23	+5.7
Apple Computer	13.9	14	+ .1
Syntex Corp.	16.3	22	+5.7
Novell, Inc.	21.9	31	+9.8

willing to pay high prices in comparison with earnings. As was previously discussed, this shows anticipation of higher earnings from Novell.

Compare the Current Price/Earnings Ratio with the Average Price/Earnings Ratio

Using the P/E ratio in a relative way, by comparing the current P/E with its average, provides a more useful indicator than comparing it with the average of the stock market or a segment of the market. *Caution:* Be certain that the P/E ratio you use is in fact based on current earnings announcements. Newspapers and electronic quote machines can occasionally be slow to update earnings. Always verify that the current earnings or P/E ratio accurately reflects the present situation.

Look at Performance Expectations and Five-Year Growth

Now back to our basic analysis of Conagra. The Objective Selector section in Table 8.3 contains the performance expectation of the objective. It is a reminder of our objective of 20 percent annual growth. The base price in the Notes is the price on which the five-year data are based. If this stock were purchased at the time, the base price would have been the cost.

Next we look at the current price and the five-year performance. A recent price for Conagra saw the stock at $41.875 per share with a $.67 dividend.

The five-year average figures show sales growth at 20.6 percent with earnings at 16.2 percent annually. Because the statistics attract new buyers of the stock, they are important. If sales and earnings increase enough, the stock price will rise. Significant increases in sales and earnings attract stock buyers.

It is difficult to define a direct relationship between the sales and earnings increase and the price increase of the stock. Stock prices are only partly based on historical increases. It must be kept in mind that stock prices are anticipating the growth of future sales and earnings.

Although the future increases can be forecast from the current trends, the mechanism is not precise. We compensate for this here by selecting stocks showing higher growth rates than our objective requires and then looking for information indicating that the stock's growth rate will continue.

Annual Return Is Our Focus

The price (including dividends) of Conagra is growing at an average rate of 22.0 percent annually. An average annual return of more than 20 percent is attractive. Figure 8.1(a) shows which years have had significant price increases.

Conagra's Price History

The price history of Conagra shows some volatility in the expected 1986–1987 area. The price growth appears to have been steady from 1989 through February 1991, although the high-to-low volatility (dollar amount between the high and low price) increased slightly in 1989 and 1990. Prices on this graph are adjusted for two stock splits: a two-for-one split in 1987 and a three-for-two split in 1989.

Stock splits such as these are difficult to evaluate. Although many investors get excited about splits, they create more accounting work for large institutions. The financial effects of stock splits are neutral—neither good nor bad. They tend to attract buyers at first, but whether or not the buyers keep coming depends on developments apart from the split. What is more important after a split is the company's ability to maintain good earnings growth.

(a) (NYSE-CAG) PRICE HISTORY

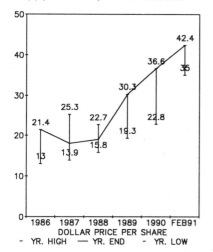

1986 1987 1988 1989 1990 FEB91
DOLLAR PRICE PER SHARE
- YR. HIGH — YR. END - YR. LOW

(b) ANNUAL SALES & EARNINGS

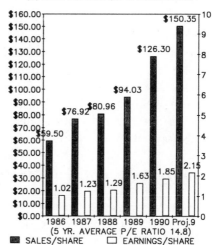

1986 1987 1988 1989 1990 Proj.9
(5 YR. AVERAGE P/E RATIO 14.8)
■ SALES/SHARE □ EARNINGS/SHARE

(c) GAIN IF SOLD AT YEAR END

1987 1988 1989 1990 FEB91
(BUY PRICE $21.40)
— DOLLAR GAIN ■ PERCENT GAIN

FIGURE 8.1   **Conagra**

Check Those Sales and Earnings

Conagra's sales and earnings graph (Figure 8.1(b)) shows that sales increased 250 percent between 1986 and the projected figures for 1991. They went from $59.50 a share to a projected figure of more than $150 a share in 1991. Earnings showed a steady but less dramatic increase, from $1.02 to an expected $2.15 (75% increase). While this is still a good increase, it is worth scrutinizing for future weakness. If future sales fall short of projections, the earnings growth could be adversely affected.

Conagra's sales and earnings have been growing at a steady pace. Earnings show a positive increase since 1986 with only a minor weakness in 1988 ($1.29 per share vs. $1.23 per share).

Since company information involves more than just numbers, let's look at more of the story on Conagra.

Analysts Predict a "Market Leader"

Analysts predicted correctly that Conagra would be a market leader in 1991 (see Notes, Table 8.3). The financial strength was affected by the purchase of another company, Beatrice. The current debt is 52 percent of the capitalization[10] (debt over 50% of capitalization is considered high by many stock analysts), but the addition of Beatrice can help the company bring the debt down to the former level of 38 percent, which is expected by the analyst. All these factors suggest that Conagra is a good candidate as a growth stock.

Even though this method of analysis and selection is based on sound financial fundamentals, remember that the stock market is not always attracted to companies just because they happen to be financially sound. A company can be in great financial shape, but still weak in price growth. Figure 8.1(c) shows the pattern of gain for Conagra stock.

Novell, the Current Group Leader

Novell, Inc. is the clear leader in terms of price growth. Figure 8.2(a) shows that much of the increase began in 1989. In 1990, the price went from just over $19 a share to a high of $34 for the year, an increase of $15 a share.

Why Are Sales and Earnings Important?

Annual sales and earnings (Figure 8.2(b)) show steady sales increases, with earnings doubling in 1990. Obviously, this is part of

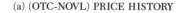

(a) (OTC-NOVL) PRICE HISTORY

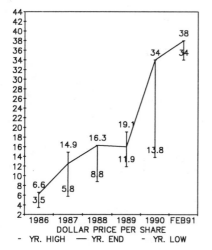

(b) ANNUAL SALES & EARNINGS

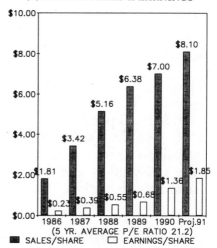

(c) GAIN IF SOLD AT YEAR END

FIGURE 8.2 **Novell**

the reason for the price increase. There is also some anticipation of further earnings growth as shown by the current P/E ratio of 31, compared with Novell's average P/E of 21.9.

We don't necessarily want to pick the stock with the best earnings, but rather with consistent earnings that we can anticipate will continue to grow. The main focus is always on the price and dividend growth (where applicable). We look to the earnings growth to support and possibly accelerate the price growth.

What's the Annual Gain?

Figure 8.2(c) shows the dollar gain and percentage gain at the end of each year for investors fortunate enough to buy Novell in 1986 at $6.25 per share. The cash gain for stock sold at the end of 1989 would have been $9.75, which amounts to a 156 percent total gain. The higher than average P/E ratio correlates to higher risk. If Novell is able to sustain the earnings growth, the risk could be worth taking.

Apple Computer

Among the five stocks, Apple Computer's P/E ratio of 14 was the low at the end of February. The fact that it traded nearly at its average ratio of 13.9 suggests there could be future value in the price of the stock. These figures also represent a strong up market, fired by lower interest rates and a positive conclusion of the Persian Gulf conflict. Stock prices move either by themselves or are driven by the current overall market situation. Because the market has been strong and Apple has not done much, there could be a growing concern as to the future earnings growth. Look at the figures displayed in Figure 8.3(a)–(c).

Look at Apple's Price History

Apple Computer shows a rather interesting price history. The price rose significantly from the base of $21.90 a share in 1986 to nearly $60.00 a share in 1987 and dropped back to the mid-$40s. Did this occur because of earnings anticipation? A look at the steadily increasing sales doesn't give us the answer. The increases are steady year after year. A look at earnings increase is a different story.

Apple's Sales and Earnings

We see significant earnings increases in 1987 (38 percent) and 1988 (87 percent), but other years are more modest. The earnings

(a) (OTC-AAPL) PRICE HISTORY

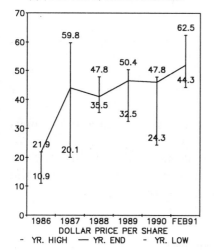

DOLLAR PRICE PER SHARE
- YR. HIGH — YR. END - YR. LOW

(b) ANNUAL SALES & EARNINGS

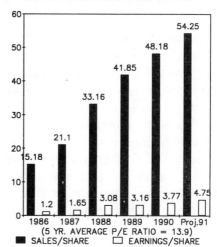

(5 YR. AVERAGE P/E RATIO = 13.9)
■ SALES/SHARE □ EARNINGS/SHARE

(c) GAIN IF SOLD AT YEAR END

(BASE PRICE $21.9 * CUMULATIVE
---- DOLLAR GAIN ■ PERCENT GAIN

FIGURE 8.3 **Apple Computer**

for Apple in 1989 were up 3 percent and 1990 shows a 19 percent increase. Earnings for 1991 are projected at 26 percent, which is certainly an improvement, but the current price shows that some investors are skeptical. Possibly, some of this doubt comes from the projected sales increase, which is below average. The projected sales increase of 13 percent compares with an average annual increase of over 35 percent.

The Earnings Growth Attraction

Earnings growth is the bottom line main attraction to most investors. This also applies to most takeover situations. It is earnings growth that gives value to a stock. High-value stocks have lower prices in relation to high earnings. Low-value stocks have higher prices and lower earnings. The only situation that contradicts this is earnings anticipation, such as in the Novell situation. Earnings anticipation can keep the price high in relation to current earnings. The risk in an earnings anticipation situation is that the actual earnings will come in lower than expected. Comparing the companies' earnings growth helps to complete the picture in selecting a fundamentally sound investment.

Stock	Annual Average Sales Growth (%)	5-Year Earnings Growth (%)
Novell, Inc.	38.0	54.2
Apple Computer	35.8	34.6
Syntex Corp.	20.6	22.8
Albertson's	14.4	22.0
Conagra	11.2	16.2

Albertson's and Conagra

These figures also suggest that both Conagra and Albertson's deserve a closer look. Conagra is showing significantly higher sales increases, but needs higher earnings. It appears as though Albertson's is showing greater efficiency by making more earnings on sales, but the company needs better sales increases to sustain that earnings growth. We can test that idea by checking the graphs shown in Figure 8.4(a)–(c).

Consider Sales and Earnings Growth

Albertson's sales and earnings graph shows that the sales increases tend to be about average (11.2%) each year. Earnings, on the other hand, are showing a slight decline in the annual percentage increase. The year 1988 had a 30 percent increase; 1989 showed a

(a) (NYSE-ABS) PRICE HISTORY

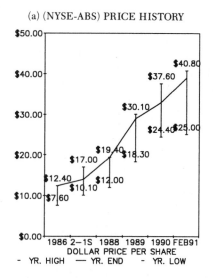

DOLLAR PRICE PER SHARE
- YR. HIGH   — YR. END   - YR. LOW

(b) ANNUAL SALES & EARNINGS

(5 YR. AVERAGE P/E RATIO 15.5)
■ SALES/SHARE   ☐ EARNINGS/SHARE

(c) GAIN IF SOLD AT YEAR END

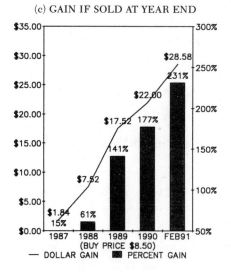

(BUY PRICE $8.50)
— DOLLAR GAIN   ■ PERCENT GAIN

FIGURE 8.4   **Albertson's**

21 percent increase; 1990 came in at only a 16 percent increase, suggesting a decline in the efficiency of earnings, which could become a future concern for investors. Since Albertson's is a grocery chain, this trend is important. The only major way the company can increase business is to take it away from someone else.

Limited markets such as this can become a downside risk as the company grows to a significantly larger size and it grows more difficult to increase market share. On the upside, food suppliers tend to be stable companies with some resistance to recession. Although growth is often slower, it is usually steady.

Steady Price Growth Is a Positive Sign

Albertson's price growth shows a steady uptrend; even the high-to-low volatility reflects this fact. This is a positive sign for a growth stock.

Syntex

Moderately narrow-line pharmaceutical companies also tend to be recession resistant. Such companies may have been established on a unique drug or product that was in enough demand to build them to a significant size. Then they must become efficient. They settle down to a steadier growth rate, taking business away from the competition. Many companies are successful at this, and occasionally they come out with a new product that again pushes sales and earnings to new highs. From the Stock Selector, we saw that Syntex depends on the product Naprosyn for 50 percent of its sales. Figure 8.5(a)–(c) provides additional insights.

Sales and Earnings Are Conservative

Syntex comes in a conservative third in average annual earnings growth, but fourth in sales growth. Although the sales are important, the earnings are even more important. It is likely that the company can maintain this efficient posture partly because of the costs of doing business. Profit margins in pharmaceuticals tend to be better than in the food industry.

Sales and Earnings Show Steady Increase

Sales and earnings for Syntex show a line of steadily increasing numbers. The price growth shows a fairly steady increase since

(a) (NYSE-SYN) PRICE HISTORY

(b) ANNUAL SALES & EARNINGS

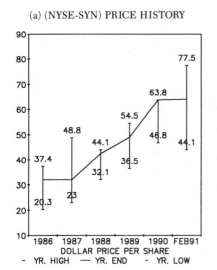

(c) GAIN IF SOLD AT YEAR END

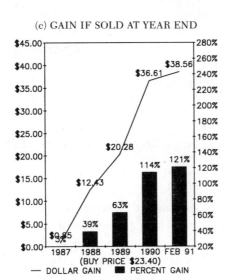

FIGURE 8.5 **Syntex**

1987. The price and dividend growth average is 24.2 percent, which is respectable. The price moved from the mid-$30s range to the $60s in 1990. The volatility in the first two months of 1991 is some cause for concern. It could reflect some doubt in the minds of investors. Sudden action such as this is often a signal to the investor to find out what might be the cause.

Look for the Meaning behind the Numbers

Analyzing financial data for growth stocks will often create more questions than it will give answers. When questions arise about the data, it can be helpful to learn the meaning behind the numbers. This information will tell the investor where the problems are and, more importantly, where the earnings growth is likely to be generated. In Table 8.2, the notes for the companies are excellent examples of such useful information.

Look for Special Information

As mentioned earlier, Conagra recently acquired Beatrice, which is expected to help it quickly become a market leader. Albertson's strong store opening program could help it significantly improve the sales-and-earnings growth picture. Apple Computer has a recession concern, but also has a big hit with the new low-cost Mac-Intosh computers. Novell has shown strong profitability since 1988 and has very little long-term debt. Syntex has strong earnings momentum with its main product but is also introducing new drugs.

Some Subjective Information Is Still Important

Although it is difficult to put a numerical value on subjective information, it is extremely important to be aware of these developments. They directly impact the future growth of the company, which affects the growth of the price of the stock.

Sometimes the information will be positive, and other times it will be negative. Frequently, it can be difficult to gauge what continuing impact this information will have on price movement. Still, the investor should be aware of the story behind the numbers.

Always Remember the Objective

Our goal is to select stocks that are in alignment with our objective—stocks with an investment rating of "B" or better and the potential to produce a 20 percent annual gain for the next five years. If we have several to choose from, it only makes sense to select the companies that appear to have the highest potential for growth.

Price Forecasting Is Difficult

Stock price forecasting is difficult at best. Business climates, industries, and economic situations can change so quickly that what is projected one month is outdated by the next. The stock market has a natural buying bias, which is why it keeps increasing through the years. Successful companies also have a natural buying bias toward their products, illustrated by their increases in revenues each year. Growth that shows a trend, punctuated by occasional, sudden increases in earnings, is fairly common in large companies. Since these increases tend to be unpredictable, analysts often do not include them in price growth forecasting. Projected growth figures are therefore on the conservative side for analysis, making it acceptable to leave some room for variance on the positive side.

Price History Carries More Weight than Forecasting

Historical data is concrete. It reflects what actually happened and therefore has more weight than projected figures. In the analysis of projected growth figures, we will compensate for historical weight by allowing a projection variance of 5 percent. If a projected growth rate is 15 percent or better and the historical

Table 8.5   Projected Growth

Stock	Recent Price	Projected Price Range		Annualized Total Gain	
(1993–1995)		High	Low	High	Low
Syntex Corp.	$64	$140	$105	23%	15%
Albertson's	33	60	45	18	10
Conagra	35	65	45	18	9
Apple Computer	52	95	65	17	7
Novell, Inc.	38	70	45	17	5

See endnotes for *Value Line* references.
Allowable variance is 5 percent.

performance is 20 percent or better, the stock will become a strong candidate for selection.

According to the *Value Line Investment Survey*, each of the five stocks is within the acceptable projected growth range of 15 to 20 percent annually. Actually, these stocks are all within 3 percent of our objective of 20 percent annual growth.

The *Value Line* estimate also gives us a low forecast number that will be a helpful reference when evaluating the growth performance.

Compare Price Growth with Forecast

When comparing the price growth history with the forecast, it is easy to see that the forecast tends to be conservative (see

Table 8.6　*Stock Picks: Growth*

Stock Picks: Growth					Objective: 20%		
Funds: $50,000		Actual Cost: $46,625			Leaves: $3,375		
Final Selection Based on Research Analysis.							
	Current Data			Averages		Next 5-Yr Analyst Forecast	X = Selected
Stock Symbol	Current Price	P/E Ratio	P/E Ratio	Price Growth			Today
AAPL	$57.250	14	13.9	49.2%	17.0%	X	3/1/91
Notes: Low P/E high competition				Buy: 100 shares = $5,725			
ABS	$38.500	23	17.3	46.2%	18.0%	X	3/1/91
Notes: Concern of market limits				Buy: 200 shares = $7,700			
CAG	$41.875	21	14.8	22.0%	18.0%	X	3/1/91
Notes: Low growth history				Buy: 200 shares = $8,375			
NOVL	$48.875	31	21.2	102.1%	17.0%	X	3/1/91
Notes: Rapid growth may slow				Buy: 200 shares = $9,775			
SYN	$75.250	22	16.3	24.2%	23.0%	X	3/1/91
Notes: Low growth history				Buy: 200 shares = $15,050			

Table 8.4). It is also interesting to observe that forecasts and history are only similar on two stocks. Syntex has a history of 24.2 percent annual growth and a forecast of 23 percent over the next five years.

Conagra's history shows 22 percent and a forecast of 18 percent annually. It will be interesting to see how these forecasts compare with the actual results. Some people might be tempted to think the forecasts are too low, but only time will tell.

Using the format of the Stock Selector allows us to quickly analyze stocks for summary information on which to base a buy decision. Basic analysis to find a growth stock doesn't guarantee an instant winner, but it provides a sound financial basis for comparing strengths and weaknesses in various stocks. We started out choosing stocks that were somewhat familiar. We ended up selecting stocks that have a reasonable chance to meet the stated objective.

Key Ideas

Select stock for growth.

Narrow the prospect list.

Look for ambitious growth:

—Be careful using average numbers.

—There are three ways to make graphs.

—Use averages for comparison.

—Be wary of undiscovered gems.

Compare the growth attributes.

Concentrate on growth.

Look at prices and dividends:

—What is the five-year average P/E ratio?

—More about price/earnings ratios.

—How do the P/E ratios compare?

—Compare the current P/E ratio with the average P/E ratio.

Look at performance expectations and five-year growth.

Annual return is our focus.

Conagra's price history:

—Check those sales and earnings.

—Analysts predict a "market leader."

Novell, the current group leader:

—Why are sales and earnings important?

—What's the annual gain?

Apple Computer:

—Look at Apple's price history.

—Review Apple's sales and earnings.

Understand the earnings growth attraction.

Albertson's and Conagra

—Consider sales and earnings growth.

—Steady price growth is a positive sign.

Syntex

—Sales and earnings are conservative.

—Sales and earnings show a steady increase.

Look for the meaning behind the numbers:

—Look for special information.

—Some subjective information is still important.

Always remember the objective:

—Price forecasting is difficult.

—Price history carries more weight than forecasting.

Compare price growth with forecast.

Notes

1. *Value Line Investment Survey,* November 23, 1990, Analyst Marjorie A. Crough.
2. *Value Line Investment Survey,* November 23, 1990, Analyst Philip S. Mulqueen.
3. *Value Line Investment Survey,* February 1, 1991, Analyst George A. Niemond.
4. *Value Line Investment Survey,* February 1, 1991, Analyst Bridget A. Collins.

5. *Value Line Investment Survey,* February 8, 1991, Analyst Rudolph C. Carryl.

6. *Value Line Investment Survey.* Target price range projections:

Syntex Corp.	2/8/91	Analyst Rudolph C. Carryl
Albertson's	11/23/91	Analyst Philip S. Mulqueen
Conagra, Inc.	11/23/90	Analyst Marjorie A. Crough
Apple Computer	2/1/91	Analyst George A. Niemond
Novell, Inc.	2/1/91	Analyst Bridget A. Collins

7. Annual average P/E ratio information can be obtained from the *Value Line Investment Survey,* which can be found at the public library, through a broker, or by subscription. Several stock analysts, including Peter Lynch, former Portfolio Manager of Fidelity Magellan Fund, recommend using an average P/E ratio as a benchmark for a stock's value.

8. Some analysts use a longer history, but we are concentrating on five-year histories.

9. P/E ratios can also be compared with those of other companies in the same industry. The *Value Line Investment Survey* shows a "relative P/E ratio."

10. Capitalization, in this sense, refers to the total market value of the company (current price times total number of shares).

CHAPTER 9

Pay Me Now and Later

Selecting Total Return Stocks—Find the Best Dividends and Growth

Total return stocks are stocks that pay a relatively high dividend (usually slightly less than income stocks) and show significant growth in value and price. They tend to be the stocks of large, usually well-known companies. Many stocks appearing on the Dow Jones averages are good candidates for total return. They are superlarge companies whose price action can easily be felt by the entire market.

The analysis of total return stocks is similar to that of growth stocks. We are looking for stocks that will pay a good dividend and are likely to grow in value and price over the next five years:

Total Return Objective Specific Statement

By investing $100,000 in common stock, I expect to achieve a 12 percent rate of return annually for the next five years. Risk will be moderated by the stock dividends, diversification into at least three different stocks in three different industries, and a minimum investment rating of B. The rate of return will be calculated by adding the annual price increase of the stock to its annual dividend payout.

Total Return Usually Means Slower Growth

Our objective is set lower because total return stocks tend to show slower growth. A larger return is possible, but we are

98

moderating risk by setting the objective at a more conservative level. These stocks tend to have lower risk than growth stocks because they are paying out that cash dividend each quarter, which is similar to the effect created with income stocks. The risk is lowered by a certain amount each time the dividend is paid out to the shareholder.

Check the Total Return Prospect List and Narrow the List

First, let's take another look at the prospect list from Chapter 4 (see Table 4.2), where we also set our total return objective. Table 9.1 shows five selected companies (identified by an X) in five industries.

In this group of total return prospects, we see yields of 3 to 6 percent and price fluctuations that should include the amount

Table 9.1 *Prospect Selector: Total Return*

Prospect Selector: Total Return
Objective: 12%
Source: Financial News Information
(*X means selected for further analysis*)   *Date: 2/28/91*

							Price History		
			Annual Dividends			Current	12 Months		
Prospect Stock Name	*Symbol*	*X*	*Paid $*	*Yield %*	*Rank*	*Price $*	*High $*	*Low $*	*Change %*
Aetna Life	AET		2.76	6	10	45.125	54	29	86
Am Home Prod	AHP	X	2.30	4	7	57.000	60	40	50
AT&T	T	X	1.32	4	6	33.375	44	29	52
Emerson Elec	EMR		1.32	3	3	43.500	45	31	45
Exxon	XON	X	2.68	5	9	55.125	56	45	24
Gen Elec	GE	X	2.04	3	2	68.000	76	50	52
IBM	IBM	X	4.84	4	5	128.750	140	96	46
Kmart	KM		1.74	5	8	35.000	37	23	61
Sara Lee	SLE		0.94	3	4	34.375	36	24	50
Woolworth	Z		1.04	3	1	32.750	37	24	54

of annual growth we expect to find. Because they are all well-known companies in industries such as drugs, telephone utility, oil, consumer products, and computers, we have reasonable diversification.

The information on the prospect list is sufficient for our first step in the selection process. We have narrowed down a list of 10 stocks to 5 possibilities. To get more information, we will look at the data appearing in the *Value Line Investment Survey* and the *Standard & Poor's Stock Guide*. *Value Line* has an advantage because it lists the data by year, whereas the *S&P Stock Guide* tends to summarize. A good business section of the public library will carry this information on a reference shelf.

Calculate the Total Return

An additional form is used to calculate the total return on the stocks being analyzed. Called the *Total Return Calculator* (Table 9.2), it is designed to simplify the calculation of a five-year cumulative annual average total return. A hypothetical buy price is established, and all dividends paid during the five-year time period are added to the current price. The current year is considered a full year for both the growth and dividend calculation.

The specific years being used for the total return calculator are the following: 1987, 1988, 1989, 1990, 1991.

Due to the dividend sensitivity of the total return objective, all of 1991 is being used, even though the dividends haven't yet been paid and we do not have a year-end price. A strong basis for year-end evaluation is thus established. All beginning prices (base price) are based on closing year prices from 1986. Graphs include 1987 through February 1991, using actual *prices* but they rely on projections for sales, earnings and, in some cases, dividends.

Table 9.3 shows three stock candidates for a total return objective in the Stock Selector.

Look at the Relative Price/Earnings Ratios

American Home Products is trading with the highest P/E ratio at 15, 1.8 points above its five-year average. General Electric is trading 1.2 points above its average P/E. Small differences here are

Table 9.2 *Total Return Calculator*

Date: 2/28/91			*Total Return Calculator*		
Stock >>>	*American Home Products*	*AT&T*	*General Electric*	*Exxon*	*IBM*
Price 5 Years Ago	$42.000	$27.900	$48.500	$37.100	$123.000
5 Years Total Dividends	$ 9.87	$ 6.29	$ 8.59	$ 11.42	$ 23.37
Add the Current Price of	$57.000	$39.670	$68.000	$55.125	$128.750
Equals	$66.870	$45.960	$76.590	$66.545	$152.120
Divide by the price five years ago (include current year as one).					
Equals	$ 1.592	$ 1.647	$ 1.579	$ 1.794	$ 1.237
Subtract 1 =	$ 0.592	$ 0.647	$ 0.579	$ 0.794	$ 0.237
Remove the decimal and round off will equal the percent total return.					
Total Return	59.0%	65.0%	58.0%	79.0%	24.0%
Divide by five years; this equals the average annual total return.					
Annual Average Total Return	11.8%	8.4%	11.6%	15.8%	4.8%

unimportant; most of these stocks are trading close to their average price/earnings ratios. A 1.8 point difference is insignificant.

There is no hard-and-fast rule that says one number is a high P/E ratio and another is low, although the investor can get a feel for where a P/E ratio should be by comparing it with the relative P/E for the industry. Relative P/E ratios for these companies are as follows:

Stock	Relative P/E Ratio
AHP	0.98
T	0.99
XON	1.01
GE	0.94
IBM	0.94

Table 9.3 *Stock Selector: Total Return*

Stock Selector Date: 2/28/91	Objective: Total Return 12%				Research from Value Line			
Stock	Current Price $	P/E Ratios 5-Yr Curr/Avg	Annual Dividend $	Price + Dividend $	5-Yr Average Annual Growth			
					Sales %	Earn's %	Price $	Divs %
AHP	57.000	15 13.2	2.30	59.300	6.6	10.6	4.97	11.8
XON	55.125	14 12.6	2.68	57.805	11.4	3.8	14.26	18.4
GE	68.000	14 12.8	2.16	70.160	14.0	14.0	5.87	12.0

Notes:

AHP Base Price = $42.000/A leading supplier of pharmaceuticals/now bringing new products to market/i.e.: birth control implant/ Financial Strength A+ market weakness in some product areas/long-term debt 66% capitalization.

XON Base Price = $37.125/World's largest integrated oil company/ Alaska oil spill costs have been worked out, shouldn't hurt bottom line/good stability in the company due to balance of exploration and production/Financial Strength A++.

GE Base Price = $48.500/One of the largest and most diversified companies in the world/several businesses sensitive to recession light recession OK/Financial Strength A++/long-term debt is 12% of capitalization.

The number 1.0 indicates that the company is trading at its industry average. A high number, such as 2.0, says a stock is trading at twice the industry average; a lower number (say 0.5) is half the industry average. The listed stocks are all about average for their individual industries.

One question to consider is why IBM is trading below its average P/E ratio when the market has been moving rather steadily upward. The figures may be reflecting a more serious problem since IBM has been showing some earnings weakness.

General Electric—Examine Five-Year Growth

According to the statistics in Table 9.4, GE has great potential as a stock investment in the total return objective category. The stock ranks number one in two of the three most important areas:

Table 9.4   *Stock Ranking: Total Return*

Stock	American Home Products	Rank	Exxon	Rank	General Electric	Rank
Avg P/E	13.2	3	12.6	1	12.8	2
Curr P/E	15.0	3	14.0	2	14.0	1
Curr Div	$ 2.30	2	$ 2.68	1	$ 2.16	3
Curr Price	$57.00	2	$55.125	1	$68.00	3
Average Annual Sales Growth	6.6%	3	11.4%	2	14.0%	1
Average Annual Earnings Growth	10.6%	2	3.8%	3	14.0%	1
Average Annual Price + Div Growth	11.8%	3	18.4%	1	12.0%	2
Objective	12.0%		12.0%		12.0%	

(Number 1 is most favorable.)

sales growth and earnings growth, and is high in price plus dividend growth.

It is trading near its average P/E ratio and has an annual dividend of $2.16 per share (represents a yield of 3.2 percent). The financial strength of the company is rated A++ by the *Value Line Investment Survey.*

General Electric is high in the five-year average sales growth. We will take a look at this in the graphs.

American Home Products Are Close to Our Objective

The table shows sales growth of 6.6 percent with American Home Products, 11.4 percent with Exxon and 14.0 percent with General Electric. If the sales stay strong and AHP can become more efficient in the earnings, the stock could be a strong total return stock.

American Home Products comes in lower than Exxon in the important sales but not in the earnings growth category. The higher average P/E ratio is not much of a problem, as was discussed earlier. A total return average of 11.8 percent annually is close enough to our objective of 12 percent to make this another candidate.

Exxon—Low Projections Invite Caution

About the only negatives with Exxon are the volatility of the oil industry and a recent increase in price. Oil prices are controlled at times and wild at other times. Higher oil prices usually mean greater profits, but not always. Market share and the cost of doing business can also be important factors in what happens to earnings and the price of the stock. The recent run-up in price has already discounted some of the potential earnings growth.

Even though the earnings is not as strong as other stocks, Figure 9.1(a) shows a steady increase in price. There is anticipation building that earnings will be showing some important growth in the next few years.

Value Line Investment Survey projects only a 9 percent annual total return on the high side and 4 percent on the low end, in the time period 1994–1996. These figures (if they are correct) are significantly lower than our objective of an annual 12 percent return. Does this opinion eliminate the stock from consideration? Absolutely not. But it does tell us where the caution is with Exxon. Looking at the information graphically might help to clarify the data (see Figure 9.1(a)–(d)).

The price growth shows fairly steady growth with only a minor weakness in 1990, based on year high, low, and end-of-year prices. Sales were projected to be weaker in 1991, but earnings were still expected to increase. Some weakness appeared in 1989, the year of the Alaska oil spill, but overall the company appears to be regaining strength. Dividends have shown a consistent increase at an 8.8 percent per year average. The gain-if-sold showed a definite weakness in 1990, but it appears to have recovered.

The information on Exxon suggests a stock that performs well, with the qualifier that it might be difficult for the company to continue to grow in value over the next few years. If the value of the stock based on sales and earnings is not increasing, the price is unlikely to grow at the previous rate.

(a) (NYSE-XON) PRICE HISTORY

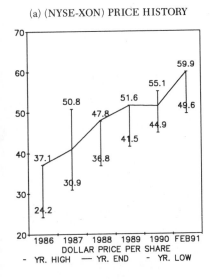

(b) ANNUAL SALES & EARNINGS

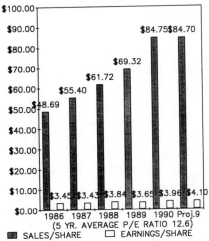

(c) ANNUAL DIVIDENDS

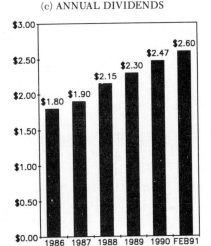

(d) GAIN IF SOLD AT YEAR END

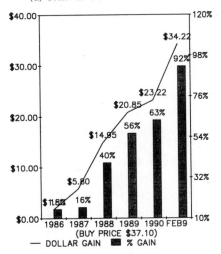

FIGURE 9.1 **Exxon**

As stated earlier, we don't necessarily want the highest earnings, but rather consistent earnings or a situation where an earnings difficulty appears to be improving and has had little or no effect on the price and dividend growth.

How Do These Companies Look on a Graph?

Now look at General Electric's numbers graphically, as shown in Figure 9.2(a)–(d).

A weakness in General Electric's sales occurs in 1988. It was an actual revenue drop of $.50 per share, below the 1987 level. Sales show some recovery for the following year, and the growth continues through the projected figures for 1991. It is also interesting to look at what happened with earnings. Earnings per share for 1988, the same year with the sales difficulty, still showed a $.55 per share increase. The weakness appears to have been resolved.

There was increased high-to-low price volatility in 1987 but the stock still closed the year with a gain. Although the stock does show some volatility year to year, it has an upward trend.

Dividend increases averaging 12.4 percent annually are impressive. The average increase is $.17 each year. The importance of dividend growth in a total return stock again recommends General Electric as a good candidate.

What Are the Historic Results?

The investor selling American Home Products, within the definitions of the model, would have earned $24.37 per share. The gain on General Electric would have been $29.87. Only a few days later, this would have changed. The point here is that it is not the day-to-day fluctuations we want to focus on with a total return objective, but rather the consistent pattern of growth. It is doubtful that any stock will ever show a perfect growth pattern, but we can compare the growth of one with another.

Now look at the graphic information on AHP (Figure 9.3(a)–(d)).

AHP Price Volatility

American Home Products shows a fairly steady amount of high-to-low price volatility. From a $7.75 high-to-low price fluctuation, in 1988, to as high as nearly $15, in the preceding year, is a

(a) (NYSE-GE) PRICE HISTORY

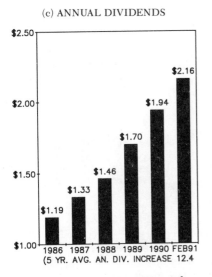

DOLLAR PRICE PER SHARE
- YR. HIGH — YR. END - YR. LOW

(b) ANNUAL SALES & EARNINGS

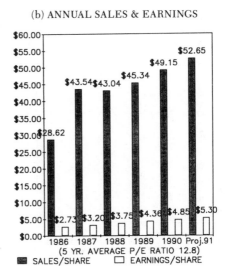

(5 YR. AVERAGE P/E RATIO 12.8)
■ SALES/SHARE □ EARNINGS/SHARE

(c) ANNUAL DIVIDENDS

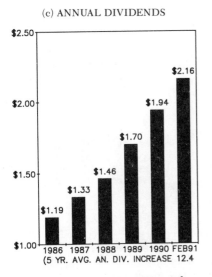

(5 YR. AVG. AN. DIV. INCREASE 12.4

(d) GAIN IF SOLD AT YEAR END

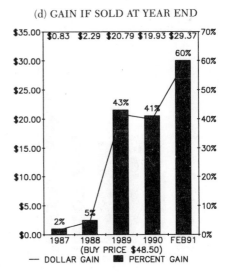

(BUY PRICE $48.50)
— DOLLAR GAIN ■ PERCENT GAIN

FIGURE 9.2 **General Electric**

considerable increase. This is probably related to the surge in income but a more modest increase in earnings. A $2.77 increase in sales led to a corresponding $.35 increase in earnings. Keep in mind that 1989 did show some volatility in the overall stock market with more than a 90-point drop in mid-October.

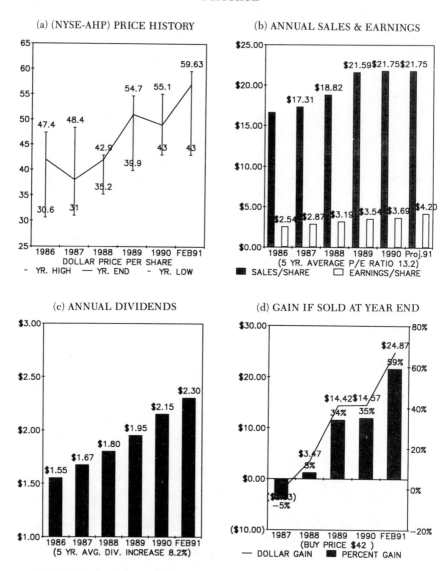

FIGURE 9.3 **American Home Products**

Sales Are a Real Concern

Sales are a bigger concern from 1989 to 1991, as they tend to go
flat with no increase expected in 1991. Notice that earnings for
1991 are projected to be nearly 14 percent higher. That is nicely
above the average of 9.2 percent and is a positive sign.

AHP's Dividend Is Growing

American Home Products shows a consistent yearly increase (8.2 percent average annual) in the dividend payment. The constancy of the dividend growth can be almost as important as the amount of increase. It is another sign of stability and the company's commitment to the dividend.

Although an investor purchasing the stock would have been disappointed in 1987, the next four years would have shown an excellent return on investment. An average annual total return of 11.8 percent is close enough to make American Home Products a good candidate.

American Home Products, Exxon, and General Electric Offer Equal Safety

In terms of safety, all the stocks are about equal at A+ or better in financial strength. The amount of debt at GE is 12 percent of capitalization (total worth), and there is some concern regarding

Table 9.5 *Stock Picks: Total Return*

Stock Picks: Total Return			Objective: 12%			
Funds: $100,000		Actual Cost: $90,063		Leaves: $9,937		
Final Selections Based on Research Analysis.						
	Current Data		5-Yr Data		Next 5 Years	
Stock Symbol	Price	P/E Ratio	P/E Ratio	Price Growth	Analyst Forecast	X = Selected Today
AHP	$57.000	15	13.2	11.8%	18.0%	X	3/1/91
Notes: Watch debt & sales growth				Buy: 500 shares = $28,500		
XON	$55.125	14	12.6	18.4%	9.0%	X	3/1/91
Notes: Watch sales & earnings				Buy: 500 shares = $27,563		
GE	$68.000	14	12.8	12.0%	22.0%	X	3/1/91
Notes: Look for weaker sales				Buy: 500 shares = $34,000		

AHP at 66 percent, although the A+ financial strength suggests it can manage that debt.

Exxon's total debt is $13.7 billion, nearly 7.7 billion of which is long term, making it a conservative 19 percent of market capitalization.

Look at Debt

As prices rise, the percentage of debt to capitalization decreases, so there will be fluctuations. A conservative rule is to consider only stocks whose debt is not more than 50 percent of market capitalization. Some other analysts believe that it's not the amount of debt, but rather the ability to service or make payments on the debt that is more important.

The difficulty here is trying to determine whether or not a company will be able to pay off loans in the next five years. Unless you are an accountant or analyst with access to all the relevant information, making such a determination is practically impossible. For most people, the company's ability to pay off debt is more of an opinion than a concrete fact.

Why Are IBM and AT&T Two Current Rejects?

Two current rejects for the total return objective are IBM and AT&T. Both stocks have run up in price without showing counterbalancing increases in earnings. It is better to wait until trend improvement can be observed than to gamble on its occurrence. Both are good, well-established companies and are likely to recover from the current earnings weakness, which make them better suited to our speculation objective. Speculation with larger company stocks is best accomplished at the lowest possible price in a recent trading range.

At the time this information was assembled, IBM was trading at relatively high prices, and AT&T was trading in a narrow range established in early February 1991. AT&T, which went from the high $20s to the high $30s, could climb back up to its pre-Gulf War mid-$40s range or drop back to the $29–$30 support level. Uncertainties in the market, the economy, and the company make this more of a speculative play.

IBM ran from about $115 a share to $140 and appears to have reversed direction, currently showing a lack of price stability. It could easily drop back to its old trading range between $100 and $110 a share.

AT&T Price Action

Figure 9.4 shows price action charts through April 1991; AT&T gained price strength while IBM fell back to its old trading range. Money could have been made on AT&T but lost on IBM. Whether the stocks are good buys at this point is still a matter of speculation. It will take improvement in the fundamentals of sales and earnings to make them good growth stock selections.

Diversification

Now that we are down to three stock picks, a question arises concerning diversification. Is the investment of $100,000 in three different industries and three companies diversified enough? While a bit more diversification is advisable, it is not essential. Remember these are three highly consistent, stable, and slow-growing companies. The main purpose of diversification is to protect your investments against severe damage from any one company that might be suffering severe financial reverses. Although these problems can still occur, they are unlikely with total return stocks. Diversification also has a negative effect in limiting the number of shares you can buy.

Ascertain Depth and Breadth

Effective investing calls for depth as well as breadth. Depth is the number of shares owned, and breadth is the diversification. Many good total return stocks are priced from $50 to more than a $100 a share. If you buy one hundred shares of stock at a hundred dollars a share, it is a $10,000 investment. If that stock suddenly rises 20 percent in price and you take the profit, you have earned

Selection

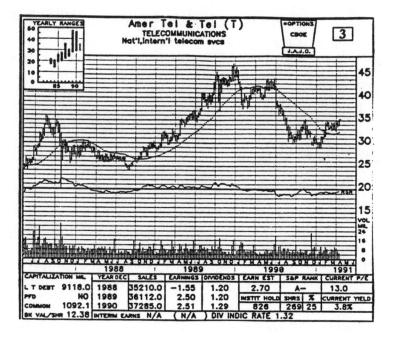

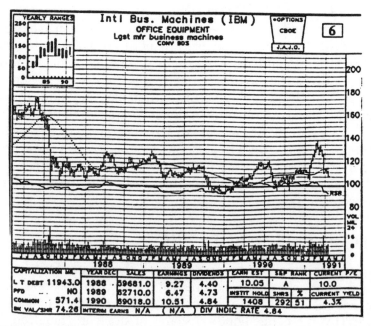

FIGURE 9.4   **AT&T and IBM** (Charts courtesy of Trendline, a division of
Standard & Poor's Corporation. *Current Market Perspectives,* April 1991,
pp. 30 and 134.)

$2,000—probably less than half that, after commissions. The profit picture is significantly improved if you own four or five hundred shares. Commissions, on a per hundred share basis, decline significantly.

Be careful that diversification doesn't create a portfolio of stock positions that are too thin to provide significant growth. Too much diversification can be just as damaging as no diversification. It is also important to keep in mind that diversification does absolutely nothing to protect the portfolio from market risk. Whether you own the stock of 3 companies or 10 companies, a decline in the stock market will likely have the same impact.

Summary

Total return stocks can be the ideal selection if you are looking for a combination of growth and income or if you desire to limit risk through the types of stock selected. Representing some of the largest companies in the world, these stocks tend to grow at slower rates than many growth or speculative stocks. They also tend to be more stable and consistent than other types of stock. The better stocks show consistency in sales and earnings growth as well as price and dividend growth. Even though they demonstrate consistency, they can also be highly volatile at times.

Because total return stocks tend to be market leaders, they often are the first to fall during a correction and the first to recover as the market stabilizes. Oftentimes, this represents selling by individual shareholders and eventual buying by institutional investors. The nervous money leaves and the smart money buys in, at bargain prices.

Determining growth potential of these stocks can be difficult. If the growth capability is obvious, the stock quickly can become overpriced in anticipation. Many may show poor growth for the preceding few years, but the opinion of analysts forecasts acceptable growth ahead. With others, it is just the opposite, good growth history but gloomy forecasts.

Analysis will not remove the necessity of making a judgment and a decision regarding the stock's future performance. Examination of the facts gives the investor a firm foundation with which to arrive at that decision, and the use of the Stock Selector simplifies and shortens the process.

Key Ideas

Selecting total return stocks—find the best dividends and growth.
Total return usually means slower growth.
Check the total return prospect list and narrow the list.
Calculate the total return.
Look at the relative price/earnings ratios.
General Electric—Examine five-year average sales growth.
American Home Products are close to our objective.
Exxon—Low projections invite caution.
How Do these companies look on a graph?
What are the historic results?
    —AHP shows price volatility.
    —Sales are a real concern.
    —AHP's dividend is growing.
AHP, Exxon, and GE offer equal safety.
Look at debt.
Ascertain depth and breadth.

Notes

1. *Value Line Investment Survey,* February 1, 1991, Analyst Thomas P. Au.
2. *Value Line Investment Survey,* April 5, 1991, Analyst Thomas P. Au.
3. *Value Line Investment Survey,* February 1, 1991, Analyst John E. Ferebee.

CHAPTER 10

Pay Me Frequently

Speculation Objective Specific Statement

I will invest $30,000 in stocks that are expected to increase in price more than 30 percent annually, over the next three years. Risk will be moderated by the amount of money invested, diversification into a minimum of three companies, and also by analysis and daily monitoring.

It is the nature of speculation stocks to have higher risk than other stock categories. As discussed in Chapter 5, it is important to understand the source of the risk. Is the stock, for example, a new company, with little or no information available, or is it about to be acquired by another company?

What Is the Speculative Situation?

Market damage	New company
New growth	Takeover
Turnaround	High dividend

Two of these speculation situations—new growth and turnarounds—are more directly involved with the company's growth fundamentals. The others certainly can be influenced by fundamentals but are more heavily impacted by difficult-to-measure anticipation factors. Our focus here will be on the growth factors.

In spite of the higher risk involved, some turnaround issues reveal better financial fundamentals than others. Although they may still be classified as speculation stocks, they may be gradually working their way up to becoming quality growth stocks.

Speculation Prospecting List

We have narrowed our prospect list (Table 10.1) to four stocks. Two of them (Amgen and Quantum Corp.) are new growth situations and the other two (Cray Research and Unisys) are turnarounds.

The Stock Selector for speculation stocks looks at information similar to that of growth stocks, with just a few differences. The main distinction is that we will look at growth on a year-to-year basis, rather than over an average five-year time frame. This will give a clearer picture of when the growth actually appeared.

Amgen

Several stock analysts and commentators have referred to Amgen as the "darling of Wall Street." A glance at the P/E ratio tells us that the stock has a lot of positive anticipation and also shows why P/E ratios become irrelevant with many speculation stocks. An

Table 10.1 *Prospect Selector: Speculation*

Prospect Selector: Speculation Objective: 30% Source: Financial News Information (*X means selected for further analysis*)								*Date: 2/28/91*
Types of Speculation: Market Damaged, New Company, New Growth, Takeover, Turnaround (& Cyclical), High Dividend, High Risk.								
					Price History			
Prospect Stock Name	*Symbol*	*Type of Speculation*	*X*	*Current Price $*	*Rank*	*$ High*	*$ Low*	*% Change*
Amgen	AMGN	New Growth	X	91.250	7	105	27	289
Cray Resch	CYR	Turnaround	X	41.250	6	51	20	155
Dekalb Gen	SEEDB	New Company		21.250	2	45	30	50
Ford Motor	F	TA-Cyclical		32.625	4	49	25	96
Gen Motors	GM	TA-Cyclical		39.500	5	51	30	70
Quantum	QNTM	New Growth	X	23.375	3	26	11	136
UAL Corp	UAL	Takeover		144.500	8	170	84	102
Unisys	UIS	Turnaround	X	4.375	1	17	2	750

average P/E of 41 and a current P/E of 113 is a big difference, but is 113 a good or bad P/E ratio and is 41 really any better? Some investors thought 41 was too high a price/earnings ratio and bailed out early. They missed out on most of the gain.

Some analysts would say that it will take years for Amgen's earnings to catch up with its current price. There is no doubt that a high P/E carries a lot of risk, but once it climbs to the heights, the P/E ratio becomes less and less relevant to stock analysis. The investors buying the high P/E ratios are anticipating higher earnings to fill the gap.

Amgen's History

To be fair to Amgen investors, let's look back to 1989, when the stock was trading with an average P/E of 43. At this time, investors bought the stock between $15.5 and $30 a share (see Figure 10.1(a)). If they held the stock until February 28, 1991 and sold at the close, they realized a gain of from 200 to more than 500 percent. What happened to Amgen that was so great? Sales per share went from just over $2.00 in 1988 to $5.46 in 1989. Earnings went from a deficit of 25 cents a share to a positive 56 cents. In 1990, earnings climbed to $1.60 a share and the price ran up even faster. Earnings for 1991 are projected at more than $2.00 a share and the price shows that a large number of investors believe they could be even better (see Figure 10.1(b)).

The price growth represents an annual average of more than 139 percent for five years. Breaking it out by year quickly shows where the main increase has been. The price growth has been consistently good for all five years but is exceptionally good in the past three years (1989 through February 1991; see Figure 10.1(c)).

Amgen's Interesting Sales and Earnings

Now look at the sales and earnings growth by year.

Sales Growth Great, Earnings Show Efficiency

Sales growth has been phenomenal, but the earnings growth shows some strong efficiency between 1989 and 1990, where

(a) (OTC-AMGN) PRICE HISTORY   (b) ANNUAL SALES & EARNINGS

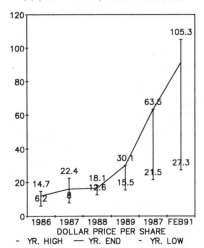
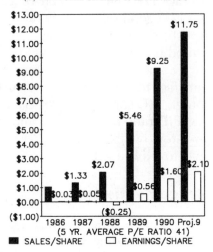

(c) GAIN IF SOLD AT YEAR END

FIGURE 10.1 **Amgen**

earnings increased more than sales. Here are some of the reasons
for the popularity of Amgen. The financial strength is rated a
B++, but the long-term debt is only 4 percent of capitalization.
This debt is based on a stock price of $74 a share. The financial
strength rating is lower than it would be for many stocks with low
long-term debt because of the extremely rapid growth in price
and earnings.

Table 10.2 *Speculation, Amgen (Detail)*

Stock Selector Date: 2/28/91		Objective: Speculation 30%		Research from Value Line					
		12-Month Prices			5-Year Price Growth				
Stock	*Current Price*	*High*	*Low*	*P/E Ratios 5 Yr Curr/Avg*	*1987 Year One*	*1988 Year Two*	*1989 Year Three*	*1990 Year Four*	*1991 Year Five*
AMGN	$91.250	$105	$27	113 41	33.0%	38.0%	150%	429%	694%

AMGN   Base Price = $12.000.

Incredible Price Growth

Amgen has had fairly steady price performance since 1988, when the high price for the year was just over $18 a share. There was a good increase from 1988 to 1989, where the stock price more

Table 10.3 *Stock Selector: Speculation, Amgen*

Stock Selector Date: 2/28/91		Objective: Speculation 30%		Research from *Value Line*					
		12-Month Prices			5-Year Price Growth				
Stock	*Current Price*	*High*	*Low*	*P/E Ratios 5-Yr Curr/Avg*	*Yr 1*	*Yr 2*	*Yr 3*	*Yr 4*	*Yr 5*
AMGN	$91.250	$105	$27	113 41	33.0%	38.0%	150%	429%	694%
5-Yr Sales Growth					5-Yr Price Growth				
Yr 1	*Yr 2*	*Yr 3*	*Yr 4*	*Yr 5*	*Yr 1*	*Yr 2*	*Yr 3*	*Yr 4*	*Yr 5*
27.0%	56.0%	64.0%	69.0%	27.0%	67.0%	0.0%	150%	186%	31.0%

Notes:
AMGN   Base Price = $12.000/State of the art biotechnology for pharmaceuticals/price appreciation due to red blood cell stimulator/new drugs coming/LT debt is 4% of capitalization/Financial Strength B++.

than doubled, (comparing the annual low to high). From 1989 to 1991 the stock took off on a steady upward climb. Notice that the sales and earnings graph shows a similar trend.

It is exciting to buy a stock at $12 a share and five years later see the price above the $100 level, but back in 1986–1987, there wasn't much reason to buy the stock. Sales were growing, but earnings didn't show any real progress until 1989, which means many investors wouldn't have purchased the stock until early 1990, at about $30 a share. Here we have a pure new growth situation: Sales more than doubled in 1989, and earnings went from negative to a positive 56 cents a share.

The positive changes attracted a flood of new investors who anticipated even higher earnings. Earnings nearly tripled in 1990, and the price more than doubled. The first two months of 1991 seem to be continuing the pattern in price increases, although earnings are projecting only a more modest 31 percent increase.

Anticipation Pushes the Price Up

So why does the price appear to be outgrowing the projected earnings increase in 1991? It's just that old anticipation. We know that the sudden growth from 1988 through 1990 came from the red blood cell stimulator, an important new product in health care. The company's announcement of the development of other such products has caused speculation investors, anticipating further earnings increases and price growth, to buy the stock.

Earnings projections usually don't reflect to-be-released products because estimating the earnings impact is difficult and many unforeseeable roadblocks can obstruct the release of a new product. It is anyone's guess how new product earnings will affect the picture. If one product caused earnings to triple in a year, we cannot know that a similar event will occur with the newer similar product. Many stock buyers are *speculating* that this will happen with Amgen.

Amgen's earnings are driven by new pharmaceutical products that have not withstood the challenge of time. Problems may be encountered that could adversely affect the stock's bottom line. Since that has not happened thus far, the outlook for the stock is fairly bright and will continue to be so as long as earnings have the ability to catch up to the soaring price.

Quantum Corporation

Now let's look at a new growth speculative situation in the computer industry.

Quantum Corporation is another company that has experienced rapid new growth. The modest average P/E ratio of 10.4, compared with the current 11, suggests that the price has not surged too far ahead of sales. Currently trading just a little bit higher, with a P/E ratio of 11, makes the current stock price quite attractive at $23.50 a share. So, what has been happening to the price of the stock?

The 12-month high and low show more than 140 percent price volatility; it is currently trading on the high side (see Figure 10.2). In a situation like this, some investors will mistakenly try to buy the stock near the 12-month low. If earnings were poor or declining significantly, this strategy might work; but if that were the case, why buy the stock? When earnings are good, it will be difficult to buy the stock at a price much lower than its current (2- or 3-month) trading high and low prices, unless something very unusual happens (such as market damage).

Good Earnings at Quantum

Earnings are definitely good at Quantum, with a better than 72 percent average annual growth. The stock also shows steady, strong sales growth of more than 60 percent annually. High-level customers such as Apple Computer and Sun Microsystems are a recommendation for the quality of the product. The financial strength of "A" is also good, especially in an industry as recession-sensitive as computer manufacturing. With little or no long-term debt, the company should be better able to withstand economic downturns. Quantum's narrow product line is a cause for concern.

What If They Lose Quality Customers?

What might happen if Apple Computer or Sun Microsystems starts buying its disk drives from another supplier? Cross-contracts like this are usually based on quality equipment, a reasonable price, and adequate supply. As long as Quantum is able to deliver, it will likely keep the contract; if it falters, serious earnings can be lost.

(a) (OTC-QNTM) PRICE HISTORY

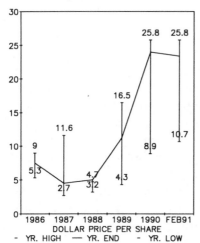

1986 1987 1988 1989 1990 FEB91
DOLLAR PRICE PER SHARE
- YR. HIGH — YR. END - YR. LOW

(b) ANNUAL SALES & EARNINGS

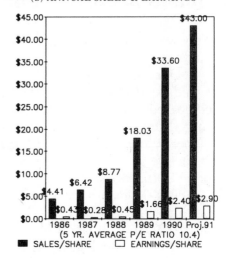

1986 1987 1988 1989 1990 Proj.91
(5 YR. AVERAGE P/E RATIO 10.4)
■ SALES/SHARE ☐ EARNINGS/SHARE

(c) GAIN IF SOLD AT YEAR END

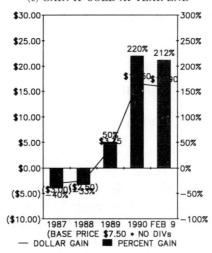

1987 1988 1989 1990 FEB 9
(BASE PRICE $7.50 * NO DIVs
— DOLLAR GAIN ■ PERCENT GAIN

FIGURE 10.2 **Quantum Corporation**

Although this is a valid question, these customers are also the source of future growth.

Price competition has been stiff in the computer industry. One of the fastest growth areas is in the low-cost personal computers. As long as Apple Computer does well in this market, Quantum should also do well. If Apple starts to have difficulties, it could wave a red flag at Quantum stockholders.

Table 10.4   *Stock Selector: Speculation, Quantum*

Stock Selector Date: 2/28/91	Objective: Speculation 30%			Research from *Value Line*					
		12-Month Prices			5-Year Price Growth				
Stock	Current Price	High	Low	P/E Ratios 5-Yr Curr/Avg	Yr 1	Yr 2	Yr 3	Yr 4	Yr 5
QNTM	$23.375	$26	$11	11 10	−40.0%	−33.0%	50.0%	220%	212%
5-Year Sales Growth					5-Year Price Growth				
Yr 1	Yr 2	Yr 3	Yr 4	Yr 5	Yr 1	Yr 2	Yr 3	Yr 4	Yr 5
46.0%	37.0%	106%	86.0%	28.0%	−35.0%	61.0%	269%	45.0%	21.0%
Notes: QNTM Base Price = $7.500.									

What Kind of Growth for Quantum?

Quantum's average annual earnings growth of 72.2 percent is obviously positive. Most of the growth occurred in 1989 when the company saw earnings increase by 262 percent, from $.45 a share to $1.66 a share. Earnings increases in 1990 and 1991 have been more modest, but still are 45 percent and 21 percent, respectively.

Strong earnings growth for the future will depend on Quantum sales staying strong. Quantum has shown a solid, steady track record in sales growth. Amgen and Quantum Corp. have experienced sudden increases in sales, earnings, and price. Now, look again at the full Stock Selector (Table 10.5) and view these companies in comparison with stocks that have had some difficulties with sales and earnings.

Compare the Growth of the Speculation Stocks

Table 10.6 shows some interesting facts in a comparison of the details. In this grouping, Quantum ranks as the most conservative speculation stock. If its present trends continue, Cray Research

Table 10.5   *Stock Selector: Speculation—All*

| Stock Selector Date: 2/28/91 | Objective: Speculation 30% | | | Research from *Value Line* | | | | |

		12-Month Prices			5-Year Price Growth				
Stock	*Current Price*	*High*	*Low*	*P/E Ratios 5-Yr Curr/Avg*	*Yr 1*	*Yr 2*	*Yr 3*	*Yr 4*	*Yr 5*
AMGN	$91.250	$105	$27	113 41	33.0%	38.0%	150%	429%	694%
QNTM	$23.375	$ 26	$11	11 10	−40%	−33%	50%	220%	212%
UIS	$ 2.000	$ 3	$ 1	11.5 12	25.0%	11.0%	−38%	−82%	−81%
CYR	$41.250	$ 51	$20	11 15	−2%	−21%	−50%	−80%	−48%

5-Year Sales Growth					5-Year Price Growth				
Yr 1	*Yr 2*	*Yr 3*	*Yr 4*	*Yr 5*	*Yr 1*	*Yr 2*	*Yr 3*	*Yr 4*	*Yr 5*
27.0%	56.0%	64.0%	69.0%	27.0%	67.0%	0.0%	150%	186%	31.0%
46.0%	37.0%	106%	86.0%	28.0%	−35%	61.0%	269%	45.0%	21.0%
43.0%	−6%	−13%	51.0%	1.0%	0.0%	0.0%	0.0%	94.0%	0.0%
13.0%	9.0%	15.0%	4.0%	11.0%	17.0%	7.0%	−40%	33.0%	6.0%

Notes:
AMGN   Base Price = $12.00/State of the art biotechnology for pharmaceuticals/price appreciation due to red blood cell stimulator/new drugs coming/L.T.debt is 4% of capitalization/Financial Strength B++

QNTM   Base Price = $7.50/Designs, manufactures and markets high capacity rigid disk drives/Winchester technology/zero L.T. debt/Financial Strength A/Supplies disk drive for Sun & Apple big demand on low end Mac

UIS   Base Price = $2.875/Unisys faces an uncertain future/long term also unclear/L.T. debt is 42% of capitalization/pfd stock 25% of cap/Financial Strength C/". . . the equity has wide price recovery potential to mid-decade."

CYR   Base Price = $80.250/Mfg. large, high-speed computers/weak world economies are a negative/L.T. debt 15% of capitalization/Financial Str. B++ Outlook better for mid-decade/Sale of one unit can alter income.

Table 10.6   *Growth, Earnings, Strength*

Stock	*Avg. 5-Yr Price Growth*	*Avg. 5-Yr Sales Growth*	*Avg. 5-Yr Earnings Growth*	*Current Financial Strength*
AMGEN	138.8%	48.6%	68.0%	B++
QUANTUM	42.4	60.6	72.2	A
CRAY RSC	−9.8	10.4	4.6	B++
UNISYS	−18.6	15.2	22.9	C

can be a good turnaround selection. Both Cray and Unisys are fine companies, but both must recover somewhat to bring their prices back up to former levels.

Cray Research

As we look at Figure 10.3(a)–(c), showing the fundamentals for Cray Research, we see a few positive signs. The price appears to have bottomed and is moving slightly upward. Annual sales are continuing to increase and earnings are showing signs of recovery. With earnings up 33 percent in 1990 and projected to be up another 6 percent in 1991, growth appears to be returning. The price was down 19 percent in 1990, but some of this could have been attributed to the bear market. The price shows good recovery in early 1991, up 28 percent by the end of February.

If we had bought Cray Research at the end of 1986 for $80 a share and still held the stock, we could have had a long wait to break even. But in 1991, the speculation investor looking for the turnaround point may have found it.

Unisys

Be particularly careful when a company has an extreme setback in the fundamentals, such as happened with Unisys (see Figure 10.4(a)–(c)). Percentages can become deceptive (either positively or negatively) when the numbers are extraordinarily low. Average numbers can easily hide problems. The analysis will be more accurate if actual annual numbers are examined.

Although we have attempted to average negative growth numbers, it is unnecessary, especially with price growth and earnings. Negative earnings are generally just counted as a zero, until they become positive.

The caution does not necessarily eliminate a stock such as Unisys as an investment. Some speculation investors actually prefer stocks with weak fundamentals, especially if the price is low yet the product line is well established. The risk is greater, but the reward can also be. A prudent approach can be to wait for the sales and earnings to recover and then consider purchasing the

(a) (NYSE-CYR) PRICE HISTORY

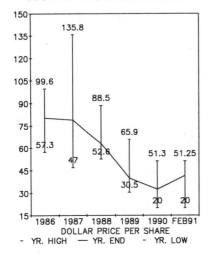

DOLLAR PRICE PER SHARE
- YR. HIGH — YR. END - YR. LOW

(b) ANNUAL SALES & EARNINGS

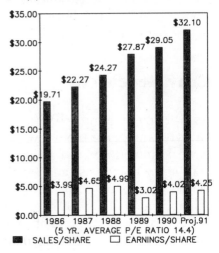

(5 YR. AVERAGE P/E RATIO 14.4)
■ SALES/SHARE □ EARNINGS/SHARE

(c) GAIN IF SOLD AT YEAR END

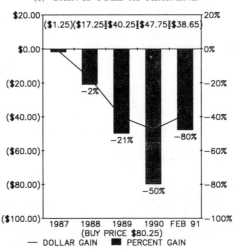

(BUY PRICE $80.25)
— DOLLAR GAIN ■ PERCENT GAIN

FIGURE 10.3 **Cray Research**

stock, even though it probably will be at a considerably higher price.

Unisys prices have declined, the sales have fallen, and earnings have dissolved into losses two years in a row. At this point, there is little in the fundamentals to answer two crucial questions:

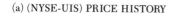

(a) (NYSE-UIS) PRICE HISTORY

(b) ANNUAL SALES & EARNINGS

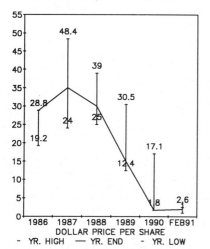

48.4

39

30.5

28.8

24

25

19.2

17.1

12.4

1.8 2.6
.1

1986 1987 1988 1989 1990 FEB91
DOLLAR PRICE PER SHARE
- YR. HIGH   — YR. END   - YR. LOW

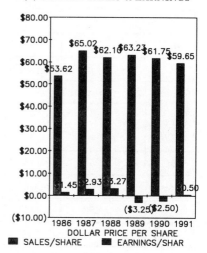

$80.00

$70.00

$65.02
$62.16 $63.23 $61.75
$59.65

$60.00
$53.62

$50.00

$40.00

$30.00

$20.00

$10.00

1.45 2.93 3.27   0.50

$0.00

($3.25)($2.50)

($10.00)
1986 1987 1988 1989 1990 1991
DOLLAR PRICE PER SHARE
■ SALES/SHARE   ■ EARNINGS/SHAR

(c) GAIN IF SOLD AT YEAR END

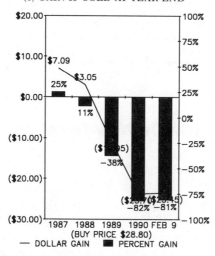

$20.00   100%

                                   75%

$10.00 $7.09
                                   50%
          3.05
    25%
$0.00   25%

    11%   0%

($10.00)

            ($ 5)   −25%
            −38%
                                   −50%
($20.00)

                                   −75%
         ($ .7)($. 5)
           −82% −81%
($30.00)
        1987 1988 1989 1990 FEB 9   −100%
           (BUY PRICE $28.80)
         — DOLLAR GAIN   ■ PERCENT GAIN

FIGURE 10.4 **Unisys Corporation**

Where is the bottom, and will Unisys recover from these difficult times? Even as a turnaround, this is a highly speculative stock. If the company shows the positive earnings projected for 1991, the picture could improve. But, at this point, everything suggests a lack of all-important growth.

Table 10.7 *Stock Picks: Speculation*

Stock Picks: Speculation				Objective: 30%			
Funds: $30,000		Actual Cost: $27,050			Leaves: $2,950		
Final Selection Based on Research Analysis.							
		Current Data		5-Yr Data		Next 5 Years	
Stock Symbol	Price	P/E Ratio	P/E Ratio	Price Growth	Analyst Forecast	X = Selected	Today
AMGN	$91.250	113	41	68.0%	27.0%	X	3/1/91
Notes: Watch new product impact.				Buy: 200 shares = $18,250			
CYR	$41.250	11	14.5	4.6%	29.0%	X	3/1/91
Notes: Watch for new sales.				Buy: 100 shares = $4,125			
QNTM	$23.375	11	10.4	72.2%	40.0%	X	3/1/91
Notes: Watch Apple Computer sales.				Buy: 200 shares = $4,675			
UIS	$ 2.000	NA	11.5	22.9%	75.0%		3/1/91
Notes: Look for stabilization.				Buy: None at this time.			0

Good Potential in New Growth

Either Amgen or Quantum could be a good new growth pick.
Both have strong fundamentals and potential areas of weakness.
Amgen might develop problems with its main product and suddenly run into sales and earnings difficulties. Quantum is ham-
strung by a single product that it sells to one big customer. The
competition could come along and take the customer away. These
kinds of questions give the speculation category its name and test
the investor's tolerance for risk.

Cray Is a Turnaround

Cray Research is a turnaround selection. The number one concern
with Cray is that it is primarily a one-product company; the sale
of one system, however, can significantly affect the bottom line.

Unisys *could* become a turnaround situation, but at this point does not appear to be making the turn.

We have selected these stocks, based on facts, financial data information, knowledge of where the growth was in the past and will likely come from in the future. With these speculation stocks, we anticipate a high rate of return. New developments and consequent price reactions happen quickly, so these investments must be constantly monitored.

Summary

A speculation stock is primarily a growth stock with greater volatility in the fundamentals. A good speculation stock favors the volatility if the numbers are rising, rather than falling. Speculative stocks can be found with hardly any volatility, low fundamentals, and very little trading activity. Such stocks may have a closing trade one day on the bid and appear to be down a half dollar. The next day, the stock might have the final trade on the offer and appear to be up a half dollar. These stocks need to be approached with great caution. There are usually definite reasons why investors don't like the stocks. In many ways, it is better to have too much buying and selling action in a stock than to have nearly no action at all.

Key Ideas

What is the speculative situation?
—Market damage
—New growth
—Turnaround
—New company
—Takeover
—High dividend
Amgen: A look at Amgen's history.
—Amgen's interesting sales and earnings.
—Sales growth great, earnings show efficiency.

—Incredible price growth.

—Anticipation pushes the price up.

Quantum Corporation:

—Good earnings at Quantum.

—What if they lose quality customers?

—What kind of growth for Quantum?

Compare the growth of the speculation stocks.

Good potential in new growth—Cray is a turnaround.

Notes

1. *Value Line Investment Survey*, February 8, 1991, Analyst Keith A. Markey.

2. *Value Line Investment Survey*, February 8, 1991, Analyst Keith A. Markey.

3. *Value Line Investment Survey*, February 1, 1991, Analyst George A. Niemond.

4. *Value Line Investment Survey*, February 1, 1991, Analyst George A. Niemond.

5. *Value Line Investment Survey*, February 1, 1991, Analyst George A. Niemond.

PART THREE

The Market

It is necessary for the investor to understand some basics of how the market moves. It can be disappointing to spend time analyzing stocks, find a perfect selection, and buy a block of shares just before the stock market falls on its face. That "perfect" stock can suddenly follow the rest of the market down. Although market risk is part of stock investing, even a small amount of analysis and understanding can help the investor avoid disappointments. So far, no one has been able to consistently predict market tops or bottoms. The reason is simple: You don't know you're there until it's past.

Predictable understanding of the market is impossible. Even though an investor may see various trends with their strong points and weak areas, an overriding event can come unexpectedly and turn the market with short notice.

Still, an understanding of the current strength of the stock market can work to your advantage. Is the market advancing steadily, breaking through old resistance points, or is it about to fall to the first major support level? Part Three will examine some market basics.

CHAPTER 11

Sizing Up the Market

The stock market is influenced by both fundamental and technical factors. It is crowd psychology at its best. If the fundamentals of low interest rates and good corporate earnings are in evidence, combined with a technically advancing market, the uptrend is strong and likely to continue. When the confidence falters, the market corrects and begins to fall.

Because it is so difficult to see a market reversal approaching, we will look at some factors that are known to have an effect on its progress. Some of these elements will be technical, such as *support* or *resistance*, whereas others will be more fundamental, such as earnings and interest rates. The analysis will not attempt to predict the market, but simply try to understand what it is doing now, and determine its weaknesses and strengths.

Which Market Are We Talking About?

When most investors talk about "the market," they are referring to the Dow Jones Industrial Average, a list of 30 industrial stocks that are believed to be representative of the entire stock market. The indicator is a simple average, which has had several modifications in the past one hundred years.

Dow Averages Have Had Many Changes

Many companies have been deleted from the original list and new ones have been added; the only company remaining on the list since the beginning is General Electric. Numerous stock splits have occurred through the years and have been compensated for by use of a special devisor.

For many years, a debate has raged about whether the Dow Average method of calculation is precise, and whether it represents the full scope of the market. Many investors believe that it would be more useful if more stocks were on the list, and argue that a calculation should be added to include the number of shares. The result would be a weighted index.

The Standard & Poor's 500 Is a Stock Index

In 1967, the Standard & Poor's Corporation assembled a stock index of 500 companies weighted by the number of shares. Many investors use the list as an indicator and also as a benchmark for portfolio analysis because it represents a broader range of stocks.

Whether you use the Dow Averages or the S&P Indexes is a matter of individual preference. Many articles have been written in praise or criticism of both. Some investors follow both, using the Dow Averages as an indicator of larger capitalization companies and the S&P 500 Index as an indicator of the broader market. If you compare the two systems on a graph (see Figure 11.1), the differences are often insignificant.

The comparison of the two indicators shows only one major difference. The up-and-down volatility of the S&P 500 Index appears to be less than the activity of the Dow. The six-month period shows a similar uptrend in both averages. If we increase the volatility in the S&P 500 Index by changing the scale, the indicators look even more similar (see Figure 11.2).

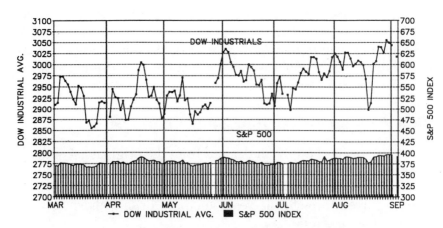

FIGURE 11.1 **Dow Industrial Average versus S&P 500 Index**

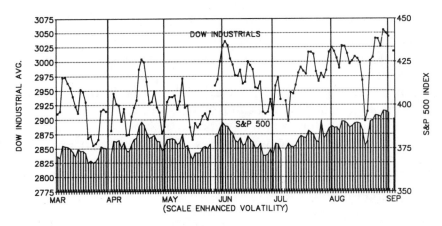

FIGURE 11.2 **Dow Industrial Average versus S&P 500 Index**

Notice the Patterns

Enhancing the volatility of the two indicators shows patterns with many similarities; in fact, it is difficult to find many differences. It is a simple matter to track both, using the Dow as a large cap narrow indicator and the S&P Index as a broad market indicator. Tracking both gives a more complete picture of the stock market.

Analyzing the Market

The great trick in analyzing the market is to understand what events can create a favorable environment for selling or buying stock. To know the events is not enough, the key is to comprehend how these events relate to the present. Even this understanding is further complicated by the market's anticipation of the future or its more immediate reaction to the here and now. The following sections describe some common influences on the market.

Corrections, When the Market Weakens

If the stock market encounters an unexpected economic crisis, real or imagined, a sudden sell will likely occur. During a sharp correction, many large institutional investors[1] can be quick to sell, pushing the market even lower.

Many factors can cause corrections. A U.S. Treasury bond auction may have had difficulty finding buyers, which increases interest rates until sufficient buyers are attracted to the auction. Increasing interest rates mean lower corporate earnings, which in turn cause stock selling. A market drop can be triggered by a report of an economic indicator being lower than expected. Surprises frequently create overreactions. In another situation, arbitrage might occur, in which futures are more attractively priced than the individual stock. Institutional traders will sell the stock and buy the futures, creating waves of selling, in turn dropping the market to lower levels.

Institutional Investors Have an Impact

Institutional investors wield great power in the stock market. Computerized, programmed trading is often their specialty, and it enables them to trade large quantities of stocks in a moment. The computers can be buying one minute and selling the next, and those computers have been blamed for much of the market volatility in the past few years. New restrictions have moderated the activity, but the institutional stock trader still has a strong impact on day-to-day trading.

Institutions can also be hesitant to buy no matter how bright and rosy the next six months look. This often creates a slow market, up a few points one day and down slightly the next. Slow doesn't necessarily mean weak; there is often a great deal of strength in a slow market. Dull markets only mean there are few sellers and not many buyers, which is usually reflected in lower than average volume. If the dull market is weak, it will soon be dropping and anything but dull.

Dividend Capture Is a Real Event

If the slow trend continues, institutions will begin buying up stock near the end of the dividend qualifying period (*EX date*) and selling the stock a few days later. The technique, referred to as *dividend capture*, is most effective when large quantities of stock are purchased. Although the individual investor can take advantage of the price fluctuations caused by the strategy, profits from a dividend capture strategy on a small scale can easily be eaten away by commissions or a subsequent drop in price. If the investor is aware of the existence of dividend capture plays on a stock being held, a profitable strategy could be to wait until the day before the EX date with a profit-taking sell order.

The great secret about institutional investors is that they are frequently wrong in anticipating future economic conditions. These incorrect assessments can create market volatility. Rapid market fluctuations illustrate the tendency of institutional stock traders to act quickly, even though their economic conclusions are imprecise. It is a "shoot first and ask questions later" kind of mentality. They want either to lighten the load of stocks currently held or to see just how far the market can be pushed.

Pushing the market down does two things for institutional investors. It shows or tests the strength of the current support level and provides stocks at bargain prices. When you're an institution trading tens of thousands of shares, short-term profits of a half dollar, quarter, or even less per share can be worthwhile. Institutional investors have an important advantage by being able to adjust quickly and make profits from smaller market changes. They can also afford to lose large sums of money over the short term, as long as they make them up in the longer term.

Most individuals will do better not trying to outguess many actions of the institutional investors. Although it is prudent to take advantage of market swings, don't wait too long, for it is more important to select investments for financially sound reasons than for institutional orchestrations.

Extended market trends of about three months to a year in length are more important than most daily movements. Longer term trends are how the market adjusts to the reality of economic developments. Some would call this the *efficient market theory,* meaning that stock prices eventually adjust to their true value. From time to time, this efficiency is probably true, but anticipation and overreactions of the buyers and sellers cancel out much of this efficiency.

Fundamental Analysis Is the Heart of Basics

Fundamental analysis of the stock market refers to the technique of looking at earnings, interest rates, and the general direction of the economy over the next six months to a year. The first two create the condition of the third; higher corporate earnings and lower interest rates create a better outlook for economic development. When the market is interested in a stock, the price of that stock is strongly influenced by changes in earnings or the anticipation of earnings.

Find Earnings Reports in Financial Newspapers

Reports of corporate earnings on individual companies appear daily in the financial newspapers. The information can be useful for tracking the progress of an individual company or observing earnings changes in some of the larger corporations. Unusual developments in earnings will often receive news coverage. If a major corporation has a strong change in its earnings, it likely will receive prominent coverage, directly affecting the price of the company involved and sending a ripple of activity throughout the entire stock market.

It is difficult to base specific trades on newspaper stories since much of the action has probably already occurred, but keeping an eye on what's happening with corporate earnings in general can help the investor better understand the current market actions.

Corporate Earnings Reports Are Issued Regularly

Quarterly corporate earnings reports come out on the traditional three-month schedule starting in January. Others may not start in January but use the same quarterly structure. Because of this reporting structure, business analysis is based on three-month figures starting with January. The analysis gives importance to the months of April, July, October, and January, when the reports are actually released.

Interest Rates Give or Take Strength to a Trend

Current interest rates also are important to the strength and direction of the stock market. Interest rate changes will make the news if they are significant or if the *prime rate* or *federal discount rate* are changed. The prime rate refers to the interest charged by commercial banks to their best customers. Changes in the prime rate also impact other interest rates, including rates for mortgages, car loans, and consumer loans. The prime rate is heavily influenced by changes in the federal discount rate. This is the rate "the Fed" charges when banks borrow funds to meet cash reserve requirements.

The federal discount rate can be changed at any time although changes tend to be infrequent. This rate should not be confused with the federal funds rate, which is the rate charged by banks when they lend money to each other. The federal funds rate is not directly controlled, but can be influenced by, the Fed. Fed funds interest rates change every day, and at times can be at quite different levels than the federal discount rate.

Figure 11.3 shows the track of the federal discount rate from 9 percent in 1984, to 5 percent in 1991. The ½ percent raise in 1987 was cited as being a major factor in the market crash. Even so, the rate was moved up even farther to 7 percent through 1989 and much of 1990. The bear market and recession that began in 1990 were enough concern to cause the Fed to begin lowering the rate to fuel economic recovery.

The Federal Discount Rate: Manipulation with a Purpose

The manipulation of the federal discount rate represents an attempt to prevent or moderate inflationary spirals by raising the rate, or to stimulate the economy out of a recession by lowering the rate. The ideal situation is for the discount rate to be moved before either an inflationary or recessionary period begins, thereby keeping the economy steady in its growth rate. As with many economic controls, the process often isn't quite that simple or efficient.

The stock market and the economy have a tendency to overreact to changes in the discount rate. The infamous crash of 1987 was believed to be an overreaction to a rise in the discount rate from 5.5 percent to 6 percent in September. If the rate is changed too early, the action can worsen the situation it was intended to help, such as increasing inflation or deepening a recession.

Day-to-day interest rates can also be influenced by the periodic auction sales of U.S. Treasury bonds, notes and bills. If the

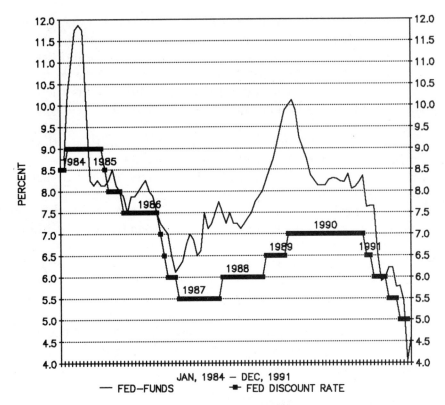

FIGURE 11.3   **The Federal Funds Rate and Federal Discount Rate**

auction is not going well, prices of the bonds or notes or bills are lowered, raising their effective interest rates. The auction results influence the Federal funds (Fed funds) rate and the stock market reacts to the information.

Fed Funds Rate Is Different, but Related

Interest rates are constantly changing during the business day. The easiest rate to track on a daily basis is the federal funds rate. The closing rate appears in the business news each day. To observe its impact on the stock market, it is necessary to study the rate by looking at a graph, as shown in Figure 11.3.

Compare the Interest Rates

In 1989, when the federal discount rate was 6.5 percent Fed funds were running above 10 percent and climbing. The discount rate then leveled off at 7 percent. Fed funds drifted back down and stabilized at about 8.25 percent, and at this point, the two rates began to parallel each other. In October 1990, Fed funds were beginning to accelerate just as the federal discount rate was lowered by a half percent. In 1991, the discount rate continued to be lowered and the federal funds rate followed the decline. The surprise in this graph is back in early 1989, when interest rates were rising and the Dow Industrial Average was also in an upward direction. The reason for this phenomenon is that these short-term interest rates are only part of the picture. Longer term interest rates were less volatile and the economy was growing. Dropping interest rates gave strength to the stock market, and it again rose to new highs.

To observe the more recent movement of the market in relation to Fed funds, look at Figure 11.4, which shows the daily closing levels of each.

Fed Funds Rate and Dow Industrials

Figure 11.4 compares the Fed funds rate with the daily closing of the Dow Industrial Average from April 1990 through June 1991. It is easy to see that the Fed funds rate dropped about a quarter of a percent just as the Dow Industrials approach the 3000 point barrier in July. The drop was not enough to give confidence to investors in the stock market. Also, the economy faced a new crisis when Iraq invaded Kuwait. The Dow began to drift lower and was classified a bear market. In mid-October, the Fed began to exert pressure to force interest rates down. The Fed funds rate began to drop, and in December the federal discount rate was again lowered.

Fed funds went to 8 percent, 7.5 percent and nearly down to 7 percent in December. The lowered rates had an obvious positive impact on the stock market. In the middle of October, the bear market turned into a bull and the market resumed its climb. The lowering of the discount rate caused Fed funds to drop even lower and the stock market to resume its climb up to the 3000 level.

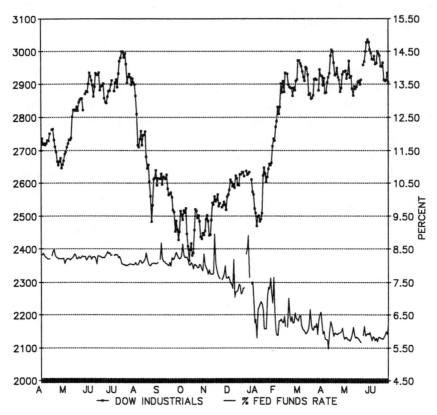

FIGURE 11.4 **Dow Industrial Average versus the Federal Funds Rate**

Leading Indicators of the Strength of the Economy

In-depth fundamental studies look at the factors that have a direct effect on economic direction. A study of these factors looks at the Index of 11 Leading Economic Indicators:

1. Average weekly hours paid to production or nonsupervisory workers in manufacturing.
2. Average weekly claims for Unemployment Insurance (inversely related).

3. New orders for consumer goods and materials in 1982 dollars.

4. Index of 500 common stock prices.

5. Contracts and orders for new plant and equipment in 1982 dollars.

6. Index of new private housing starts.

7. Percentage of purchasing agents in greater Chicago area who experience slower deliveries in current month.

8. Index of consumer expectations.

9. Change in manufacturer's unfilled orders for the durable goods industry.

10. Change in index of 28 sensitive materials prices.

11. Money supply (M2 in 1982 dollars).[2]

The composite of this list will often be referred to in the news as "The Government List of Leading Economic Indicators" or the "Index of Leading Economic Indicators." Most news reports also will discuss specific areas within the list that are showing dramatic changes. The government report on these indicators is released monthly.

The report on leading economic indicators can affect the stock market if the changes from one month to the next are large enough.

Fundamental Analysis Summary

This is a brief look at some of the important factors used in a fundamental analysis of the stock market. It is also possible to calculate and follow earnings or P/E ratios of one or more of the stock market indexes. Information of this nature is available on the Dow Averages as well as the Standard & Poor's 500 Index. Although such information can give some insight into the fundamental strength of the market, it often is difficult to forecast from such figures. Just keeping up with the changes in corporate earnings, interest rates, and economic indicators will give the investor some perception of the strength or weakness of the current trend in the stock market.

Technical Analysis

What's the Trend?

The main idea behind technical trading is that the stock market and individual stocks move in trends. When charted on a graph, these trends show patterns that many people believe indicate signals of strength or weakness in the direction of the stock market, or with individual stocks. The technical stock trader takes advantage of the signals from the market and stock trends, then tries to buy the stock on weakness and sell at the peak of strength.

Purist technical stock traders follow only the price trends or market levels and their signals, and do not consider the fundamentals of earnings, interest rates, or economic trends. In fact, they often will state that they do not want to be "confused" by fundamental information. The major difficulty with this approach is the frequent disagreement on interpreting the signals.

Technical Analysts Can Be Wrong, Too

Many technical traders missed the crash of 1987 and the major correction of 1989. The signals were there although many analysts debated their meaning and chose not to believe their warnings.

Many other investors saw weakness developing in the market fundamentals. They noticed the interest rates creeping up, especially the short-term rates. This started in early spring. Another major interest rate surge came in August, when the federal discount rate was raised. The Dow Industrial Average hit its peak in late August and made the turn. It was already down several hundred points when the crash of October 19 took the market by "surprise." Apparently, the technical analysts also were ignoring a few signals.

Both Fundamental and Technical Analysis Can Be Useful

It is possible to benefit both from technical and fundamental analysis. Many stock traders use technical analysis, with fundamentals in mind, to examine the overall market and then base specific stock investment decisions on fundamentals. Even Charles Dow spoke of both technical and fundamental approaches to the stock market, back in 1902.

Charles Dow's Theory of Market Trends

Charles Dow created technical analysis with his origination of the Dow Jones Industrial Average and Railroad Average (now called the Transportation Average) to reflect current trends of the stock market. In some of his early writings, which appeared in the "Review and Outlook" section of *The Wall Street Journal,* Dow spoke of trends of the stock market as suggesting future events. One of his favorite sayings was ". . . the present is always moving toward the future." His views were refined and enhanced by later *Journal* editors, primarily William Hamilton. The approach was eventually called "The Dow theory."

An investor can follow fundamental, technical, and Dow theory analysis to the letter or choose certain elements from each to learn about strength and weakness in the stock market. A feel for what the market is doing and might do next, based on analysis, helps the investor look at the stock market from the viewpoint of anticipation.

The Dow theory of market analysis does not apply to individual stocks. The main concepts of the Dow theory are trend classification, confirmation, and the view that stocks tend to move as a group.

Trend Classification into Different Types

Primary Trend is the main direction of the market. It is usually measured in months and years, although a Primary Trend move can be almost any time frame.

Secondary Trend is the shorter term trend of the market, which runs contrary to the primary trend. It is usually measured in days and weeks, and occasionally in months.

Tertiary Trend is the day-to-day fluctuations of the stock market.

Trend Confirmation—One Average Follows the Other

Trend confirmation refers to the primary and secondary trends of the Dow Industrial and Transportation Averages. The theory says that the two averages must have a similarity of direction. When confirmation exists, it is signaling strength to the current primary trend. If both averages turn together, it is a strong signal of a change in the primary trend. Divergence, in which one average makes a move and the other does not follow, is a signal of weakness in the move.

If the Dow Industrials have moved up 100 points over the past month and the Transportation Average has dropped 20 points, it is a signal of weakness in the market. Eventually one of the averages will turn to join the direction of the other.

Knowledge of market trend classification and confirmation can help the individual investor analyze the strength of the market in a general way. A glance at the price charts in the financial newspapers can quickly give the investor some idea of the direction and strength of the stock market.

Stock Prices Move as a Group

This is the one concept agreed on by stock market analysts. There can always be individual stock exceptions, but as a general rule stock prices move as a group (in addition to their individual price movements). If the Industrial Average moves up 50 or 60 points in a day, most of the stocks traded during that day, will also be up.

Price trading ranges that show the current main trend, resistance, and support can be helpful to timing a stock purchase or sell.

Resistance—No One Wants to Buy More

The price high, which the stock price just can't seem to break through, so it begins to drop. This can be looked at either for the short term (past few days or weeks) or the longer term (a year).

Support—No One Wants to Sell More

At the price low, the price of the stock stops falling, and buyers begin to push the price back up to former levels. This can be looked at for the short or longer term. Figure 11.5 illustrates the concepts of support and resistance.

The *main trend* is the price trend of a stock during the past 44 days. In Figure 11.6, the somewhat unrealistic prices are added merely as a reference to illustrate a main trend.

From these graphs, we can tell that the movement of the stock has been upward for the past 44 days, even though it has shown periods of advancing and declining.

Another aspect of technical analysis would involve drawing a straight line from the lowest low (the asterisk) to the highest low (asterisk).

Connect the lowest high numeral sign to the highest high numeral sign; this forms a trading "channel" that gives a somewhat clearer picture of where the stock is going.

A logical approach can be to draw a line from the lowest low (@) to the highest high (@) and see where the stock has been trading relative to this line (see Figure 11.7) This procedure shows

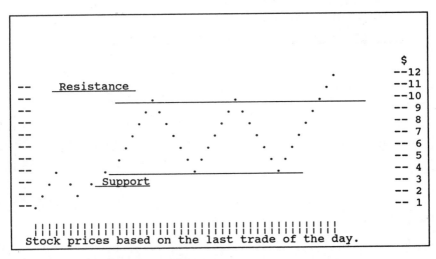

FIGURE 11.5 **Support and Resistance**

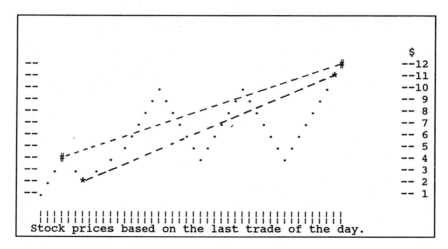

FIGURE 11.6 **The Main Price Trend**

where the stock has progressed in the past 44 days and where it stands in relation to the main trend. This type of line is called an *internal trendline.*

Whether the investor takes the time to draw the lines or just looks at a price graph to see what the trend is doing is not as important as the observation. In the majority of situations, anyone can see a trend just by looking. Areas of support and resistance

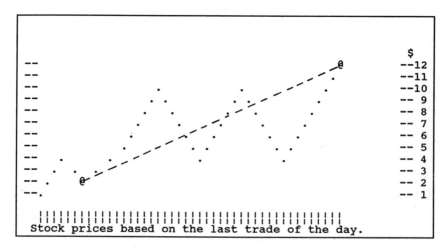

FIGURE 11.7 **Internal Trendline**

are usually quite evident. Looking and understanding are what matter most.

A limited amount of technical analysis of individual stocks can be an advantage, but too much analysis or attempts to predict price movements too closely can cause missed opportunities and disappointment. Choosing a good stock is more important than tight timing of the buy or sell.

Hit-and-Run Analysis

Hit-and-run analysis is used by both sophisticated and beginning investors. It has the advantage of quick action and the disadvantage of higher risk. The investor hopes to make a significant profit in a short period of time.

This form of analysis involves a short look at information on the market and an individual stock. It might be a stock recommended in the newspaper or in a magazine. The investor reads the article, checks what the market is doing, and if favorable conditions exist, places an order to buy.

They Act on Assumptions

Hit-and-run investors must assume that the conclusions in the news article are correct and that there still is time to get in on the stock move. Another assumption is that other investors will read the same article and take a similar action. The final assumption is that the hit-and-run analyst will be able to sell and take a profit before everyone else does.

Hit-and-Run Analysis Is Often Hit and Miss

Hit-and-run analysis is discussed here because thousands of individual investors consistently use this approach. Sometimes, they are able to take advantage of a stock move, and turn a quick profit. Other times, the stock either does nothing or drops in price.

Some fast-action investors do well. They only have to be right about half the time to be profitable. Their "talent" lies in the decisiveness of their actions. They approach the stock market knowing that they will make money on some stocks and lose money on others.

They see the information, decide how much risk to take (in terms of dollar size of the order), and make their move. If the situation fails to develop as expected, they sell and get out of the stock; they do not depend on hopes and wishes to pull them through a bad stock purchase. Conversely, they do not fall in love with a stock that has just made them a profit. They take the profit and move on to the next opportunity.

Lack of emotion in making or losing money is the strength of the hit-and-run analytical approach. The ability to decide quickly and make the buy or sell without getting bound up in worries is this investor's greatest strength.

The weakness to a hit-and-run approach is the damage it can do to the investor's money. Hit-and-run analysis investors tend to be attracted to the stock market near the high and use a simple strategy of "buy high and sell higher." The strategy works until the market decides to make a secondary correction.

Beginner's Luck Makes It Worse

Early successes can contribute to the problem. When a hit-and-run investor begins to pick stocks for the short-term profit success, a feeling of *I can do not wrong* occurs. Successes often will continue as long as the market is moving upward.

The number of shares in each transaction begins to increase, putting larger sums of money at risk. The focus tends to tighten to one or two stocks at a time. These are often high-flying stocks that are vulnerable to market swings. The market suddenly enters a secondary correction phase, but this investor makes no adjustment. The losses mount until this unemotional investor begins to get nervous. If an investor starts with $20,000 and now has $10,000 left, it becomes difficult to continue putting more money at risk.

Just as the market secondary correction hits bottom and turns up to continue the primary trend, the inexperienced hit-and-run analyst has often pulled to the sidelines. At this point, the investor either believes that the market is headed for doom or that understanding it is impossible. Thus, just when this investor should be getting back into the market, he or she sits on the sidelines frustrated and confused. Confidence might return, but probably not until the market begins to reach new highs.

If an investor has the ability to buy and sell stocks, taking profits and losses without allowing emotions to control the activity, the hit-and-run strategy can be effective.

The overwhelming disadvantages can be the lack of understanding of primary and secondary market cycles and the total lack of individual stock analysis. Nevertheless, investors who develop a cold, logical approach with enough market and individual stock analysis can take advantage of this approach.

Key Ideas

Which market are we talking about?

—Dow Averages have had many changes.

—The Standard & Poor's 500 is a stock index.

—Notice the patterns.

Analyze the market:

—Corrections occur when the market weakens.

—Institutional investors have an impact.

—Dividend capture is a real event.

Fundamental analysis is the heart of basics:

—Find earnings reports in financial newspapers.

—Corporate earnings reports are issued regularly.

—Interest rates give or take strength to a trend.

—The federal discount rate represents manipulation with purpose.

—Fed funds rate is different but related.

—Compare the interest rates.

—Compare the Fed funds rate and Dow Industrials.

—Study the leading indicators of the strength of the economy.

Technical analysis

—What's the trend?

—Technical analysts can be wrong, too.

Both fundamental and technical analysis can be useful:

—Charles Dow's theory of market trends.

—Trends are classified into different types.

—Trend confirmation—one average follows the other.

—Stock prices move as a group.

—Resistance—no one wants to buy more.

—Support—no one wants to sell more.

Hit-and-run analysis:

—They act on assumptions.

—Hit-and-run analysis is often hit-and-miss.

—Beginner's luck makes it worse.

Notes

1. These include managers of large stock portfolios for corporations, pension funds, insurance companies, mutual funds.

2. *Source: Business Conditions Digest 1990,* U.S. Department of Commerce, Bureau of Economic Analysis.

CHAPTER 12

Analysis of Bulls and Bears

Strength Is an Upward Direction—Buyers and Sellers Determine the Prices

Think of strength as the ability of advancing market to continue its current trend. A weak market is hesitating to advance or is declining. Trends and the strength of trends can be observed in many ways, but the source of strength comes from the balance between buyers and sellers of stock.

Stock prices and the stock market rise because of many factors, but the mechanics of rising prices is based on just one activity: There are more buyers of stock than sellers. Most investors buy on anticipation—the belief that corporate earnings will continue to increase. When corporate earnings increase, additional buyers come to the market and stock prices rise even higher. This is why most stock prices tend to move as a group.

Market Strength

Market strength, that is, the momentum behind the current market trend, can be assessed by analyzing various technical (trend analysis) and/or fundamental (earnings analysis) indicators. For example, moderate to high volume is normally associated with a strong upward moving market. A decrease in the market trading volume can signal growing weakness.

Fundamental market strength can be estimated by the earnings reports coming from the corporations. Strength can be deceptive at times, but it is usually more easily determined than high and low market fluctuations.

An investor can also learn about market strength through a study of market trend analysis. It is possible to understand the current market just by mastering some of the basics of trend analysis. Learning about primary and secondary trends can give an investor information about the strength or weakness of the market. Primary market trends are described as bull or bear markets.

Riding the Bull Market Up

A *bull market* is a period when most stock prices are rising. The primary trend is upward, not for just a day or a few weeks, but rather for at least three months.

Historically, bull markets fall into three distinct phases. The first is a steady uptrend among the market leaders, the large capitalization companies. The second phase has a broader-based growth, extending to a large number of different stocks. The third phase shows buying with wild abandonment and is punctuated by periods of volatility and "buying frenzy" that continue to push the market to new highs.

An Extended Phase

Figure 12.1 shows the progress of the bull market of 1988–1990. Many market analysts say that this period represented part of an extended second phase (since 1982) and that the bull market never reached the third stage of buying frenzy. This is confirmed by the halt in the advance of the Transportation Average. The bull market here appears to have ceased at the October correction.

Dow Industrial and Transport Averages

Figure 12.2 shows the daily closing levels of the Dow Jones Industrial Average and Transportation Average for three years (July 1988–July 1991). The primary uptrend in 1988 and through most of 1989 is easy to see in this graph, as the two averages are moving in concert. Then in October 1989, a strange thing occurs. The Dow Transportation Average experiences a sudden powerful surge

FIGURE 12.1 **Primary Bull Market**

that is only partially experienced by the Industrial Average. This reflects the takeover attempt on UAL Corp. (United Airlines); later, on October 13, 1989, the financing on the buyout was turned down.

Anatomy of a Correction

A bull market will continue as long as there is a predominant belief that corporate earnings will be better in the near future (six months to a year) than they are at the present. Anything, real or imagined, that threatens the anticipation of corporate earnings

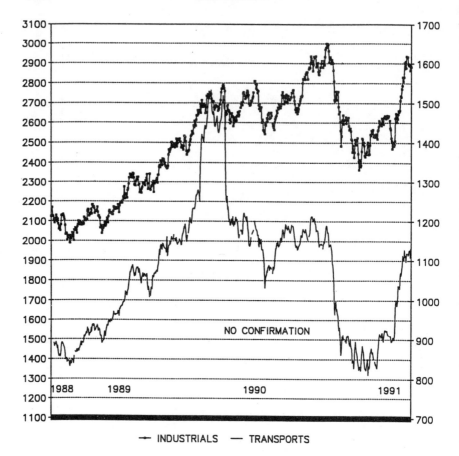

FIGURE 12.2 **Dow Industrial and Transportation Averages**

can stop the advance of a bull market. Many times, this halt is only temporary; after a modest decline, the market again begins its climb. At other times, the interruption can be lengthier.

Enthusiasm Gets Ahead

Buying enthusiasm can cause stock market prices to run ahead of conservative anticipation, and this can create a sudden upswing in prices followed by a severe market decline known as a *correction*. Stock market corrections can be as short as a single day, a few days, or longer. If the market drop continues for a few days or weeks, it will eventually be called a secondary trend. As long as the economic outlook remains strong and corporate earnings continue to improve, the bull market will return. Periods of correction and secondary downtrends also can be marked by volatility with wide up-and-down price fluctuations.

Friday, October 13, 1989 a Difficult Day

A closer look at the correction of October 13, 1989, reveals some interesting facts. As shown in Figure 12.3(a), the Dow Industrials had been drifting lower since Labor Day. In the later weeks of September, the Industrials formed a technical double bottom, confirmed by the Transportation Average. Double bottoms are perceived as a signal of strength and will often be followed by a rally. The rally itself was more than 100 points, from just under 2700 to slightly over 2800 on the Dow. The Transportation Average confirmed the rally, but a weakness signal appeared in the total New York Stock Exchange volume (Figure 12.3(b)).

Low Rally Volume

The volume showed only a small increase during the rally; in fact, it dropped below 100 million shares at the peak. Low volume on market advances is a signal of weakness in the stock market. It means the number of buyers has declined and also that the broad market is not likely participating in the runup. Combine this technical weakness with fundamental bad news and the correction can be severe.

On the day before the correction, nothing much was happening. The Dow Industrials were showing a minor decline, but nothing to get excited about. The Transportation Average and Utility Average (Figure 12.4(a)–(b)) were both up just a small amount. Total volume on the New York Stock Exchange was running about average.

A Quiet Day

News stories the following Monday indicated that many professional money managers left work early due to the quietness of the market and the fact that it was a sunny afternoon. Friday was

(a) INDUSTRIAL & TRANSPORTTION AVG.

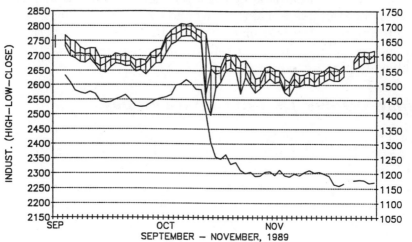

SEPTEMBER — NOVEMBER, 1989

(b) NYSE TOTAL DAILY VOLUME

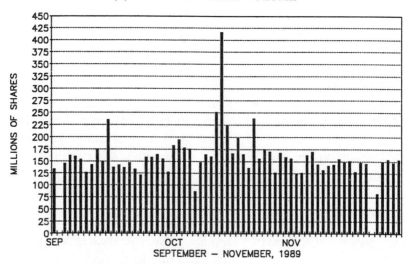

SEPTEMBER — NOVEMBER, 1989

FIGURE 12.3   **Anatomy of a Correction**

(a) DOW INDUSTRIAL & TRANSPORTATION AVG.

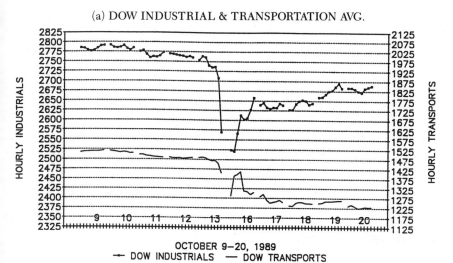

OCTOBER 9–20, 1989
—▪— DOW INDUSTRIALS — DOW TRANSPORTS

(b) DOW UTILITY AVG. & NYSE VOLUME

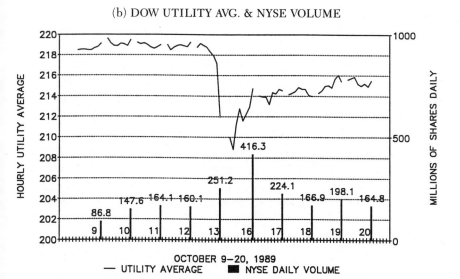

OCTOBER 9–20, 1989
— UTILITY AVERAGE ■ NYSE DAILY VOLUME

FIGURE 12.4 **Anatomy of a Correction—Hourly Averages**

business as usual up to the final trading hour. Then, according to one of the floor traders, ". . . all hell broke loose."

Sudden and severe selling began in earnest. All three averages dropped in an almost free-fall manner. Volume suddenly shot up, closing Friday the 13th with total volume of 251 million shares traded, more than 100 million in the last hour. Stock market "circuit breakers" put in place after the 1987 crash failed to modify the plunge. Several NYSE stocks, among them UAL Corporation, AMR Corporation, BankAmerica, Walt Disney, Philip Morris, and Pacific Telesis, stopped trading due to order imbalances and did not resume until the following Monday. When the quantities of buy-and-sell orders become severely out of proportion to each other, trading can halted to attempt a reestablishment. This is part of the reason that all three Dow Averages show *gap openings,* at which the opening levels on Monday are significantly lower than at the close on Friday.

Nearly a 200-Point Drop in One Day

The Dow Industrial Average dropped more than 190 points on that one day, a sharp correction. The Transportation Average dropped only 78 points but continued downward for the next week. Five days later, it was down 186.48 points before leveling off. It is interesting to note that the bubble in the Transportation Average ended at nearly the same level it began, when the UAL buyout was first announced.

The Industrials quickly resumed their advance, while the Transports remained in a rather narrow range in what appears to be below the correction level. The picture is deceptive because the bubble in the Transportation Average was caused primarily by one stock.

The buyout offer on the UAL stock nearly tripled its asking price. That Friday the 13th brought an announcement that loans for the takeover were not approved. This obviously caused the price of UAL Corp. to decline but also sent a signal of a possible tight money future to the rest of the financial community. Tight money generally means higher interest rates, and the market reacted accordingly. The Industrial Average apparently overreacted, as it showed by a short time of fluctuation (consolidation) before resuming an upward primary trend.

The Aftermath of Correction

The following Monday was more encouraging for the Industrial and Utility Averages. By the end of the trading day, they had regained more than 50 percent of the Friday sell off. The Transportation Average recovered in the first three hours of trading but fell back for the remainder of the day, largely due to the declining price of UAL.

The setback in Transports was felt by the Industrials, but only for a short time. The Industrial Average renewed its climb to another new high. Notice that the Transportation average significantly slowed its advance at this point. Remember, stocks tend to move as a group. If there is a divergence in the averages, it is considered to be a signal of weakness in the market advance. Industrials closed just under the 3000-point barrier in mid-July 1990, at the exact same level for two consecutive days.

It Turned on a Dime

After the Industrial Average achieved a new high, things began to change. Both Dow Averages turned on a dime and began to drop. A few days later, Kuwait was invaded by Iraq, and the turn in the primary trend continued to push the averages into a bear market and the economy into a recession.

These times of high volatility can be difficult for the individual investor who becomes frustrated by stock prices that rise a few dollars one day, only to fall back the next. Additional frustration comes from the fact that a *secondary downtrend* eventually can become a bear market trend (see Figure 12.5).

A secondary trend is a market trend running contrary to the primary bull or bear trend. It may last a few days or a few weeks, and it can be the beginning of a turn in the primary trend. Secondary trends can be frustrating to investors because they are so difficult to distinguish from turns in the primary trends. One of the main differentiating characteristics of a secondary trend is volume.

If a bull market begins to slow and sell off for a few days with declining total volume, it is likely a secondary trend. Using the same principle, if the market has been declining for several weeks and suddenly begins to rally on lighter total volume, the rally is probably a secondary trend.

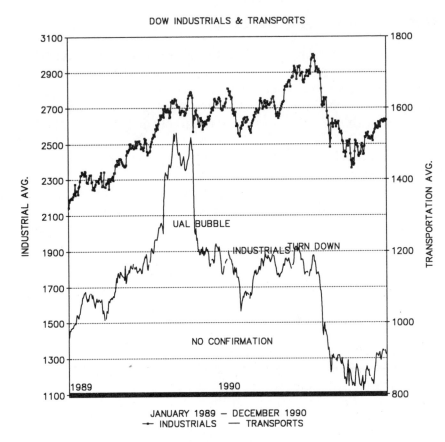

DOW INDUSTRIALS & TRANSPORTS

FIGURE 12.5 **Long-Term Market Averages**

The volume indicator by itself is not absolute. Checking other indicators, such as the advances versus declines or new highs and new lows, can help to confirm the strength of any market move. Another good backup to indicators is to find news information on what is happening to weaken the market.

The Frightened Bear Market

Figure 12.6 shows the movement of the stock market in 1990 from April to mid-October. The two secondary trends illustrated are both on declining volume. The downtrend in late April was

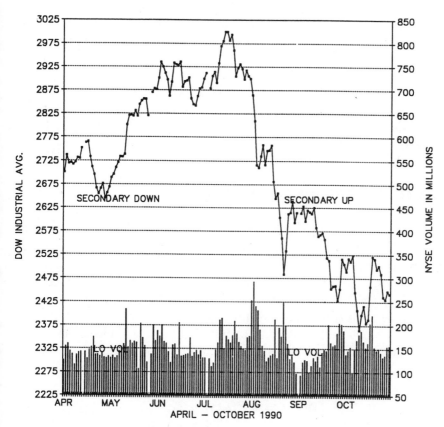

FIGURE 12.6 **Secondary Trends**

followed by a strong rally in May and part of June. Volume surged with the rally, not on the downtrend.

The market peaked near the 3000-point level and began to drop on increasing volume. The increasing volume and the uncertainty created by the Kuwait invasion strongly suggested that this was more than just a secondary trend. The market continued to drop until mid-August, when a significant rally occurred.

Look at the volume on the August rally—it is again declining. Rallies are difficult to sustain with lower than average or declining volume because they lack momentum on the buy side and eventually run out of stock buyers. Even a later, shorter term, secondary uptrend also is on lowered volume.

Business news and NYSE volume can be useful in providing information about and indicating a secondary trend. Although secondary trends can cause the investor concern, they should not be so alarming as to generate an overreaction. They are capable of becoming a turn in the primary trend, but in most cases they do not. Investors should be patient with secondary trends to see how they develop. Think of them more as a caution signal rather than a sign to hurriedly buy or sell.

Hunting the Bear for Profits

A *bear market* is a period of time when most stocks are dropping in price, and the primary trend is downward. Prices fall because there are more sellers than buyers of stock.

There are many definitions of a bear market, but it is generally described as a 20 percent or more reduction or a decline lasting more than three months in the Dow Jones Industrial Average. Some bear markets are more pronounced or more clearly defined than others. A well-defined bear market will generally have three phases.

The Bear Has Different Phases

In the first phase, distribution begins to outweigh accumulation. The market shows increased volatility with heavier volume on days the market is dropping.

The second phase is either a slow- or fast-selling episode leading to a certain amount of panic. The market tends to drop the greatest amount in this phase.

The third phase occurs when the market is near bottom although it can still experience further declines. In this phase, the market will often experience brief rallies but then will fall back. It will last as long as the economic news continues to be negative.

A One-Day Bear Market

On October 19, 1987, the Dow Industrial Average fell 508 points in one day. That represented a 22.61 percent decline and by definition was a bear market. Others will define a bear market as a two-month, or longer, period of time when most stocks are dropping in price.

Since 1946, there have been 10 bear markets, and most were accompanied by a recession. The average length of a bear market is 17.7 months. The longest bear was May 1946 through June 1949, for a total of 37 months. The shortest was August 1987 through December 1987.

Bear Markets since World War II

1.	May 1946 through June 1949	37 months
2.	August 1956 through October 1957	14
3.	August 1959 through June 1962	34
4.	February 1966 through October 1966*	8
5.	November 1968 through May 1970	18
6.	January 1973 through October 1974	22
7.	September 1976 through March 1978*	18
8.	November 1980 through August 1982	21
9.	August 1987 through December 1987*	5
10.	July 1990 through October 1990	3

(* Bear markets with no recession.)

From July to mid-October 1990, the Dow Industrials dropped more than 600 points, more than 22 percent in a little more than three months. It was not a textbook bear market, as it did not go through the traditional phases, and it just barely made the basic definition.

Figure 12.7 shows that the market sell-off was slow and orderly. It did not have the "panic selling" phase shown in previous times, such as the more than 500-point drop in 1987.

When the Sellers Appear

Sellers appear in a bear market, anticipating lower corporate earnings. The selling will continue until investors believe the stock prices are more in line with the present earnings situation and future potential.

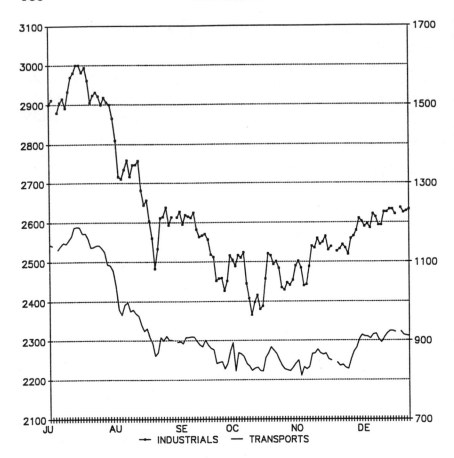

FIGURE 12.7   **Primary Bear Market**

As anticipation in the bull market example causes the market occasionally to get ahead of itself, overskepticism sometimes will cause a bear market to sell off too quickly. When this happens, the bear market can make a sharp drop, then experience a rally. Bear market rallies are quite common and, as illustrated previously, can become a secondary trend. On Figure 12.7, we see several rallies and at least one well-defined secondary uptrend during September. This is the same secondary trend discussed earlier. Historically, there are more bear market rallies than bull market corrections.

The terms bull and bear have been used to describe rising and falling markets for many years. The traits of the two animals have been applied to the actions of investors as well as the markets. The bull is aggressive, moving forward, seldom giving ground. The bear will often run to the woods and hide. Also, the bear market can eat up profits as the stock prices fall. Both the bull or the bear can be strong at times and weak in other situations.

A Charging Bull and the Retreating Bear

While the bull market is nearly always charging forward, seldom giving ground, the bear market has many investors selling their stock and putting the funds into temporary, more conservative investments.[1] Their aim is to prevent the bear from quickly eating up all the profits. As the market continues to drop, these investors will look for new buying opportunities.

Taking Advantage of a Bull or Bear

Taking advantage of the bull or bear market should be based on the current market situation, rather than on a future possibility. In other words, avoid trying to predict what the stock market will do in the future. The lengths of bull and bear trends are difficult to forecast. An investor who sets a strategy of waiting for the next bear market could wait several years, and miss out on many profit opportunities. Many investors missed out on the market advance from the end of 1987 to mid-1990 because of predictions that the bear market would go lower, when actually it had turned up.

A Time to Buy Stock

An ideal time to buy stock is when a bear market nears its bottom. Buy when prices are low, but gaining strength.

The next best times to buy stock are during a bull market correction, when the stock market suddenly drops after several advances, or during a secondary downtrend as the market is drifting lower but also showing some signals of strength, in technical levels of support, growing volume on up days, positive moves in so-called *bellwether*[2] stocks, or a positive fundamental economic outlook.

A Time to Sell Stock

The best time to sell stock is as soon as possible after a turn in the bull market trend, when the stock market is continuing to show weakness. This downturn is often a difficult judgment call, because of the anticipation and optimism that helped to create the bull market.

The 1990 Bull Peak

As shown in Figure 12.8, the bull market peak of 1990 did not occur until July, even though there had been little positive economic news all year. Corporate earnings were disappointing, the savings and loan crisis was beginning to spill over into the banks, and other problems were beginning to appear. Many analysts were announcing the beginning of a bear market two and three months before the

FIGURE 12.8 **Dow Industrial and Transportation Averages**

top. Buying enthusiasm, fueled by earnings anticipation, pushed the Dow Jones Industrial Average all the way up to the 3000-point level.[3] The move was exciting at the time, but the Dow Industrial Average has since far exceeded the 3000-point level.

Obviously, it is better to sell early than to wait for either a 20 percent decline or three months of steadily declining prices. Waiting to decide whether or not the market has turned can be expensive.

The second best time to sell stocks is during a market rally. There is a tendency for more short rallies (prices moving up) in a bear market than there are short corrections (prices moving down) in a bull market. Selling into a rally is nearly always a good strategy.

These are just a few market trend considerations for buying and selling stock. Investors can improve their profit potential by learning the basics about the market and forming a strategy based on analysis of the current situation.

Planning a Market Strategy

Ask Questions

In planning market strategy, the investor must analyze and identify the current market trend. Answer the question: "What is the market doing now?"

Is the primary trend bull or bear? Is there a secondary trend in effect? Is the market showing signs of strength or weakness?

Make a Market Statement

After the market question is answered, formulate a market statement describing the current trend and strength of the market. Then make a list of possible strategies for action as shown in Table 12.1.

The statements and strategies in Table 12.1 are merely examples. There can be any number of approaches to a given situation. The important thing is that the investor analyzes and writes down a statement of the market trend and strength, then decides on a strategy for action.

Table 12.1 *Market Statements and Strategies*

Market Statement
The market is in a prolonged bull market trend.

Strategy

1. Look for signs of weakness and prepare to sell (conservative).
2. Look for a secondary market correction and a buying opportunity (aggressive).

The market is showing weakness.

1. Sell stock positions. Move funds to Money Market until the stock market shows signs of strength (conservative).
2. Hold stock, but buy protective put options (conservative).
3. Take profits, on the next rally (aggressive).
4. Sell short (aggressive).

The bear market is showing further weakness.

1. Wait for buying opportunities (conservative).
2. Buy on a further sharp drop and take advantage of recovery rally (aggressive).

The investment market strategy should be based on the current primary trends—bull or bear—or secondary trends of the stock market. These long- and short-term trends are easily observed in the charts appearing in the financial newspapers, such as *The Wall Street Journal,* the *New York Times* or *Investor's Business Daily.*

Stock market charts also appear in many daily newspapers. Current trends are relatively easy to observe; turning points are often illusive.

Key Ideas

Strength is an upward direction—Buyers and sellers determine the prices.

There are several ways to assess market strength.

Ride the bull market up:

—An extended phase.

—Dow Industrial and Transport Averages.

Anatomy of a correction:

—Enthusiasm gets ahead.

—Friday, October 13, 1989, a difficult day.

—Low rally volume.

—A quiet day.

—Nearly a 200-point drop in one day.

—The aftermath of correction.

—A turn on a dime.

Learn how the frightened bear market reacts.

Hunt the bear for profits:

—Different phases of the bear.

—A one-day bear market.

—When the sellers appear.

The bull charges and the bear retreats:

—Taking advantage of a bull or bear.

—A time to buy stock.

—The 1990 bull peak.

Plan a market strategy:

—Ask questions.

—Make a market statement.

Notes

1. The cash might be put into money market funds, U.S. Treasury bills and bonds or conservative utility stocks. When this cash movement is heavy, it will cause the prices of these investments to rise, an action referred to as a "flight to quality."

2. *Bellwether* is a term used to describe the stocks of some of the largest companies such as IBM, General Motors, or AT&T. Many investors believe that these stocks lead the direction of the entire stock market.

3. The Dow Jones Industrials closed at a level of 2999.75 on July 16 and again on July 17, 1990. The Dow went above the record 3000 level, but closed just a quarter of a point below. Many saw this as significant resistance.

CHAPTER 13

Putting Risk in Its Place

All of us have the capacity to accept risk in our lives. But, the race car driver and the schoolteacher will likely have different reactions to risk. The airline pilot accepts and deals with risk in a different way than the computer analyst.

The stock market always has an element of risk. Even though we must accept some risk, investing should never be the same as gambling. Gambling is wagering money on a random selection. Investing requires study, planning, and understanding, as well as a businesslike approach to be successful. Investing is the acceptance of a calculated risk based on reasonable fundamental or technical information about the stock and the current market.

Dealing with Risk

Investors can handle risk with acceptance, avoidance, or a combination of both. Acceptance of risk usually takes the least amount of planning time. Acceptance should not replace analysis and planning. The investor merely determines the risk, accepts it, and proceeds with the strategy.

The second method for dealing with risk, avoidance, attempts to evade, modify, and limit the risk. There are many ways to avoid risk in the stock market. It can be partly avoided by investing in stocks that appear to have lower risk, based on the analysis. Risk can also be modified with hedging maneuvers, by the quantity of shares purchased, protective sell orders, and diversification of shares owned.

Find Stocks with Lower Risk

Lower risk stocks tend to be well-established, widely known companies that are leaders in their industry. They often are stocks that pay some dividend and have a history of earnings and price increases year after year. These companies frequently will have little or manageable long-term debt. In fact, in highly competitive industries, they can be companies with little or no long-term debt. The risk-aversive investor needs to consider such leaders of industry.

Use Strategies to Modify Risk

Strategies such as *hedging* help modify risk. Hedging strategies can involve using contrary investing, stock options, or other options and diversification (asset allocation).

Contrary Hedging

An example of contrary hedging would be an investment in the stocks of oil companies, say 500 shares of Chevron or Exxon, with the belief that oil prices will rise.

Oil prices are often difficult to forecast. The price of oil might begin to drop, and this would cause the price of the stocks to decline. As a contrary hedge, the investor could also buy 100 or 200 shares of a good automobile manufacturer, such as Ford or General Motors.

Since the stock prices of car manufacturers generally run contrary to oil company stock prices, the risk will be hedged. If oil prices remain stable and the economy grows steadily, both oil and automobile stocks likely will do well.

Options Hedges

Used with understanding, options also can be a hedge on an investment position. Buying *puts* can provide protection against a drop in the stocks price, much like buying insurance against a loss. The purchased put will allow the investor to sell the stock at a predetermined price for a set period of time.

The only risk is the money paid, the *premium*, for the put. The investor might buy a put that allows a sale of 100 shares of

Ford Motor stock at $30 a share for the next three months (depending on the actual put expiration date).[1] This effectively guarantees a minimum sell price for the stock during the life of the option. The two disadvantages to buying a put are cost (the premium paid) and the limited time for the life of the option.

Covered Calls

The most conservative option strategy is to sell *covered calls*[2] on the stock currently owned. This strategy sells someone else the right to buy the stock at a set price in a specific period of time. The stock owner receives cash (the premium) for selling the option.

For example, an investor owns 500 shares of Ford Motor Company at a purchase price of $26 a share. Ford is currently at $27 a share. The investor sells five covered call contracts (for 500 shares) at a "strike price"[3] of $30 a share.

The investor is selling someone else the right to buy the stock at $30, no matter what the current market price might be. The market stock price might go to $35 or $40, but the investor only receives $30 per share if the stock is purchased by someone else (*called away*). In compensation for selling this option, the investor receives $1 per share premium, for a total of $500.

The option will expire in three months. If the option expires without being exercised (the stock is not bought away), the option contract becomes worthless and the covered call seller gets to keep the $500 premium.

If the market stock price stays below the $30 level, the option will expire without the stock being called away. The call buyer has no reason to call the stock at $30 a share if it can be purchased at the market for a lower price. The original investor still has the 500 shares of Ford and an additional $500 for selling the option.

If the stock price of Ford drops lower, the investor effectively has $1 per share (total $500) protection, since the cash has been received for selling the covered call. This means the stock price would have to drop below $25 per share before the investor begins to have any loss.

Original stock price per share   = $26
 - Option premium received   = $ 1
Stock break-even price, with decline = $25

The investor has hedged a purchase of 500 shares of Ford $1 a share. If the stock price rises and the stock is called at $30 there will be a profit of $5 per share.

Stock sold (called away) at   = $30
+ Option premium received   = $ 1
 - Original stock price per share   = $26
= Total profit per share $ 5
= Total profit ($5 × 500 shares) $2,500/19%

Risk hedging obviously requires planning, but many investors believe it is worth the additional work. The number premium shown here is a realistic example. Actual premiums depend on current market conditions.

Planning, which makes use of specific objectives and set strategies, can also help to limit risk. When the investor follows a clear plan, it becomes easier to decide whether or not a particular stock will fit into the portfolio.

Acceptance and avoidance are key factors in dealing with stock market risk. To achieve objectives, accept a certain amount of risk, avoid the excessive risk, and plan the strategy to limit or contain the risk.

Dealing with risk is a matter of degree. All investing contains some element of risk. Even the U.S. Treasury bond (considered to be the lowest risk) has the relatively minor risk of missing out on a higher interest rate when held to maturity.

Protective Measures Can Help

The following sections describe four helpful policies: careful analysis, diversification, use of stops, and option protection.

Careful Analysis

The best protective measure in the stock market is careful analysis and selection. Taking some time to analyze the strength of the market and learn the financial status of the stock selected will help the investor select stocks that have a reasonable chance for success. Be a good stock picker and choose stocks for financially sound reasons. Growth in earnings, growth in price, and manageable debt are the three best recommendations a stock can provide.

Diversification

Diversification can be defined as investing in companies of different industries or different subgroupings of the same general industry. Whereas computers is a general industry sector, software, disk drives, or network systems would be subgroupings. The food industry is a general sector that can be divided into groups of restaurants, processors, and suppliers.

The most protective diversification is to invest in different industries. Computers, food, defense, automobiles, and insurance are different industry groupings. Investing in companies from each of the five, at the same time, will provide the investor with some protection from weak financial times in any one specific industry.

Buying stock in different subgroupings of the same industry will also provide a level of protection, but not as much as the general industry grouping. Diversification can also be established simply by buying the stock of more than one company, even in the same industry or subgrouping. This approach will provide more protection than investing in only one company.

Investment diversification can be a strong form of protection for an investment portfolio. It is a version of the old idea, "Don't put all your eggs in one basket." Investment advisers and mutual funds base most of their approach on the idea of safety through diversification. They have, in fact, created an entire industry with that approach.

Diversification is low-maintenance protection. The maintenance is handled automatically by regular stock analysis and portfolio adjustments. The strength of its protection comes from spreading the risk among different industries. But it has one key weakness. Diversification will do nothing to protect an investor's portfolio from a severe stock market decline.

Remember, stocks tend to move as a group. If most of the stocks traded are dropping in price, diversification will not prevent or lessen the decline of an investor's portfolio. The best an investor can hope for is to see the market weakness approaching and take more specific protective measures.

Careful, Specific Use of Stops

Stop orders for exchange-traded stock can be used as a specific protection against a price decline of individual stocks. A stop order (also called a stop loss order) will automatically sell a stock when the preset stop price is traded on or through. Stop orders cannot be used on over-the-counter (OTC) stocks.

If an investor places a sell stop order on IBM at $115 a share, with IBM currently trading at $119 a share, the order will just sit idle until IBM drops and does a trade at or less than $115 a share. When that occurs, the sell stop order becomes a market order and sells the stock at the "best available price." The best available price might be $115, lower or higher.

The biggest advantage to a sell stop order is its automatic nature. The stock is sold when the price of the stop is touched or penetrated. But that automatic trigger also is the biggest disadvantage to the sell stop.

The stock price may drop just low enough to trigger the sell, then rebound to former levels. This brings another psychological disadvantage. Many investors are hesitant to buy back a stock that has been sold with a stop order.

The disadvantages can be dealt with in part by only using sell stop orders in special circumstances and by being careful to place the stop price low enough. Special circumstances would be signs of new market weakness, going on vacation, or protecting significant profits. Most investors have more to do than watch the stock market every minute of the trading day. Whether it is the demand of a person's profession or retirement activities, monitoring the stock market throughout the day is often burdensome.

Much of the time this is not a concern. Watching the business news on television or reading the financial news will be enough monitoring of the stock market. Occasionally, situations will arise in which more attention to the market will benefit the investor. Investors who cannot give this special attention, should consider sell stop orders.

A primary concept to keep in mind when placing a sell stop order is that it is one the investor prefers not to have filled. The sell stop price should be low enough that it is unlikely to be executed unless there is a severe decline in the price of the stock.

Percentage Nonsense

A common belief is that sell stop orders should be placed 10 to 15 percent below the current trading price. Many experienced traders and brokers will tell you that this strategy almost guarantees a stock portfolio that will consistently lose 10 to 15 percent. Another old and mostly unreliable rule of thumb is to place sell stop orders $2 below the current trading price. Neither strategy will hold up well under close examination. In many cases, the sell stop will be too close to the current trading price and the order will be executed disadvantageously.

The arbitrary figure of $2 has been around for more than a hundred years. Charles Dow wrote about the $2 sell stop in 1900. Volatility in the market as well as individual stocks has increased significantly in the past hundred years. It is not unusual for high-quality stocks to fluctuate $2 or $3 in a day or two. In fact, it is fairly common to see stocks take a swing of 10 to 15 percent in just a few weeks or months.

Rather than using a set formula for placing a sell stop, it makes more sense to look at a stock price trading range for the past few months. This will graphically show the investor where a stop order can be placed. In an ideal placement, the stop is not likely to be executed, but if it is and the stock is sold, the price will probably drop even further and the stock can be repurchased at a bargain (assuming it is worth repurchasing).

Special Circumstances for Stop Orders

- Leaving on a vacation, especially if stock has been purchased with a margin loan.

- Recent signs of market weakness, in which the investor really doesn't want to sell the stock. In most cases, the stock should just be sold.
- Unusually strong advance in the price of a stock.

If the belief exists that a stock price will fall in the next few days or weeks, the stock should be sold rather than toy with a sell stop. There is no point in giving up the extra dollars per share by placing a sell stop order. This is also why it doesn't make sense to place a sell stop order too close to the current trading price.

Used carefully, a sell stop can be a useful tool for protecting an investor's stock portfolio. If a stop order is in place for two or three weeks and the potential risk appears to have dissipated, the order should be canceled. There is no point to leaving it sit there where it might be forgotten.

Using Option Protection

Two types of options also add some protection to the investor's stock portfolio:

1. Selling the covered call, in which the investor sells call options on stock that is currently owned.
2. Buying put options. A put option allows the buyer to sell a specific amount of a specific stock at a set price for a limited time.

Say an investor purchased 500 shares of IBM at a price of $110 per share. If the investor buys five puts with a strike price of $115 and that is also the current sell price, the stock can be "put" at that price up to its expiration date. The investor will pay commission and a premium representing the remaining time value of the option. If, for example, the premium is $5, and the commission is $40, and the option will expire in another three months, the investor will pay $2,540 for the five put[4] contracts. If the price of IBM drops just over $5 a share to $110, the investor will about break even when putting the stock. If the put option still has considerable time left to run, the investor may also sell the put for a profit.

Key Ideas

Deal with risk:
    —Find stocks with lower risk.
    —Use strategies to modify risk.
    —Consider using contrary hedging.
    —Consider an options hedge.
Protective measures can help:
    —Using careful analysis.
    —Using diversification when possible.
    —Careful, specific use of stops.
    —Percentage nonsense.
    —Special circumstances for stop orders.
    —Using option protection.

Notes

1. All stock options have a set expiration month. They actually expire at 11:59 A.M. New York time, on the Saturday following the third Friday of the designated month.

2. It is referred to as a "covered call" because the investor owns the same quantity of stock on which the option is sold. The risk is covered by the stock.

3. The strike price is the price the investor has agreed to accept for the stock.

4. One put contract is for 100 shares.

PART FOUR

Action—
Evaluation—
Adjustment

Action consists of the activities we use to track the economic changes, market changes, and stock changes that occur as time passes. Evaluation is an in-depth look at our portfolio, to search out weaknesses and serious problems. Adjustments will be the changes we make in the portfolio.

The frequency of full-performance evaluation is up to the individual. Some investors analyze performance on a daily basis. Others keep an eye on certain areas, but do a monthly evaluation. Still other investors do an in-depth evaluation only quarterly or semiannually. Whatever schedule you follow, the same information areas will be important.

The following analyses are essential:

1. Overall market performance.
2. Portfolio performance.
3. Individual stock performance.

Ideally, we'd like all three of these areas to be doing well, with the market, the portfolio, and the individual stocks all growing steadily and achieving the portfolio performance objective.

Second choice is to have two of the three doing well. If only one of the three is doing well, it is either time to realign the entire portfolio or exit the market.

If the overall market, whether the S&P 500 Index or the Dow Jones Industrial Average, is doing well, it should be pulling along stock portfolio performance, as well as the individual stocks.

Good market performance also assumes a favorable investing climate. A favorable investment climate has declining or stable interest rates, increasing corporate profits, and moderate volatility in the stock market—this is a bull market.

In Part Four, we will do three portfolio evaluations:

1. Six Months. An in-depth look at price performance and analyst opinions, looking for existing and potential weaknesses.

2. December 1. Another look at price performance, with some reevaluation of long-term potential. We want stocks to sell—for a profit in some cases or take advantage of tax losses in other situations.

3. Year End. A price-and-dividend performance check. What was our total gain at the end of the year if we sold all our stocks? We will not do a 12-month evaluation, as most investors focus on the actual profits at year end.

The adjustment focus for Part Four will be on those underperforming stocks that show little chance of improvement. This is normally also the time to select new stocks to replace the old; we will only suggest the stocks to be sold. New stocks can be selected using the stock selection methods discussed earlier.

We will "sell the losers and let the winners run." The only time to sell a winner is when you have strong reasons to believe that a negative change is coming. Find the problem stocks, get rid of them, and buy some stocks that are behaving more in line with the current market.

On the other hand, if the market is doing poorly (especially if it is declining and the climate is turning less favorable) but the portfolio performance is exemplary, it's time to get ready to sell some positions. Eventually, the portfolio's individual stock prices will follow the market down. Seldom will an individual stock continue to rise in price while the market is falling.

CHAPTER 14

Go for It!

Taking Action

Daily or weekly tracking is acceptable for analysis when an investor is charting stock prices on a graph. While tracking should not be a substitute for full portfolio evaluation because it doesn't provide enough information to evaluate an entire portfolio in depth, price and information tracking will help focus your attention on results.

Although you should always be ready to react to sudden changes, it is important not to overreact. Tracking should serve to look for signs of strength and weakness, or for apparent changes in the long-term trend. You are looking for a set amount of growth within a well-defined time period. Because achieving the growth objective depends on more than day-to-day market fluctuations, you should note daily changes but they should not be the only determining factor in a call to action.

Track Prices

Individual stock price reactions to market changes are to be expected, but countermarket moves should be examined closely for causes. Price tracking can be done by service subscription, by computer, or by hand. All these methods can produce equally acceptable results.

Try Not to Overreact

As can be seen in the hand-drawn price graphs in Figure 14.1, it is important to avoid overreacting to price changes. All good

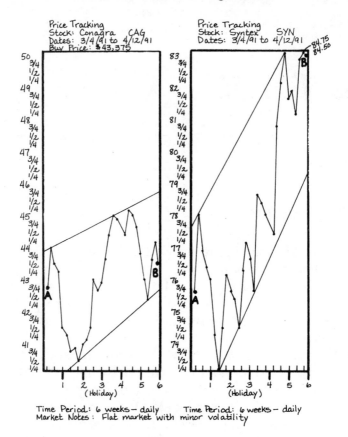

FIGURE 14.1 **Conagra and Syntex (hand drawn)**

stocks will show volatile reactions to market swings. Their prices will rise as the market rallies and fall as the market corrects. If the conclusions drawn from the stock analysis are correct, a market-driven price decline is usually not the time to sell.

Most often, the cause of the change and the ensuing price stability will assume greater importance than the market swing itself. Why did the market drop 50 points yesterday, and what is it doing today? As regards a specific stock: Why did Conagra drop $1.50 yesterday? Was it due to the market or something more serious?

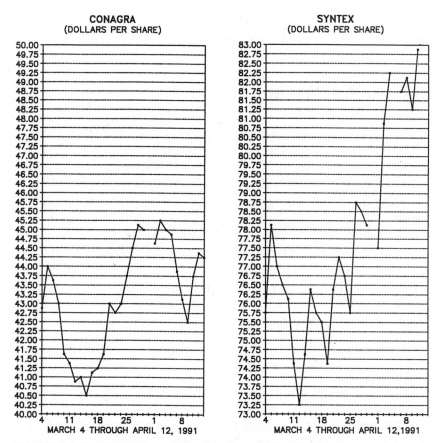

FIGURE 14.2 **Conagra and Syntex (computer drawn)**

Look for Divergences

A more serious problem might be occurring if a divergence occurred where the stock price is down while the market moves up,
suggesting a problem with the stock. These kinds of observations
can bring patience and understanding to market fluctuations.
Overreacting to these changes can result in frustrations and unnecessary losses.

An investor could have been tempted to sell Conagra when it
dropped more than 8.5 percent ($44 to $40.50). Many investment

advisors claim that they cut the loss at 8 percent. In this specific situation, that sell would not have been a good strategy.

Playing to Win Big

Jessie Livermore, one of history's more successful stock traders, is said to have followed a course of patience, ". . . when you believe your conclusions to be correct." This assumes that conclusions are based on solid facts that can be observed and evaluated.

Mr. Livermore had exceptional good luck on at least one occasion. He is said to have sold short 2,000 shares of Union Pacific railroad stock only a few days before the 1906 San Francisco earthquake. He held this short position even though the stock did not drop until a few weeks later, which was where patience paid off. Many of his business friends encouraged him to close out the position and take the loss, but Livermore believed his original conclusions to be correct.

As the stock turned and began to fall, Jessie continued to sell short. Although the exact figure is not known, it is believed that he profited more than a quarter of a million dollars from his speculation. His other guiding market philosophy came into play at this point: "Whenever you win, win big."

When these two philosophies are applied to the early March decline of Conagra, the suggested course of action is to buy more stock, rather than sell and take the loss.

Watching Stock Market Indicators with the Help of Graphs

For analysis purposes, hand-drawn graphs are as accurate and clear as those generated on a computer. The amount of time for either method is about the same, and either version provides us with helpful information. Both Conagra and Syntex reacted to the early market drop and are showing a general uptrend for the six-week time period. The trend with Syntex is considerably more dramatic and is worth further investigation into the reason for the price acceleration. The final two prices were off the scale at

$84.75 and $84.50 at the close of the six-week time period (see Figure 14.2).

The price of Conagra is moving up, but it is more in line with what the overall market is doing. Syntex runs ahead of the market in the third week and keeps on going; in fact, it shows an increase of $ 8.50 (10 percent) in a three-week period. Sudden surges like this are worth researching to learn the cause. Some analysts attribute this strength to the contributions of Beatrice Foods, an acquisition in August 1990.

In the first two weeks, the Dow Jones Industrial Average and Transportation Average (see Figure 14.3) were also declining, showing a general weakness in the market. The sudden downturn could become a concern if it had continued, but we must remember, since October 1991, the attitude of the Fed has been to force interest rates lower.

The attitude was backed up with action on February 1, 1992, when the federal discount rate was lowered a half percent to 6 percent even. Long-term Treasury bonds yields increased slightly with the market dropping, but the change was not particularly dramatic.

The brief look at the market in Figure 14.3 indicates some definite signs of weakness, but the deficiency at this point is not severe enough to warrant any action. The individual stocks are mixed in their reactions. Conagra is on a course similar to that of the market. Syntex is behaving in a positive but unusual manner and is worth checking further for possible additional purchases. Price strength with Syntex was being fueled with strong sales of their pharmaceuticals, including some new successful products.

Stock Investing with Focus

Stock investing has long-term *growth* as its main focus. Every action should be contemplated in light of the stated time period. Whether the stock market is up or down on any given day is not nearly as important as the current trends and other conditions affecting the market progress. Sudden volatile changes can catch anyone by surprise; it's part of the risk. But looking for signals of technical or fundamental weakness can help to lessen the surprise and provide facts on which to base a course of action.

INDEX TRACKING   Objective: Growth
Dates: 3/4/91 to 4/12/91

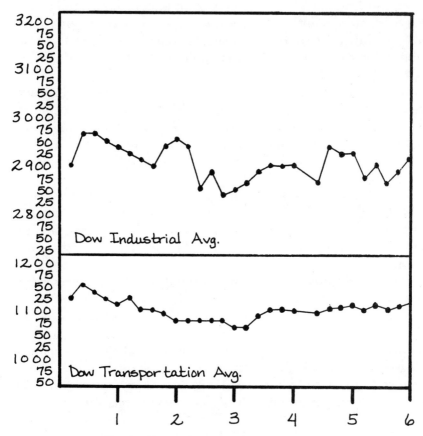

Time Period: 6 weeks daily

Market Notes: Flat market with minor volatility.

FIGURE 14.3 **Dow Averages (hand drawn)**

Analysis such as this can be invaluable to you as a growth or total return investor. The study is not difficult or time consuming and even in the short term can quickly point out important details of strength in the market, as well as individual stocks.

Stock Trading, Short-Term Speculation

Stock *trading* is the speculative buying and selling of the same stocks on a short-term basis. Transactions can be as frequent as every day or as infrequent as a few times a year. Stock trading is based on profiting from short-term market swings and price fluctuations, rather than from growth over a three- to five-year period.

Speculative stock trading depends on volatility in the market, the lack of which translates to a lack of opportunity to the stock trader. Speculative traders count on market corrections to provide buying opportunities and will help fuel rallies to take some profits. Too many individual stock speculators do just the opposite.

Speculative Difficulties

If we look back to the six-week price graphs on Conagra and Syntex (Figure 14.2), it is easy to see where the speculative traders began to repurchase the stock. A correction, stabilization rally occurs three times with Conagra and as many as five times with Syntex. The speculative trader will use this pattern to sell, buy, buy more, using predetermined price levels to trigger the transactions. The difficulties arise in three areas:

1. Selling soon enough in the correction.
2. Determining stabilization.
3. Estimating the duration of the rally.

These are real difficulties for all speculators. The institutional investor gains some advantage with a staff of researchers who constantly monitor the progress of the market. Some individual investors can also pursue this advantage, but many do not have the time. An alternative approach can be to buy, buy, sell. In other words, buy stock on the correction stabilization and sell into the rally.

Speculation Requires Constant Attention

Speculative stocks or situations need constant attention, the more the better. The frequent trading investor must live with those stocks and know them inside and out. Although the primary focus should be technical price activity, information of a fundamental nature can also be helpful. Price movement is the first reality of importance. Why the price is moving is secondary. Understanding why a stock price is moving will provide facts on which to base a projection of movement duration.

If a positive report is issued, form an opinion as to its future impact. Project where a weakness might next appear. When a negative report appears, predict how much influence it can create and for how long. Conclude whether or not you can take advantage of a temporary weakness by selling and buying back at a later date.

Summary

All stock investing needs to be actively watched. We live in a time when the economy, the market, and individual stock situations can change in an instant. Taking action to watch over your investments will allow you to evaluate and make adjustments with greater speed and accuracy. It means you will be better prepared to make more money and avoid losing it on a sudden change.

Key Ideas

Taking action:
   —Track prices.
   —Try not to overreact.
   —Look for divergences.

Playing to win big.

Watching stock market indicators with the help of graphs.

Stock investing with focus.

Stock trading, short-term speculation.

Speculative difficulties:

  —Sell soon enough in the correction.

  —Determine stabilization.

  —Estimate the duration of the rally.

Speculation—the need for constant attention.

CHAPTER 15

How Am I Doing?

Six-Month Evaluation for an Income Objective

If the objective is income, meaning current income from quarterly dividends, has anything occurred to alter the income? Has the dividend been reduced or increased? How does the investor's yield (based on the original purchase price) compare with the current yield of other investments CDs or T-bills)?

Income-producing utility stocks have a tendency to drop in price as interest rates rise because investors sell the stock to buy higher-yielding treasury investments. Although this can be frustrating for the investor to observe, it is not necessarily a reason to sell the stock. A selling decision should be based on a direct threat to the business of a specific company or any other condition that could lead to a lowering of the dividend. If the stock retains the same investment quality, even though the price has dropped, the investor should actually consider buying more.

Keeping an eye on information relating to the stock's business condition and price stability is really the only necessary evaluation for the income objective. The yield (ROI) was locked in at the time the stock was purchased and will need recalculation only if the dividend payout has changed or additional shares of the stock have been purchased.

Income Objective Specific Statement

I will invest $50,000 in two or three high-quality (B+ or better) gas or electric utility common stocks that pay annual dividends of 7 percent or more. This rate is presently 1 percent or more higher than current fixed income Treasury bill rates.

Evaluation of the income objective is primarily a safety check. Has any development placed the dividend or the price at higher risk? The easiest way to implement the evaluation is simply to go back to the Stock Selector for the income category and update the relevant information.

Checking the price to see if it is about the same or higher than when we bought the stock will quickly point out developing problems. If the price is showing a sharp decline, we first need to check for an increase in interest rates and then search information for a possible threat to the dividend. We do not want to see the dividend reduced or eliminated, as this will cause the price to drop accordingly.

Again, if a price drop is caused by upward moving interest rates, it will not affect our return on the investment, but it could eventually become a factor in slowing the rate at which the dividend increases in the years to follow. Prices hurt by interest rate increases are not quite as serious as prices that drop due to problems within the company.

Detroit Edison

When we complete the information on the Stock Selector and compare it with our analysis back in March, it is easy to see a reliable, factual picture (see Table 15.1). Interest rates are continuing to fall. The short-term T-bill rates went from 6.01 percent down to 5.34 percent, which is positive for utility stocks.

Expect Earnings to Be Higher

Earnings with Detroit Edison are expected to be up in 1991 year and continue to grow at a favorable rate in 1992. The analyst believes that dividend growth will continue to be above average.

Rating, Financial Strength, and Price Are Good

The investment rating and financial strength have not changed in this six-month period. The price of Detroit Edison is showing about a 4 percent increase. Not much to worry about at this point.

Table 15.1　Stock Selector: Income, Detroit Edison

Stock Selector Date: 2/28/91	Objective: Income 7%				Research from Value Line		
Stock	Current Price $	S&P Rating	Annual $ Paid	Dividend % Yield	Current T-Bill % Yield	5-Yr Average Annual Dividend Increase $　%	Dividend Paid Since
DTE	29.375	A−	1.88	6.4	6.01	.04　2.13	1909

Notes: Elec. to Detroit & 400 SE Michigan cities/nuclear concern/auto sales concern/plants good shape/dividend growth potential/financial condition fair/Financial Strength B.

Stock Selector Date: 9/3/91	Objective: Income 7%				Research from Value Line		
Stock	Current Price $	S&P Rating	Annual $ Paid	Dividend % Yield	Current T-Bill % Yield	5-Yr Average Annual Dividend Increase $　%	Dividend Paid Since
DTE	30.500	A−	1.88	6.0	5.34	.04　2.13	1909

Notes: Due to weather, earnings are way up this year. Earnings rise expected in 1992. Dividend growth expected above avg. financial condition fair/Financial Strength B.

　　　Checking this information is important because it enables us to evaluate some aspects of the strength of the company, and, therefore, the strength of the dividend that provides our income.

Otter Tail Power Shows Questionable Diversification

The price of Otter Tail Power has increased $3, which is more than 11 percent, somewhat surprising for a company that is not a growth stock (see Table 15.2). Earnings appear to be strong, and the analyst believes this to be a good conservative stock.

Table 15.2   *Stock Selector: Income, Otter Tail Power*

Stock Selector Date: 2/28/91	Objective: Income 7%				Research from Value Line		
Stock	Current Price $	S&P Rating	Annual $ Paid	Dividend % Yield	Current T-Bill % Yield	5-Yr Average Annual Dividend Increase $ %	Dividend Paid Since
OTTR	26.500	A−	1.60	6.0	6.01	.04 2.50	1938

Notes: Elec. to West Minnesota, N&S Dakota/ agricultural customers who are doing well low/ debt/stock repurchase plan near done finances in good shape/Financial Strength B++.

Stock Selector: Date: 9/3/91	Objective: Income 7%				Research from Value Line		
Stock	Current Price $	S&P Rating	Annual $ Paid	Dividend % Yield	Current T-Bill % Yield	5-Yr Average Annual Dividend Increase $ %	Dividend Paid Since
OTTR	29.500	A−	1.60	6.0	5.34	.04 2.50	1938

Notes: Recently purchased radio station KFGO in diversification. Looking for good 3rd quarter earnings/appeal conservative accts./ somewhat less prone to nasty surprises/Financial Strength B++.

Otter Tail is attempting to diversify and has recently purchased a radio station. Although this move is difficult to evaluate at this point, investors seem to like the idea. The fundamentals are still strong, no apparent problems here, either (see Table 15.3).

The diversification of buying an AM-FM radio station is a concern because it differs significantly from their primary business. While the company might be great at managing the electric power business with all of its intricacies, it might be a weak manager in a different industry. Generally, the most effective diversification for a company is to ". . . stick to the knitting." In other words, to stay with industries in which it has shown proficiency.

Table 15.3   *Stock Selector: Income, Union Electric*

Stock Selector Date: 2/28/91		Objective: Income 7%				Research from Value Line		
Stock	Current Price $	S&P Rating	Annual $ Paid	Dividend % Yield	Current T-Bill % Yield	5-Yr Average Annual Dividend Increase $ %		Dividend Paid Since
UEP	30.250	A−	2.16	7.0	6.01	.06	2.78	1906

Notes: Elec. & gas to St. Louis area/some nuc, 6 coal plants to finance construction with internal generated $/Financial Strength A/ Clean air act may be heavy expense in mid-decade.

Stock Selector Date: 9/3/91		Objective: Income 7%				Research from Value Line		
Stock	Current Price $	S&P Rating	Annual $ Paid	Dividend % Yield	Current T-Bill % Yield	5-Yr Average Annual Dividend Increase $ %		Dividend Paid Since
UEP	31.500	A−	2.16	7.0	5.34	.06	2.78	1906

Notes: May soon acquire Arkansas Power's electric assets in Missouri Compliance with clean Air Act poses no problem. Record earnings expected this year/avg. div. growth 94-96/Financial Strength A.

Union Electric Shows Good Diversification

In Table 15.4, we see that UEP prices have increased slightly, partly due to a continuing overall decline in interest rates. We also see some diversification in Union Electric as we did at Otter Tail Power. Many utilities have been diversifying over the past few years in an attempt to moderate the stock price fluctuations during economic changes.

Union Electric is in the process of buying Arkansas Power, another electric company. On the surface, many analysts consider this to be a more effective method of diversification. The new acquisition can have a synergistic effect on the company, significantly contributing to the bottom line.

Table 15.4 Six-Month Evaluation: Income

| Stock Evaluation | | | Income Objective: 7% | | | | | Currently: 6.5% |

September 1991

Stock Symbol & Dates	Qty #	Div $	Current Price	Begin Price	Return on Investment			Market Progress
					Divs $	Gain $	Gain %	
Detroit Edison								ONE
DTE	400	$1.88	$30.500	$29.375	$564	$450	3.8%	Indu 3.7%
	6.4% = Annual yield based on buy price							Tran 4.0%
Notes: Figured with 3 dividends; gain calculated without dividends.								S&P 5.9%
Dates Start: 3/1/91 Today: 9/3/91								
Action: Hold or buy more stock.								
Otter Tail Power								TWO
OTTR	300	$1.60	$29.500	$26.500	$360	$900	11.3%	Indu 3.7%
	6.0% = Annual yield based on buy price							Tran 4.0%
Notes: Figured with 3 dividends; gain calculated without dividends. Recently purchased radio station KFGO (diversification) Looking for good 3rd quarter earnings/conservative appeal B++.								S&P 5.9%
Dates Start: 3/1/91 Today: 9/3/91								
Action: Hold or buy more stock.								
Union Electric								THREE
UEP	1000	$2.16	$31.500	$30.250	$1,620	$1,250	4.1%	Indu 3.7%
	7.1% = Annual yield based on buy price							Tran 4.0%
Notes: Figured with 3 dividends; gain calculated without dividends.								S&P 5.9%
Date Start: 3/1/91 Today: 9/3/91								
Action: Hold or buy more.								

Conclusions: Six-Month Income Evaluation

At the six-month evaluation, our income stocks appear to be stable, with reasonably secure dividends and moderate price increases (Table 15.5). Safe money interest rates have been dropping, thereby making these stocks more attractive. T-bills have dropped more than a half percent, which has gently nudged the prices higher. The dividends appear stable during the first six months, which is the way we want our income portfolio to look at evaluation time.

Prices of our income stocks are doing quite well. They are all showing modest gains, which is a positive signal telling us the dividends are currently secure.

There is concern about the strength of the whole stock market. Gains of 4 percent through the first of September are not much to get excited about. The slowness of the market is due to the current recession. The market is forecasting a recession which could easily last another six months to a year.

Growth Objective Evaluation

When evaluating individual stocks, we look for the unusual. The focus of our attention will be on the prices of stocks that are not in line with our current objective. If the price growth is below our expectations we need to find out as much as possible about the situation and decide whether or not to sell the stock.

Table 15.5 *Portfolio Evaluation: Income*

Portfolio Evaluation							
Objective: Income 7% (Annual Dividends)							
	Annual Dividend		*Portfolio Performance*				*Market*
Date:	*Income $*	*Yield %*	*Invested $*	*Value $*	*Gain $*	*Gain %*	*Indu. %*
3/1/91		6.8	49,950				
9/3/91	2,544	6.8		52,550	2,600	5.2	3.7

The second priority of analysis is stocks with prices performing above our expectations. Close analysis will give us some idea whether the prices are increasing on better earnings or just the anticipation of earnings. Again, we must decide whether to buy more, hold the current position, or sell and take the profits. We don't want to fire our best employees unless we believe they are too expensive. Too expensive simply means that the stock's price has increased so much that earnings are unlikely to catch up in the next six months to a year. A quick review of our growth objective tells us what to look for in individual stock performance:

Growth Objective Specific Statement

By investing $50,000 in common stock with an investment grade rating of B or better, I expect to achieve a 20 percent rate of return annually for the next five years. This return will be based on the total amount of price growth in the stock selected, including any dividend payments. I will enhance safety by investing in at least three to five companies in three different industries. Any losses will be subtracted from profits to arrive at a calculation of the net gain.

The Stock Selector provided us with five stocks that have a five-year history of this minimum growth performance. Look again at the original information on Novell (Table 15.6).

Initially, Novell, Inc., far exceeded the minimum growth objective of 20 percent annually. The five-year figures show strong

Table 15.6 *Stock Selector: Growth, Novell*

Stock Selector Date: 2/28/91	Objective: Growth			%	Research from Value Line			
					5-Year Average Annual Growth			
Stock	Current Price $	P/E Ratios 5-Yr Curr/Avg	Annual Dividend $	Price + Dividend $	Sales %	Earn's %	Price & Divs $	%
NOVL	48.875	21.2 31	0.00	48.875	36.0	54.2	6.35	102

Notes: Base Price $ 6.25
Designs and services local area networks for personal computers profitability increases since 1988 / Financial Strength A
Long term debt is 1% of capitalization.

price growth, making the stock borderline speculative. The price growth, however, is backed up by the financial strength of Novell. Sales and earnings growth was enough to make this stock a buy, keeping in mind that the risk is higher than the rest of the growth portfolio. The following six-month performance analysis shows that the risk was worth taking.

Novell, Better than the Dow

In the Stock Selector evaluation (Table 15.7) for growth stocks, we will look at the figures on the first trading day in September 1991. When the Dow Averages were up a modest 4 percent in six months, Novell showed a price increase of 38 percent. This represents annualized growth of 76 percent. Increased earnings have given some support to this price growth, but the P/E ratio of 35 also shows growth in earnings anticipation.

The rapid price growth makes Novell a stock to be concerned about, but it doesn't seem to be too expensive at this point. We just want to keep an eye on the earnings and price growth to see that they keep pace with each other, as well as look closely for any weakness in the building of anticipation.

Using Table 15.7, we will evaluate each stock and point out strengths and weaknesses.

What about Apple?

Only one stock, Apple Computer, is not in line with the objective after a six-month period; it shows a loss of 8 percent. The loss does not necessarily mean that we should dump the stock, but it indicates that our analysis here should focus on Apple's difficulties. Apple is the stock we most want to find out more about. What have sales and earnings been doing for the last six months and where are the problems?

Find Out Why: Check the Research

Checking the *Value Line Investment Survey* reveals that Apple's difficulties come primarily from narrowed profit margins, as a

Table 15.7 Six-Month Stock Evaluation: Growth

Stock Evaluation Growth			Objective: 20%					Currently: 14.6%

September 1991

| Stock Symbol & Dates | Qty # | Div $ | Current Price | Return on Investment | | | | Market Progress |
				Begin Price	Divs $	Gain $	Gain %	
Conagra								ONE
CAG	200	$0.69	$47.125	$41.875	$104	$1,154	14%	Indu 3.7%
Dates Start: 3/1/91	Notes: Figures include 3 dividends; ". . . in our recommended list, because of pattern of above avg. earnings."							Tran 4.0%
								S&P 5.9%
Today: 9/3/91	Action: Hold or buy more.					P/E 22		Avg. P/E 14.8
Albertson's								TWO
ABS	200	$0.56	$42.500	$38.500	$84	$884	12%	Indu 3.7%
Dates Start: 3/1/91	Notes: Figures include 3 dividends; ". . . Financial Strength relatively high, shares will outleg market for 3–6 years."							Tran 4.0%
								S&P 5.9%
Today: 9/3/91	Action: Hold or buy more.					P/E 23		Avg. P/E 17.3

Table 15.7 (Continued)

Stock Evaluation Growth			Objective: 20%			Currently: 14.6%		
					Return on Investment			Market Progress
Stock Symbol & Dates	Qty #	Div $	Current Price	Begin Price	Divs $	Gain $	Gain %	
Apple Computer								THREE
AAPL	100	$0.48	$52.500	$57.250	$36	−$439	−8%	Indu 3.7%
								Tran 4.0%
								S&P 5.9%
Dates Start: 3/1/91 Today: 9/3/91	Notes: Figures include 3 dividends; ". . . cut prices to win a bigger share of PC mkt. Good earnings gains to '94–'96." Action: Hold, prepare to sell.						P/E 19	Avg. P/E 13.9
Novell								FOUR
NOVL	400	$0.00	$33.750	$24.438	$0	$3,725	38%	Indu 3.7%
								Tran 4.0%
								S&P 5.9%
Dates Start: 3/1/91 Today: 9/3/91	Notes: No dividends; 2–1 split; ". . . top choice for year ahead . . . rich P/E holds little appeal as long-term capital gain."						P/E 34	Avg. P/E 21.2
Syntex								FIVE
SYN	400	$0.92	$44.125	$37.625	$221	$2,821	19%	Indu 3.7%
								Tran 4.0%
								S&P 5.9%
Dates Start: 3/1/91 Today: 9/3/91	Notes: Figures include 3 dividends; 2–1 split; "L-T profits should benefit from additional new medications . . . should add 40 to 60 cents a share by '91–'96." Action: Hold or buy more.						P/E 23	Avg. P/E 16.3

result of more competitive pricing. Although this is a concern, it is not necessarily a strong negative. The *Value Line* analyst now believes the price appreciation potential will be "about average" to the 1994 through 1996 time period, based on earnings estimates. The total growth projected into 1994 through 1996 is at a high of 21 percent and a low of 11 percent annually. Our objective is 20 percent annually, which suggests that we will do well to watch Apple closely and be ready to make some changes.

Can Improvement Be Made Soon?

It is not likely that the problems can be solved in the next six months; it will take a year or more. We can afford to be patient with Apple's performance for awhile, but if the price continues to drop, it could begin to damage the overall portfolio performance. Earnings surprises from the new notebook model personal computer or the high-end Mac could make a difference, but that is more of a speculation objective. Based on the evidence and opinion, we should seriously consider selling Apple Computer if the performance continues to slide for the next six months.

Conclusion: Six-Month Growth Evaluation

The remaining stock show good results and favorable opinions from the analysts. Conagra is on track with an annualized price growth rate of 13 percent while the P/E ratio has barely increased. Earnings growth appears to be keeping up with price growth, and that's what we want to see.

Albertson's shows a six-month growth rate of 11 percent (annualized to 22 percent), with an unchanged P/E ratio. So far, it's in line with our 20 percent objective.

Novell's performance has been excellent, up 38 percent for six months. This also brings a caution as the P/E ratio is now at 34, up from when we purchased the stock. The analyst's opinion is that the stock will be likely to do well for the next year, but acceptable price performance over the longer term will be doubtful. *Value Line* projects the 1994 through 1996 return at a high of 14 percent and a low of 3 percent annually. This is a serious concern; we should look to take profits over the next year, unless dramatic

changes improve the long-term outlook of Novell. Syntex is showing a six-month gain of 19 percent, with a minor increase in the
P/E ratio. The mainline pharmaceutical products are doing well,
and good new products are expected to contribute significantly to
the bottom line over the next five years.

At this point, these stocks are living up to our expectations.
Unless we are planning changes, such as adding more Syntex to
the portfolio, further analysis is unnecessary.

Now look at the growth of the entire portfolio (Table 15.8).
After six months, we are well on our way to achieving our first-
year objective.

An annual running rate (growth if the trend continues at the
same speed) of 35 percent[14] is well above our 20 percent objective. While this is positive, there likely will be times when the
picture is not so positive. At this point, we will keep our objective
at the same level and keep a close eye on Apple Computer, the one
losing stock, and Novell, Inc., the fastest growing stock.

Another concern at the six-month point is the market. Other
than Apple, all these stocks are growing faster than the Dow Averages. This suggests that weaknesses in the growth of many other
companies could cause a severe correction or secondary downtrend. The Fed began to address these weaknesses by lowering
the federal discount rate to 4.5 percent in November 1991. When
interest rates continue to decline, it is unlikely that a secondary
downtrend will turn into a bear market.

Table 15.8   *Portfolio Evaluation: Growth*

Portfolio Evaluation								
Objective: Growth 20%								
		Portfolio Performance						Market
Date:	Invested $	Current $	Gain $	Gain %	Dividend $	Total $	Gain %	Indu. %
3/1/91 9/3/91	46,725	54,325	7,600	16.3	445	8,045	17.2	3.7

Total Return Objective Evaluation

Our total return objective is looking for 12 percent annually in a combination of price growth and dividends paid:

Total Return Objective Statement

By investing $100,000 in common stock, I expect to achieve a 12 percent rate of return annually for the next five years. Risk will be moderated by the stock dividends, diversification into at least three different stocks in three different industries, and a minimum investment rating of B. The rate of return will be calculated by adding the annual price increase of the stock to its annual dividend payout.

According to the original Stock Selector (Table 15.9), General Electric has maintained this average at exactly 12 percent for the past five years. Let's see if the return continued to increase for the next six months (Table 15.10).

General Electric Is Doing Well

The GE section of the Stock Selector evaluation (Table 15.10) shows a total return for General Electric of 11 percent for the first six months, which means the total return for General Electric is running at an annualized rate of 22 percent, well above our

Table 15.9 *Stock Selector: Total Return*

Stock Selector Date: 2/28/91	Objective: Total Return 12%				Research from Value Line			
		P/E				5-Yr Average Annual Growth		
	Current Price	*Ratios 5-Yr*	*Annual Dividend*	*Price + Dividend*				
Stock	*$*	*Curr/Avg*	*$*	*$*	*Sales %*	*Earn's %*	*Price & Divs $*	*%*
GE	68.000	14 12.8	2.16	70.160	14.0	14.0	5.87	12.0
Notes: $48.500/Base Price = One of the largest and most diversified companies in the world/Several businesses sensitive to recession/light recession OK Financial Strength A++/Long-term debt is 12% of capitalization.								

Table 15.10 Six-Month Evaluation: Total Return

Stock Evaluation				Total Return Objective: 12%				Currently: 12%
				September 1991				
					Return on Investment			
Stock Symbol & Dates	Qty #	Div $	Current Price	Begin Price	Divs $	Gain $	Gain %	Market Progress
American Home Product								**ONE**
AHP	500	$2.30	$64.000	$57.000	$863	$4,363	15%	Indu 3.7%
								Tran 4.0%
Dates Start:	Notes: Figures include 3 dividends; ". . . lowering '91 earnings estimate,							S&P 5.9%
3/1/91	June Qtr. below expectations/drop to less than 10% after June '92							
Today: 3/1/91							P/E 16	Avg. P/E 13.2
	Action: Watch carefully. Consider sell.							
Exxon								**TWO**
XON	500	$2.68	$58.000	$55.250	$1,005	$2,443	8.9%	Indu 3.7%
								Tran 4.0%
Dates Start:	Notes: "Figures include 3 dividends; ". . . overseas presence major blessing/							S&P 5.9%
3/1/91	and natural gas . . . still on hook for '89 oil spill . . . can cover cleanup costs.							
Today: 9/3/91							P/E 12	Avg. P/E 12.6
	Action: None at present.							
General Electric								**THREE**
GE	500	$2.04	$74.125	$68.000	$765	$3,828	11%	Indu 3.7%
								Tran 4.0%
Dates Start:	Notes: Figures include 3 dividends; "Earnings gains probably will remain							S&P 5.9%
3/1/91	strong second half. Strengths outweigh weaknesses."							
Today: 3/1/91							P/E 15	Avg. P/E 12.8
	Action: Hold or buy more.							

12 percent objective. This provides a dollar return of $3,572.50. Of that amount, $575 represents dividends. The P/E ratio went from 14 to 15, indicating a minor growth-of-earnings anticipation. When this is compared with the five-year average P/E ratio of nearly 13, it does not appear to suggest overanticipation.

Exxon Has the Lowest Return

Exxon has the lowest six-month return at 8.9 percent, but it is still within our 12-month objective. Notice that the P/E ratio is running below the five-year average. There could be good growth here in the next few months, even in a moderately favorable market.

American Home Products Is in the Lead

American Home Products is leading the returns at a 15 percent return. The P/E ratio barely moved, from 15 six months ago to 16 currently, which is still close to the average 13.2 for five years. Of the $4,075 total return, only $575 comes from the dividend. We are seeing some good growth in the stock.

The Stocks Are Ahead of the Dow Averages

Again, we have some concern that the returns on these stocks are ahead of the Dow Averages. If we remove the impact of the dividends and show only price growth, then American Home Products is up 12 percent for the six months, Exxon is up 5 percent (more in line with the market), General Electric is up 9 percent, and the market (based on Dow Averages) is up only 4 percent in the first part of September.

Although it is a positive sign to see conservative stocks such as these outperforming the market, it suggests the possibility of weakness in other stocks. If the market encounters a sharp correction or secondary down trend, these stocks are likely to show a decline as well. If the market continues its slow growth, simple logic suggests that this group of stocks is likely to stay on track and achieve or exceed the first-year objective of 12 percent annual return.

Conclusion: Six-Month Total Return Evaluation

The six-month portfolio evaluation of the total return, illustrates that we are ahead of schedule in achieving our 12 percent annual total return objective (Table 15.11). On $100,000 invested, we have a total return of $9,755, which represents 11 percent for six months and a running rate of 22 percent for a year (if the return continues to grow at the same speed). We will still keep the objective at 12 percent even though we are currently far ahead. This will help make up for possible difficulties in the future.

Speculation Objective Evaluation

Speculative stocks are high risk and should be followed daily and weekly on an individual basis. If they become less speculative, the investor may want to move them to the growth category. This can become a reason to get rid of them if the growth slows enough to jeopardize the achievement of our objective:

Speculation Objective Statement

I will invest $30,000 in stocks that are expected to increase in price more than 30 percent annually over the next three years.

Table 15.11 *Portfolio Evaluation: Total Return*

Portfolio Evaluation								
Objective: Total Return 12%								
		Portfolio Performance						Market
Date:	Invested $	Current $	Gain $	Gain %	Dividend $	Total $	Gain %	Indu. %
3/1/91	90,063							
9/3/91		98,064	8,001	8.9	2,633	100,697	11.8	4.0

Risk will be moderated by the amount of money invested, diversification into a minimum of three companies, and also by ongoing analysis and daily monitoring.

Amgen Is Still Hot

One of our hottest speculative stock selections is Amgen. The original Stock Selector (Table 15.12) shows Amgen's phenomenal growth performance in the past three years. Our conclusion, from the original stock selector analysis, was that Amgen would continue a similar price growth trend due to its current pharmaceutical product, as well as the development of a new, similar drug. If the conclusion is correct, Amgen should be showing a price growth of more than 200 percent annually.

Month	Monthly	Quarterly	Six-Month	Annual
April	°41.0%	164%	246%	492%
May	41.0		123	252
June	33.0	33	66	132
July	28.0		56	112
August	72.0		72	144

° Monthly price growth compared with the buy price.

Price Growth Has Been Uneven

Amgen starts out strong but then slows for a couple of months, regaining strength in the sixth month.

There Are Some Concerns

There are two concerns regarding this information:

1. Is the growth in line with the objective?
2. Is the accelerated growth a sign of emerging weakness?

The six-month growth of Amgen is considerably better than our speculation objective of 30 percent, which shows the stock to be an excellent selection for this time period. If our objective had

Table 15.12   *Stock Selector: Speculation*

Stock Selector Date: 2/28/91	Objective: Speculation 30%				Research from Value Line				
		12-Month Prices			*5-Year Price Growth*				
Stock	*Current Price*	*High*	*Low*	*P/E Ratios 5-Yr Curr/Avg*	*Yr 1*	*Yr 2*	*Yr 3*	*Yr 4*	*Yr 5*
AMGN	$91.250	$105	$27	113 41	33.0%	38.0%	150%	429%	694%
5-Yr Sales Growth					*5-Yr Price Growth*				
Yr 1	*Yr 2*	*Yr 3*	*Yr 4*	*Yr 5*	*Yr 1*	*Yr 2*	*Yr 3*	*Yr 4*	*Yr 5*
27.0%	56.0%	64.0%	69.0%	27.0%	67.0%	0.0%	150%	186%	31.0%

Notes: Base Price = $12.000/State of the art biotechnology for pharmaceuticals price appreciation due to red blood cell stimulator/new drugs coming/LT debt is 4% of capitalization/Financial Strength B++.

been the more conservative 12 percent for growth, this exceptional performance would bring into play the consideration of high risk. Since our objective is speculation, we accept the risk and want to see our objective surpassed whenever possible.

Daily Price Tracking

The first month of daily tracking graphs (Figure 15.1) shows the buy timing to be quite good with Amgen, terrible with Cray Research, and acceptable with Quantum Corporation. The Dow Industrials have been trading in a range between 2850 and 2975, a range that continued with some small growth through August. By the end of six months, Amgen is still doing well, Cray Research has recovered, and Quantum Corporation is down 39 percent from when we bought it.

Table 15.13 Monthly Evaluation: Speculation

Stock Evaluation		Speculation Objective: 30%				Currently: 24.3%	
		April 1991					
					Return on Investment		Market Progress
Stock Symbol & Dates	Qty #	Current Price	Begin Price	Divs $	Gain $	Gain %	Market Progress
Amgen							ONE
AMGN	200	$128.750	$91.250	$0.00	$7,500	41%	Indu −1.0%
Dates Start: 3/1/91	Notes: Price graph shows strong surge early March +$35/traded in a narrow range of $116-130 and ended the month just above $130.						Tran −4.3%
							S&P 0.2%
Today: 4/1/91	Action: Hold or buy more.				P/E 73.7		Avg. P/E 41
Cray Research							TWO
CYR	200	$37.875	$41.250	$0.00	−$675	−8%	Indu −1.0%
Dates Start: 3/1/91	Notes: Quick rise to $44 resistance level in early March, then a decline to just under $38, small rally at month end to $39. The P/E isn't showing weaker earnings/ looks like a trading pattern.						Tran −4.3%
							S&P 0.2%
Today: 4/1/91					P/E 9		Avg. P/E 11
Quantum Corp.							THREE
QNTM	100	$25.250	$23.500	$0.00	$ 175	7%	Indu −1.0%
Dates Start: 3/1/91	Notes: Three-point resistance 1st half of March/Slow rise in the last 2 weeks of the month/could be an early weakness signal/3–2 split might have a negative effect.						Tran −4.3%
							S&P 0.2%
Today: 4/1/91					P/E 9		Avg. P/E 10

Table 15.13 (Continued)

Stock Evaluation				Speculation Objective: 30%			Currently: 24.3%
				May 1991			
				Return on Investment			
Stock Symbol & Dates	Qty #	Current Price	Begin Price	Divs $	Gain $	Gain %	Market Progress
Amgen							**ONE**
AMGN	200	$129.750	$91.250	$0.00	$7,700	42%	Indu 0%
							Tran 1.2%
							S&P 1.2%
Notes: Trading range $125-135/three cycles in a month could be institutions taking ten dollar swings/encouraging to see increase on cycle bottoms. swings/encouraging to see increase on cycle bottoms.							
Dates Start: 3/1/91 Today: 5/1/91					P/E 113		Avg. P/E 41
Action: Hold or buy more.							
Cray Research							**TWO**
CYR	200	$37.875	$41.250	$0.00	-$675	-8%	Indu 0.7%
							Tran 1.2%
							S&P 1.2%
Notes: Sharp decline in early April to 33/up $3 rallied toward $40 and fell. Looks more like a short cycle than trend.							
Dates Start: 3/1/91 Today: 5/1/91					P/E 9		Avg. P/E 15
Action: Hold & watch.							
Quantum Corp.							**THREE**
QNTM	100	$25.250	$23.500	$0.00	$175	7%	Indu 0.7%
							Tran 1.2%
							S&P 1.2%
Notes: 3-2 split looks like attempt to shore up price from a weak earnings announcement/stock likely to trade in lower range and should be sold.							
Dates Start: 3/1/91 Today: 5/1/91					P/E 8		Avg. P/E 10
Action: Sell.							

DOW INDUSTRIAL & TRANSPORTATION AVG.
JANUARY THROUGH APRIL, 1991

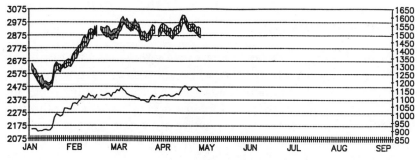

STOCK DAILY PRICE TRACKING
AMGEN (OTC–AMGN)

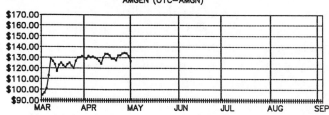

CRAY RESEARCH (NYSE–CYR)

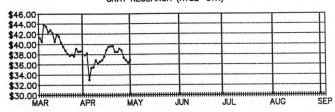

QUANTUM CORP. (OTC–QNTM)

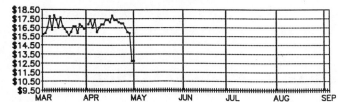

FIGURE 15.1   **Dow Averages and Stock Graphics**

Quantum Problem

The Impact of a Split

Quantum became a rather serious problem when a three-for-two split occurred in April. All the prices shown here are adjusted for the split. The stock immediately went to a lower trading range and stayed there through August. Quantum had two stock splits back in 1989; the first was a three-for-two split, and the second was a two-for-one split. The additional split at the end of April was obviously not well received.

A factor contributing to the drop may have been that many institutional investors dislike splits, possibly because of the additional accounting work they create. Institutional ownership went from 67.4 percent of the outstanding shares to 63 percent in a few days. By August 1991, institutional ownership was down to 52 percent of the shares outstanding.

Split Wasn't the Only Reason for Decline

The decline in Quantum's price was not only due to the split. A reduced earnings announcement and weakness in the personal computer market were undoubtedly even more critical factors. Recall that evaluation of the growth stock portfolio showed slower growth for Apple Computer. Since Apple represents one of Quantum's most important customers, it is logical to assume a slower growth ahead for Quantum. The severe price decline in April would have been enough for many speculative investors to cut their losses and move on to something more promising.

Where Is the Market Going?

A graph of the market (Figure 15.2) to the first part of September 1991 shows a slowly increasing market. It has been rather balanced since the rally in the early part of the year. Both the 30 Dow Industrials and 20 Transportation stocks are trading in a narrow range, with an occasional rally or correction. Even the S&P 500 Index is trading in a similar fashion. Although markets like

Table 15.14 Monthly Evaluation: Speculation

Stock Evaluation				Speculation Objective: 30%			Currently: 15.3%
				June 1991			
				Return on Investment			
Stock Symbol & Dates	Qty #	Current Price	Begin Price	Divs $	Gain $	Gain %	Market Progress
Amgen							**ONE**
AMGN	200	$121.500	$91.250	$0.00	$6,050	33%	Indu 4.3%
Notes: Prices showing downtrend, market up a bit/low in May was $115, and June $110/nervous profits? Speculative wait & see. P/E too high to be meaningful.							Tran 7.9%
							S&P 4.7%
Dates Start: 3/1/91 Today: 6/3/91						P/E 156	Avg. P/E 41
Action: Hold or buy more.							
Cray Research							**TWO**
CYR	200	$35.750	$41.250	$0.00	-$1,100	-13%	Indu 4.3%
Notes: Without any change in earnings, looks like investors are pushing the stock for short-term profit. Even though stock is down 13%, not the best time to sell.							Tran 7.9%
							S&P 4.7%
Dates Start: 3/1/91 Today: 6/1/91						P/E 9	Avg. P/E 15
Action: Hold & watch.							
Quantum Corp.							**THREE**
QNTM	150	$12.125	$15.666	$0.00	-$531	-28%	Indu 4.3%
Notes: Should have sold earlier/3-2 split/stock likely to trade in lower range and should be sold.							Tran 7.9%
							S&P 4.7%
Dates Start: 3/1/91 Today: 6/1/91						P/E 8	Avg. P/E 10
Action: Sell.							

Table 15.14 (Continued)

Stock Evaluation			Speculation Objective: 30%				Currently: 9.5%
			July 1991				
				Return on Investment			
Stock Symbol & Dates	Qty #	Current Price	Begin Price	Divs $	Gain $	Gain %	Market Progress
Amgen							**ONE**
AMGN	200	$117.000	$91.250	$0.00	$5,150	28%	Indu 1.7%
Notes: Uptrend becoming well-defined look for sign of resistance and profit taking.							
Dates Start: 3/1/91							Tran 2.1%
							S&P 2.0%
Today: 7/1/91						P/E N/A	Avg. P/E 41
Action: Hold or buy more.							
Cray Research							**TWO**
CYR	200	$33.000	$41.250	$0.00	-$1,650	-20%	Indu 0.7%
Notes: July looks to have halted the short-term cycle/establishing a real trend/will appear more real if it tests the resistance at $44 per share.							
Dates Start: 3/1/91							Tran 1.2%
							S&P 1.2%
Today: 7/1/91						P/E 13	Avg. P/E 15
Action: Hold & watch.							
Quantum Corp.							**THREE**
QNTM	150	$10.625	$15.666	$0.00	-$756	7%	Indu 0.7%
Notes: Newly defined trading range.							
Dates Start: 7/1/91							Tran 1.2%
							S&P 1.2%
Today: 5/1/91						P/E 7	Avg. P/E 10
Action: Sell.							

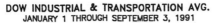
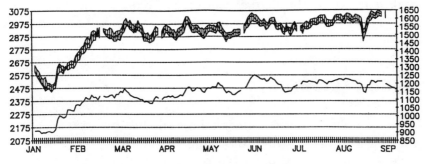

STOCK DAILY PRICE TRACKING
AMGEN (OTC—AMGN)

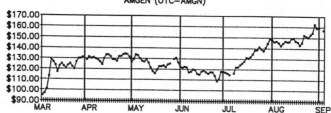

CRAY RESEARCH (NYSE—CYR)

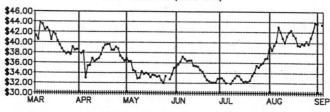

QUANTUM CORP. (OTC—QNTM)

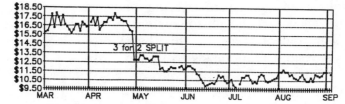

FIGURE 15.2 **Dow Averages and Stocks**

this are slow and a bit lethargic, they are usually not considered weak markets. If the market were truly weak, it would be dropping. This is why it is usually not a good idea to sell short a "dull market."

Sell on Quantum

If the speculative investor decided to sell Quantum, the most logical time was back in mid-May at about the $12 price. The stock price staged a couple of feeble rallies near the $13 level, didn't attract any interest, and dropped to $12 for the next couple of weeks. Selling at this point would have resulted in a $550 loss, but the bulk of the investment could have been reinvested in a more promising stock.

Stock Splits

Actually, the only thing increased by a stock split is the total number of outstanding shares. The real effects on the stock are neutral. All the numbers relating to the stock are recalculated to match the split. If a stock pays a one-dollar dividend and splits two for one, it then pays 50 cents per share. Earnings and sales figures are adjusted accordingly.

The commonly held belief about stock splits says that they are always a positive influence on the price of a stock, which probably originated from getting more shares without paying any more money. Although some stock prices are accelerated by the announcement of a split, this theory often does not stand up to close examination (Tables 15.15 and 15.16).

Table 15.15 is a study of over-the-counter stocks from April 1987 through April 1991, showing the effects of stock splits on prices during the next six-month period. If a price remained the same, it was counted as being down.

You would expect 1987 to be down because of the crash. The following year was about even, which still does not support the theory that all stock splits are positive. The next two years (1989 and 1990) were good years, but look at the differences in the splits. Although these figures seem to suggest that a stock price is

Table 15.15 *Effects of Stock Splits on OTC Six Months Later*

Number of Occurrences									
1987		1988		1989		1990		1991	
Up	Down	Up	Down	Up	Down	Up	Down	Up	Down
6	59	20	21	33	46	17	37	3	2

Total Splits:	244
Total Up:	79
Total Down:	165

likely to fall after a split, this is not a reliable conclusion. The next five years might show opposite figures.

The only dependable conclusion is that the direction of a stock price after a split depends more on what is happening with the company than on the split itself. Companies have many reasons for deciding to split their stock: Boosting or supporting the price can easily be one of them.

Table 15.16 shows stock splits on exchange traded (listed) companies.

If the 1987 figures are removed, according to the stocks surveyed, the chances of seeing a rising price six months after a split are about fifty-fifty. Again, this confirms that a stock split has a positive impact on stock price initially, but it won't necessarily stay up during the next six months. Price strength usually depends on factors other than a stock split.

Table 15.16 *Effects of Stock Splits on Exchange-Traded Stocks Six Months Later*

Number of Occurrences									
1987		1988		1989		1990		1991	
Up	Down	Up	Down	Up	Down	Up	Down	Up	Down
4	135	51	39	63	60	43	54	12	5

Total Splits:	466
Total Up:	173
Total Down:	293

Cray Research May Have Hit Bottom

Although Cray Research may have hit bottom at $30 back in January, it had a tendency to head in that direction several times in the March through July time period. The price quickly ran up to $44, then dropped back to establish weak support at $41 (Figure 15.2). The next support at $38 held only for about a week.

Sell and Take a Loss Is One Strategy

Would the speculative investor have sold at the end of March and taken a loss? It would have been a good strategy, but notice the similarity between the movements of Cray's prices to the movement of the Dow Industrials. Many speculators would believe the weakness of the stock to be caused by the weakness in the market and would likely have held on to the stock. They would likely have held their breath three days later as Cray plummeted to $33, a modest support level from January.

The quick recovery obviously provided many investors with a sell target, which accounts for the resistance at $39.50, and also a similar resistance level back in January. The sell-off at this point pushed the stock to a new support level of $32, two dollars above the previously well established $30 level (from December and January).

Cray's price (Figure 15.2) attempted one big rally in June, followed by two smaller ones and another successful rally beginning in the last half of July, running into August (Table 15.17). The unsuccessful rallies kept returning to the $32 level, strengthening the support. The stock then proceeded with a strong rally, returning to the trading range established back in February. August showed a strengthening of the trend, with the stock at $ 37.875 and up to $ 43.50 in September. For the March through September time period, the strongest support is $32 and the toughest resistance is $44 a share.

Is Cray Being Traded Speculatively?

The volatility of the price pattern with Cray Research suggests that a number of speculative traders are buying on price corrections and

Table 15.17 Monthly Evaluation: Speculation

Stock Evaluation				Speculation Objective: 30%			Currently: 34.1%
				August 1991			
				Return on Investment			
Stock Symbol & Dates	Qty #	Current Price	Begin Price	Divs $	Gain $	Gain %	Market Progress
Amgen							ONE
AMGN	200	$146.250	$91.250	$0.00	$11,000	60%	Indu 0.7%
Dates Start: 3/1/91	Notes: Stock in well-defined uptrend Hang on.						Tran 1.2% / S&P 1.2%
Today: 8/1/91	Action: Hold or buy more.					P/E 150	Avg. P/E 41
Cray Research							TWO
CYR	200	$37.875	$41.250	$0.00	−$675	−8%	Indu 0.7%
Dates Start: 3/1/91	Notes: Better definition of the uptrend/Former resistance at $44.						Tran 1.2% / S&P 1.2%
Today: 8/1/91						P/E 8	Avg. P/E 11
Quantum Corp.							THREE
QNTM	150	$11.250	$15.583	$0.00	$ 649	29%	Indu 0.7%
Dates Start: 3/1/91	Notes: Trading range becoming defined. Without a positive change in the stock, it could be here for awhile.						Tran 1.2% / S&P 1.2%
Today: 8/1/91	Action: Sell/Too soon to consider buying.					P/E 7	Avg. P/E 10

Table 15.17 (Continued)

| Stock Evaluation | | | | Speculation Objective: 30% | | | Currently: 45.1% |

| | | | | September 1991 | | | |

Stock Symbol & Dates	Qty #	Current Price	Begin Price	Return on Investment			Market Progress
				Divs $	Gain $	Gain %	
Amgen							**ONE**
AMGN	200	$157.250	$91.250	$0.00	$13,200	72%	Indu 1.7%
Notes: August Value Line "Timeliness #1 (highest) Royalties Epogen & Neupogen licenses should help sales bottom line over the next 3–5 years. 1991 earnings est. $.90"							Tran 2.1%
							S&P 2.0%
Dates Start: 3/1/91 Today: 9/3/91							
Action: Hold or buy more.				P/E N/A			Avg. P/E 41
Cray Research							**TWO**
CYR	200	$43.500	$41.250	$0.00	$450	5%	Indu 0.7%
Notes: "again, Cray . . . has to turn in a strong finish to post an annual earns gain in 91. A good advance for 92 . . . will maintain position into mid 90's."							Tran 1.2%
							S&P 1.2%
Dates Start: 3/1/91 Today: 9/3/91							
Action: Hold & watch.				P/E 14			Avg. P/E 15
Quantum Corp.							**THREE**
QNTM	150	$11.250	$15.666	$0.00	–$662	–28%	Indu 0.7%
Notes: "Sales boomed fiscal 91/strong sales to Apple Computer. Production of new families of product will cut profits/recently introduced 2½-inch drives."							Tran 1.2%
							S&P 1.2%
Dates Start: 3/1/91 Today: 9/3/91							
Action: Sell.				P/E 7			Avg. P/E 10

selling near price resistance points. Since the price activities of July reinforced the $32 support level, the ensuing rally didn't have a sell-off until the $43 to $44 dollar resistance area was reached. Resistance at these levels goes back to July 1990, when the stock was moving lower from the $50 level.

What Does Cray Price Tracking Show?

Theoretically, a speculative stock trader of Cray Research could have used the following buy-sell agenda:

Date:	Bought	Date:	Sold At	$ Gain	% Gain
3/01	$41.25	3/05	$43.875	$ 2.625	6%
3/10	40.50	3/13	41.875	1.375	3
3/21	37.75	3/26	39.125	1.375	3
4/03	33.00	4/18	39.625	6.625	20
5/08	33.00	6/11	36.500	3.500	11
6/26	32.13	8/14	42.375	10.250	32

Total Dollar Gain: $25.75 = 62% (Does not consider commission costs)

Keep in mind these prices are based on the end of the day. Trades made during the day could have been higher or lower. The main difficulties in trading a pattern like this are tied to exactness. In some cases, too much precision is expected and in other cases not enough. Although support and resistance levels are observable, they are not always exactly the same; judgment and decisive action are needed to anticipate where the next level will be. If a turning point is missed by only a small amount, a significant loss could result.

Trading on Technical Moves

Nevertheless, many institutional, as well as individual, investors trade on these technical stock price fluctuations. The buy-and-hold speculator is looking for a turnaround with Cray Research.

When the numbers are considered, the progress at the end of six months doesn't look good, but the picture does improve when you track prices. Although the stock is unlikely to achieve the 30 percent growth objective, early September is time to hold and watch. The $43 to $44 resistance level is likely to remain for awhile, but improvement in the overall market or earnings fundamentals could make a big difference.

Amgen Is Doing Exceptionally Well— Early Sellers Missed Out

Amgen, with only three good months, is the primary growth of the entire portfolio. As Figure 15.2 shows, Amgen went from the $91 to $95 area to just above $130 a share in March (the scale for Amgen is based on $5 a share). It rode a $10 roller coaster in April, showed a $20 fluctuation in May, and dropped $10 in June. The recovery began in the last week of June and ran up to more than $50 a share, $30 higher than the early March increase.

Investors who were tempted into selling in May and June would have missed out on significant profits. Some of the more conservative investors took profits as more speculators bought into the stock. The stock was becoming more and more speculative, as shown by the P/E ratio, which was above 200 (based on reported earnings through July).

What can an investor do in a situation like this? On one hand, the stock price increases make it overvalued; and on the other, the buying enthusiasm maintains a lot of earnings anticipation in the stock. If significantly stronger earnings come in to fill the gap, the price could go even higher.

Strategies for Outperforming Stocks

There are some simple strategies for such a situation:

1. Sell the stock on a rally and buy back on a stabilized correction.
2. Sell half the stock and keep a close watch on the rest.
3. Place a sell stop order low enough that it is not activated by minor fluctuations, yet high enough to bring decent profits (remember, stop orders cannot be placed on OTC stocks).
4. Buy protective put options.

5. Learn more about the stock. Call the company and talk to investor relations; ask for literature concerning their products, operations, and plans.

6. Research the stock as a new selection.

7. Find people who use the company's products. Ask their opinion of the company, the product, and future developments.

We don't want to dump our top performer unless it has become too expensive and hanging on could turn against us. Learning more about the stock can help, but ultimately we are faced with a judgment call.

Research tells us that a three-for-one stock split will occur on September 10, but as discussed earlier, it is difficult to say whether the effects will be positive. Neupogen, the newest drug, took off quickly, indicating acceptance from the medical profession.

The rapid price rise suggests that many investors believe that earnings will increase enough to fill the large gap in the P/E ratio, which has been bouncing between 150 and 200 based on the current situation. In a rapid-growth situation such as this, you have to look at the facts, reach a conclusion, and take decisive action.

Table 15.18 *Portfolio Evaluation: Speculation*

Portfolio Evaluation					
Objective: Speculation 30%					
		Portfolio Performance			Market
Date:	Invested $	Current $	Gain $	Gain %	Indu. %
3/1/91	28,838				
4/1/91		35,850	7,012	24.3	−1.0
5/1/91		35,013	6,175	21.4	0.7
6/3/91		33,269	4,431	15.3	4.3
7/1/91		31,594	2,756	9.5	1.7
8/1/91		38,675	9,837	34.1	3.7
9/3/91		41,838	13,000	45.1	3.7

Speculation Shows High Profit but Weak Diversification

Our speculation stock portfolio is up 45 percent for the first six months, but this gain is due almost entirely to the price growth of Amgen. The situation strongly suggests that the current portfolio has weak diversification. At this point, we should seriously consider selling some of the Amgen and replacing the other stocks with better speculation candidates.

Speculative traders who trade frequently likely would have made changes earlier, possibly back in April and May; the longer term investor should now be concerned as well. If Amgen begins to tumble, there are no other stocks in the portfolio to take up the slack. Unless the investor has some strong understanding of the other two companies, it's time to go shopping again.

Comparing Market and Performance Portfolio—Outperforming the Market

How does price performance match the stated objective and the current progress of the stock market? These are the two benchmarks by which to measure price performance.

While our most important benchmark is our original objective, it is also important to compare our performance to the entire market. The market comparison gives us a relative growth position and can point out possible signs of weakness.

Outperforming the Market

All three non-income portfolios are outperforming the market. The growth portfolio is up 17 percent (objective 20 percent annual), total return is up 11 percent (objective 12 percent annual), and our speculation stocks are up a whopping 45 percent (objective 30 percent annual) for six months. This is excellent performance in all three objectives.

Although as discussed earlier, some individual stock situations are begging for some decisions, we are doing quite well. We might even be doing *too* well.

Table 15.19 *Portfolio Results for Six Months*

Time Period: 3/1/91 to 9/3/91 (Six Months)

	Closing Levels		Changes		
Market Indicator	Then	Now	Points	%	Notes
Dow Industrial Avg.	2,909.90	3.017.67	+107.77	+4%	
Dow Transportation	1,150.74	1,196.76	+46.02	+4%	
Other Indexes					
S&P 500 Index	370.47	392.10	+21.98	+6%	S&P ahead of Dow 2%
S&P Indust. Index	438.58	462.08	+23.50	+5%	
Interest Rates					
Fed Funds	6.4%	5.79%	N/A	−.6%	Short-term rate, .5%+
Discount Rate	6.0%	5.5%			
T-bond Index	3,693.12	3,956.53	+263.21	+7%	
T-bond Index Ylds	8.46%	8.16%	N/A	−.3%	Long-term rate, .3%
Our Results					
Income	6.9% annually (price growth not considered)				
Growth	+18.0% for six months				
Total return	+12.0% for six months				
Speculation	+45.0% for six months				

Dow Averages—Is It Possible to Be Doing Too Well?

The Dow Averages have shown only a 4 percent gain and the S&P 500 Index, which shows a broader and more precise gain, is up only 6 percent for the same six-month period. This difference poses some question as to the strength of our advances. Stocks tend to move as a group, but our portfolios are considerably ahead of the market. With continued low interest rates, this is not the time to panic, but it is a caution light. The most important fact still is that our portfolios are all meeting the requirements of their respective objectives within the first six months.

Look for Sells in December, and Buy with Caution

In December, we are looking for stocks to sell. This is the month we decide which stocks to get rid of before the end of the year. Deciding to take losses will give us a tax write-off or lessen the tax impact of previously taken profits.

The market usually gets volatile in December because two counteracting forces are at work. Tax-loss sellers are trimming their stock portfolios of underperforming assets, and investors with cash are looking for stocks to buy before the "Santa Claus rally" appears. December is the month to look for stocks to sell. If the sell candidates can be sold into a short rally before Christmas, all the better.

Key Ideas

Six-Month Evaluation for an income Objective:
Detroit Edison—
 —Expect earnings to be higher.
 —Rating, financial strength, and price are good.
Otter Tail Power shows questionable diversification.
Union Electric shows good diversification.
Conclusions: Six-month income evaluation.
Growth objective evaluation:
Novell figures are better than the Dow.
What about Apple?
 —Find out why, check the research.
 —Can improvement be made soon?
Conclusions: Six-month growth evaluation.
Total Return objective evaluation:
 —General Electric is doing well.
 —Exxon has the lowest return.
 —American Home Products is in the lead.

The stocks are ahead of the Dow Averages.

Conclusions: Six-month total return evaluation.

Speculation objective evaluation:

Amgen is still hot—

　—Price growth has been uneven.

　—There are some concerns.

Daily price tracking.

Quantum problem—

　—A split caused difficulties.

　—Split wasn't the only reason for decline.

Where is the market going?

Sell on Quantum.

Cray Research may have hit bottom—

　—Sell and take a loss is one strategy.

　—Is Cray being traded speculatively?

　—What does Cray price tracking show?

　—Trading on technical moves.

Amgen is doing exceptionally well—early sellers missed out.

There are strategies for dealing with outperforming stocks—many believe in the future earnings potential.

Speculation shows high profit but weak diversification.

Compare market performance with portfolio performance—stocks that outperform the market.

Dow Averages: Is it possible to be doing too well?

Look for sells in December; buy with caution.

Notes

1. *Value Line Investment Survey,* January 18, 1991, Analyst Paul E. Debbas.
2. *Value Line Investment Survey,* October 18, 1991, Analyst Paul E. Debbas.
3. *Value Line Investment Survey,* January 18, 1991, Analyst Alan N. Hoffman.
4. *Value Line Investment Survey,* October 18, 1991, Analyst Alan N. Hoffman.

5. *Value Line Investment Survey,* January 18, 1991, Analyst Arthur H. Medalie.

6. *Value Line Investment Survey,* October 18, 1991, Analyst Arthur H. Medalie.

7. *Value Line Investment Survey,* October 18, 1991, Analyst Alan N. Hoffman.

8. *Value Line Investment Survey,* February 1, 1991, Analyst Bridget A. Collins.

9. *Value Line Investment Survey,* August 23, 1991, Analyst Peter Azcue.

10. *Value Line Investment Survey,* August 23, 1991, Analyst Philip S. Mulqueen.

11. *Value Line Investment Survey,* August 2, 1991, Analyst George A. Niemond.

12. *Value Line Investment Survey,* August 2, 1991, Analyst Bridget A. Collins.

13. *Value Line Investment Survey,* August 9, 1991, Analyst Rudolph C. Carryl.

14. Be careful with annualized figures; they can be misleading. Many would annualize the running rate at the current 17.6 percent average.

15. *Value Line Investment Survey,* February 1, 1991, Analyst John E. Ferebee.

16. *Value Line Investment Survey,* August 9, 1991, Analyst Thomas P. Au.

17. *Value Line Investment Survey,* October 4, 1991, Analyst Thomas P. Au.

18. *Value Line Investment Survey,* August 2, 1991, Analyst John E. Ferebee.

19. *Value Line Investment Survey,* February 8, 1991, Analyst Keith A. Markey.

20. *Value Line Investment Survey,* August 9, 1991, Analyst Keith A. Markey.

21. *Value Line Investment Survey,* August 2, 1991, Analyst George A. Niemond.

22. *Value Line Investment Survey,* August 2, 1991, Analyst George A. Niemond.

CHAPTER 16

Looking for Sells in December

Most individuals base their fiscal year on the calendar year. For this reason, December is the time to start looking for sell candidates. Selling in December will allow the individual to take possible tax advantages, particularly with underperforming stocks. During this month, we want to either sell the losing stocks and move on to better selections or watch them carefully. If an underperforming stock is showing an upward price trend, it might be best to wait and watch. We can sell it up to and including the final stock trading day of the year.

December 1 Income Evaluation

Dividends Appear Secure

A review of our individual income stocks shows them to be doing quite well in terms of price growth (Table 16.1). At this point in time, the dividends appear to be secure. Detroit Edison is showing a 15 percent price increase, Otter Tail Power is up 12 percent,

Table 16.1 *Buy-and-Sell Information*

	Buy Information			Sell Information			Gain	
Date	Stock	Qty	Price	Date	Qty	Price	$ °	%
3/1/91	DTE	400	$29.375	12/2/91	400	$33.875	$1,800	+15%
3/1/91	OTTR	300	26.50	12/2/91	300	29.75	975	+12
3/1/91	UEP	1000	30.25	12/2/91	1000	36.125	5,875	+19

° Profits do not include dividends. Commissions not included.

and Union Electric is leading with a 19 percent increase since our purchase back in March.

Look for Problems

As stated, in December we are looking primarily for problems in our portfolio. With income stocks, we have two concerns: the strength of the dividend and the price of the stock. If the dividend is cut or reduced, the price will drop due to investor mistrust.

As we see, our income stocks are holding strong during the first part of December. At this point, there are no indications for caution with these three. The market is still weak, but has held firm for most of the year. It is reflecting the difficulties of climbing out a recession, which is often a slow process.

Close to Income Objective

A review of the entire income portfolio (Table 16.2) indicates we are coming closer to our objective of 7 percent annual income yield. Because interest rates have been dropping since last March, this has become an even more attractive yield.

As of December 1991, no "safe" money investments are paying a comparable amount. We will still miss our first-year income objective by one-half of a percent; however, if we see the dividend growth we expect, this half percent will be made up easily in the income from year two.

The price growth here is telling us that our dividends appear to be secure, which is what we want to know. The individual stocks in our income portfolio are showing similar enough results that we don't need to sell any of them at this point. Because the U.S. economy remains in a recession, we are concerned with Detroit Edison's reliance on the automobile industry and we will need to keep an eye on that stock, but for now things appear stable. Our income portfolio is reasonably secure (Table 16.3).

December Growth Results Mixed

Our December 1 check of the growth portfolio (Table 16.4) reveals somewhat mixed results. At present, we are not checking on

Table 16.2 December 1 Stock Evaluation: Income

Stock Evaluation				Income Objective: 7%				Currently: 6.6%
				December 1991				
					Return on Investment			
Stock Symbol	Qty #	Div $	Current $	Begin Price	Divs Price	Gain $	Gain %	Market Progress
Detroit Edison								**ONE**
DTE	400	$1.88	$33.875	$29.375	$752	$1,800	15.3%	Indu 0.9%
Dates Start: 3/1/91	6.4% = Annual yield based on buy price							Tran 4.2%
Today: 12/2/91	Notes: Figures include 4 dividends; gain calculated without dividends.							S&P 3.0%
	Action: Hold or buy more.							
Otter Tail Power								**TWO**
OTTR	300	$1.60	$29.750	$26.500	$480	$975	12.3%	Indu 0.9%
Dates Start: 3/1/91	6.0% = Annual yield based on buy price							Tran 4.2%
Today: 12/2/91	Notes: Figures include 4 dividends; gain calculated without dividends.							S&P 3.0%
	Action: Hold or buy more.							
Union Electric								**THREE**
UEP	1000	$2.24	$36.125	$30.250	$2,180	$5,875	19.4%	Indu 0.9%
Dates Start: 3/1/91	7.4% = Annual yield based on buy price							Tran 4.2%
Today: 12/2/91	Notes: Figures include 4 dividends; gain calculated without dividends.							S&P 3.0%
	Action: Hold or buy more.							

Table 16.3 *Portfolio Evaluation: Income*

Portfolio Evaluation							
Evaluation: Income 7% (annual dividends)							
	Annual Dividend		Portfolio Performance				Market
Date:	Income $	Yield %	Invested $	Value $	Gain $	Gain %	Indu. %
3/1/91	848	6.8	49,950				
9/3/91	2,544	6.8		52,550	2,600	5.2	3.7
12/2/91	3,412	6.8		58,600	8,650	17.3	1.8

the comments of analysts because our main concern is price performance, not analyst opinion. We may want to check opinion if we are having trouble with a sell decision, but first we are just comparing price growth with our objective and the market.

Most Stocks Are Up and Running

Conagra is up 8 percent since March 1. Novell is up a remarkable 110 percent for the same time period. Syntex is up just 8 percent, which isn't exceptional when compared with the others, but has some chance to achieve the growth objective. Conagra and Syntex require some patience at this point in time. Both stocks are significantly outperforming the market, even though they are currently not on track for objective attainment. We don't really have any good reason to sell.

Apple Still Has Problems

Apple Computer is still a disappointment. The financial condition of the computer industry is growing unstable. Apple must cut prices to remain competitive. When they cut prices, earnings drop. This could be the time to take the small loss and move on to another growth stock. Albertson's is more of a toss-up. It still has competition to deal with, but as a food retailer it has some insulation from recession.

The growth portfolio is on track for the 20 percent objective (Table 16.5), but much of that comes from the strong showing of

Table 16.4 December 1 Stock Evaluation: Growth

Stock Evaluation			Growth Objective: 20%					Currently: 25.3%
			December 1991					
					Return on Investment			
Stock Symbol & Dates	*Qty #*	*Div $*	*Current Price*	*Begin Price*	*Divs $*	*Gain $*	*Gain %*	*Market Progress*
Conagra								ONE
CAG	300	$0.54	$32.000	$27.917	$131	$1,154	13.8%	Indu 0.9%
Notes: Figures include 4 dividends; 2–3 split.								Tran 4.2%
								S&P 3.0%
Dates Start: 3/1/91								
Today: 12/2/91					P/E 24			Avg. P/E 14.8
Action: Hold or buy more.								
Albertson's								TWO
ABS	200	$0.58	$33.750	$38.500	$84	–$884	–11.5%	Indu 0.9%
Notes: Figures include 4 dividends.								Tran 4.2%
								S&P 3.0%
Dates Start: 3/1/91								
Today: 12/2/91					P/E 20			Avg. P/E 17.3
Action: Hold or buy more.								
Apple Computer								THREE
AAPL	100	$0.48	$51.750	$57.250	$48	–$439	–7.7%	Indu 0.9%
Notes: Figures include 4 dividends.								Tran 4.2%
								S&P 3.0%
Dates Start: 3/1/91								
Today: 12/2/91					P/E 20			Avg. P/E 21.2
Action: Hold, prepare to sell.								

Table 16.4   (Continued)

Stock Evaluation				Growth Objective: 20%				Currently: 25.3%
				December 1991				
Stock Symbol & Dates	Qty #	Div $	Current Price	Begin Price	Return on Investment			Market Progress
					Divs $	Gain $	Gain %	
Novell								FOUR
NOVL	400	$0.00	$51.250	$24.438	$0	$10,725	109.7%	Indu 0.9%
Dates Start: 3/1/91	Notes: Figures include 4 dividends; 2-1 split.							Tran 4.2%
								S&P 3.0%
Today: 12/2/91	Action: Hold/prepare to sell.					P/E 52		Avg. P/E 13.9
Syntex								FIVE
SYN	400	$0.92	$40.000	$37.625	$267	$ 1,217	8.1%	Indu 0.9%
Dates Start: 3/1/91	Notes: Figures include 4 dividends; 2-1 split.							Tran 4.2%
								S&P 3.0%
Today: 12/2/91	Action: Hold or buy more.					P/E 21		Avg. P/E 16.3

Table 16.5 *Portfolio Evaluation: Growth*

Portfolio Evaluation								
Objective: Growth 20%								
		Portfolio Performance						Market
Date:	Invested $	Current $	Gain $	Gain %	Dividend $	Total $	Gain %	Indu. %
3/1/91	46,725							
9/3/91		54,325	7,600	16.3	445	8,045	17.2	3.7
12/2/91		58,025	11,300	24.2	558	11,858	25.3	0.9

Novell. Novell has shown truly phenomenal performance throughout the year. A two-for-one split didn't seem to even slow the growth for a minute. We are showing 110 percent growth in our ownership of this stock. This is a perfect example of the high performer who might be getting too expensive to keep. The positive anticipation of the market has truly favored the stock. Some protective strategies are now in order.

Consider Protective Strategies

When a stock has an existing price increase of 110 percent, it is time to plot defensive strategies. One choice at this point is to place a target sell order low enough so that it is not broken through by normal market swings, yet high enough that the price will be likely to drop significantly after the sell. This is best accomplished by scrutinizing a price movement graph.

Since the stock is OTC, we can't use a sell stop order. Because Novell, Inc., does trade options, profits can be partly hedged by selling covered calls, or nearly insured by buying puts.

The risk in selling the call is that the stock might be called away, forcing a sell, or the price may suddenly weaken severely. The risk with buying puts is the cost of those puts, keeping in mind their expiration date. Even with their risks, these strategies would offer some protection to the profits in Novell. Selling all or some of the stock at the current price to protect profits is an alternative course. There seems to be some growth left in Novell, Inc., but also growing risk. By selling only some of the stock, the investor would realize some profit and still benefit from future growth.

Total Return in December

Keeping in mind that total return stocks are similar to growth, but tend to be more conservative, we want to be close to or higher than our objective. Once a total return stock starts to lose ground in price, due to weakened sales or earnings, it becomes difficult to turn around quickly. So, investors should be more conservative in their evaluation (Table 16.6).

Our primary concern is problems in price performance:

- Has the stock price increased since our purchase?
- How does the price increase compare to our objective?
- Is the stock on target?

Dividends are important and make a significant impact on the return, but they are not our main focus for this evaluation. We will factor them into the total return growth figures. Although we might not see any dividend growth by the first December evaluation, it is a factor to watch in subsequent examinations.

American Home Products Is Exceptional

American Home Products is showing exceptional performance. If the stock were sold on December 2 (the first trading day of the month), the return on investment would have been 38 percent (not counting commissions), which would have included price appreciation and $1,150 in dividends. At this point, we won't worry about American Home Products.

Table 16.6 December 1 Stock Evaluation: Total Return

Stock Evaluation					Total Return Objective: 12%			Currently: 15.8%
					December 2, 1991			
					Return on Investment			
Stock Symbol & Dates	Qty #	Div $	Current Price	Begin Price	Divs $	Gain $	Gain %	Market Progress
American Home Products								ONE
AHP	500	$2.30	$76.375	$57.000	$1,150	$10,838	38.0%	Indu 3.7%
Dates Start: 3/1/91 Today: 12/2/91		Notes: Figures include 4 dividends. A 38% increase in this time period is excellent for any stock. The P/E ratio is rising so watch earnings. P/E 18						Tran 4.0%
								S&P 5.9%
								Avg. P/E 13.2
Action: Hold or buy more.								
Exxon								TWO
XON	500	$2.68	$59.375	$55.250	$1,340	$3,465	12.3%	Indu 3.7%
Dates Start: 3/1/91 Today: 12/2/91		Notes: Figures include 4 dividends. A gain of 12% is on target for our objective. P/E ratio is holding steady. P/E 12						Tran 4.0%
								S&P 5.9%
								Avg. P/E 12.6
Action: Hold or buy more.								
General Electric								THREE
GE	500	$2.20	$65.750	$68.000	$1,040	–$85	–.3%	Indu 3.7%
Dates Start: 3/1/91 Today: 12/2/91		Notes: Figures include 4 dividends; to be down at this point is a big concern. P/E ratio is holding now, but needs to be watched along with earnings. Price could drop quickly, watch carefully. P/E 13						Tran 4.0%
								S&P 5.9%
								Avg. P/E 12.8
Action: Hold or buy more.								

Exxon Is on Track

At a 12.3 percent return, Exxon is on track to achieving the objective. Although lower interest rates can certainly be favorable to a company such as Exxon, some of the positive impact is neutralized by a softening of oil prices. Since the Iraq conflict, oil-producing nations have been unable to control the production of oil. Too much oil means lower prices, which is not necessarily good for Exxon at this time, but could be positive in the future. Lower energy prices will help to stimulate the stalled economy.

General Electric Might Be a Problem

GE is the main problem stock. If we are looking to sell, it would be the logical selection at this point. It is the only stock in the total return portfolio that is showing a decline. There does not appear to be any obvious reason for this decline, as earnings do not seem to be weak. Although this would be the stock to sell if you just had to sell one of the three, it is not advisable to sell it without a more definite reason.

Only the Price Is Down

If the price had fallen lower, earnings were showing a decline, or the overall market were stronger, this would be a good time to sell the stock and take the loss. The only immediate observable factor is the lower price, which is likely to show a rally before the end of the year. If a sell is to be made, this would be an ideal place for a limit sell order. Put a sell order in at a price just slightly higher than is currently showing, a price that will at lease cover the commission on the sell, perhaps somewhere around $67 a share. A look at a recent price graph could provide an even better sell price.

If the stock does not sell at the limit price before the end of the year, change the sell to a market sell order and be done with it. It must be sold before the end of the year for any tax considerations.

Total Return Portfolio Is on Target

The complete total return portfolio is essentially on target to objective with a 13 percent actual total return at the first of December (Table 16.7). Taking into account poor performance on the
market, we can afford to wait and see if our lower performing
stocks will catch up as the market improves.

American Home Products Is Exceptionally Good

We have one stock showing exceptionally good performance
(AHP +38 percent), one that has nearly reached the 12-month
objective (XON +10 percent) and one that shows less than satis-
factory performance (GE −3 percent). We must remember, however, we have held these stocks for only nine months. During this
time, the Dow Jones Industrials are up 2 percent, Dow Transports
are up 6 percent, and the Standard & Poor's 500 Index is up only
4 percent since the first of March. The lack of performance
strongly suggests that the present problems are with the overall
market, rather than individual stocks. A sell of one of the Total
Return stocks, therefore, could be premature.

Table 16.7   *Portfolio Evaluation: Total Return*

Portfolio Evaluation								
Objective: Total Return 12%								
		Portfolio Performance						*Market*
Date:	*Invested $*	*Current $*	*Gain $*	*Gain %*	*Dividend $*	*Total $*	*Gain %*	*Indu. %*
3/1/91	90,063							
9/3/91		98,064	8,001	8.9	2,633	100,697	11.8	4.0
12/2/91		100,751	10,688	11.9	3,530	104,281	15.8	0.9

With interest rates continuing to drop, it is reasonable to expect the investment climate to improve in spite of the current recession. It will be better to analyze performance of these stocks in a market that is showing some growth.

Speculation Is up One-Sidedly, with Amgen

Our speculative stock portfolio is up significantly thanks again to the strong performance of one stock, Amgen. The portfolio is up 61 percent on an objective of 30 percent annual return (Table 16.8). The profits here would provide us with two years' growth, if we sell all the stock and go to cash. That is a tempting proposition to any investor, but do we want to sell our best performer just yet? If earnings come in to spark the fuel of anticipation, the stock still has a ways to go (Table 16.9).

December 1 Evaluation: Speculation

As we go into the last month of 1991, it is with no little amount of frustration. The market has not favored any kind of speculation, in

Table 16.8 *Portfolio Evaluation: Speculation*

Portfolio Evaluation					
Objective: Speculation 30%					
		Portfolio Performance			Market
Date:	Invested $	Current $	Gain $	Gain %	Indu. %
3/1/91	$28,838				
4/1/91		35,850	7,012	24.3	−1.0
5/1/91		35,013	6,175	21.4	0.7
6/3/91		33,269	4,431	15.3	4.3
7/1/91		31,594	2,756	9.5	1.7
8/1/91		38,675	9,837	34.1	3.7
9/3/91		41,838	13,000	45.1	3.7
12/2/91		46,588	17,750	61.6	0.9

Table 16.9 December 1 Stock Evaluation: Speculation

Stock Evaluation				Speculation Objective: 30%			Currently: 61.6%

				December 1991			
Stock Symbol & Dates	Qty #	Current Price	Begin Price	Return on Investment			Market Progress
				Divs $	Gain $	Gain %	
Amgen							**ONE**
AMGN	600	$59.750	$30.417	$0.00	$17,600	96%	Indu 0.9%
Notes: Stock in well-defined uptrend. Hang on.							Tran 4.2%
							S&P 3.0%
Dates Start: 3/1/91 Today: 12/2/91	Action: Hold or buy more.					P/E 77	Avg. P/E 41
Cray Research							**TWO**
CYR	200	$43.500	$41.250	$0.00	$450	5%	Indu 0.9%
Notes: Better definition of the uptrend/Former resistance at $44.							Tran 4.2%
							S&P 3.0%
Dates Start: 3/1/91 Today: 12/2/91	Action: Hold and watch carefully.					P/E 15	Avg. P/E 15
Quantum Corp.							**THREE**
QNTM	150	$11.250	$15.583	$0.00	-$650	-28%	Indu 0.9%
Notes: Not encouraging.							Tran 4.2%
							S&P 3.0%
Dates Start: 3/1/91 Today: 12/2/91	Action: Sell.					P/E 7	Avg. P/E 10

fact it has been an almost impossible market for the stock speculator. It hasn't gone up by much, nor has it shown enough weakness to produce profits by selling short or buying on weakness. Successes and failures track an individual course rather than that of the market.

Cray Is Doing Better

Although it is certainly encouraging to be up nearly 100 percent with Amgen, another good sign is seeing some positive performance in Cray Research. The fact that it was down for most of the year but is now up 13 percent gives us reason to expect better performance. Unless the stock weakens severely between now and the end of the year, we could do well to hang on to Cray Research.

Quantum Corporation continues its slide. Technically, our plan sold out of it earlier, but we discuss the stock here for example. It appears to have hit bottom around the $9.25 level and could settle down to be a speculative, growth stock. As a speculative stock, it should have been sold long ago, at least back in September. If a poor-performing stock like this is held in a speculative portfolio until the end of the year, that is the time to unload it and move on to something more interesting. The awkward split did little to support the price and in fact may have been a contributing factor in the price decline.

Quantum Is a Problem for Now

At this point, there is only one argument for possibly keeping Quantum Corporation for a longer time. The actual dollars we can obtain from the sell aren't enough to do much reinvesting in a better selection. We could only get a little over $1300 for the stock. It would be difficult to find any stock with this amount of money. Many speculators would put it on the back burner and let it sit until it recovers or use the loss to trim a gain from elsewhere.

Sell the Losers in December

December is definitely an important time to look for stocks to sell in any category. The sells can help cut back on earlier profits or can be taken as a loss for income tax purposes. One strategy can be to pick the sell candidates early in December, then look for the traditional *Santa Claus rally* to get the best possible price for the stock.

Key Ideas

December 1 income evaluation:
  —Dividends appear secure.
  —Look for problems.
Investments are close to income objective.
December growth results mixed:
  —Most stocks are up and running.
  —Apple still has problems.
Consider protective strategies.
Total return in December
Our primary concern is problems in price performance:
  —Has the stock price increased since our purchase.
  —How does the price increase compare to our objective?
  —Is the stock on target?
American Home Products is exceptionally good.
Exxon is on track.
General Electric might be a problem.
Total return portfolio is on target.
Speculation is up one-sidedly, with Amgen.
Cray is doing better.
Quantum is a problem for now.
Sell the losers in December.

CHAPTER 17

What's Our Score at Year End?

Most individual investors set up evaluations to coincide with the individual tax calendar, January 1 through December 31 every year. We will therefore add a progress evaluation through December 31, 1991.

The Stock Market of 1991

As we are well aware, the year could only be rated fair for the overall stock market. Much of the modest increase for the entire year actually came in the last couple of weeks in December, in true Santa Claus fashion. The Dow Industrial average was up only 9 percent at the close of trading on December 31, 1991. Transports were double that, or up 18 percent, which is an interesting divergence, suggesting the presence of strength in the market.

The Standard & Poor's 500 Index was much better, up 14 percent, reinforcing the idea of underlying strength in the overall stock market. Transports normally increase at a slower rate than the Dow Industrials. The S&P 500 Index is also usually slower to increase than the 30 Dow stocks. When these indicators are outperforming the Dow Industrial Average, it shows that there exists a broad buying strength in the current market. How long this strength will continue is uncertain, but it is considered a positive indicator.

Income Stocks Are Doing Well

Our income stocks are still doing well (Table 17.1). Declining interest rates create an especially favorable situation for utility

Table 17.1 Year-End Stock Evaluation: Income

Stock Evaluation					Income Objective: 7%			Currently: 6.8%
				Year End 1991	Return on Investment			
Stock Symbol & Dates	Qty #	Div $	Current Price	Begin Price	Divs $	Gain $	Gain %	Market Progress
Detroit Edison								**ONE**
DTE	400	$1.88	$34.750	$29.375	$752	$2,150	18.3%	Indu 8.9%
6.4% = Annual yield based on buy price								Tran 18.0%
Notes: Figured with 4 dividends; gain calculated without dividends.								S&P 12.6%
Dates Start: 3/1/91								
Today: 12/31/91			Action: Hold or buy more.					
Otter Tail Power								**TWO**
OTTR	300	$1.60	$31.000	$26.500	$480	$1,350	17.0%	Indu 8.9%
6.0% = Annual yield based on buy price								Tran 18.0%
Notes: Figured with 4 dividends; gain calculated without dividends.								S&P 12.6%
Dates Start: 3/1/91								
Today: 12/31/91			Action: Hold or buy more.					
Union Electric								**THREE**
UEP	1000	$2.24	$38.625	$30.250	$2,180	$8,375	27.7%	Indu 8.9%
7.4% = Annual yield based on buy price								Tran 18.0%
Notes: Figured with 4 dividends; gain calculated without dividends.								S&P 12.6%
Dates Start: 3/1/91								
Today: 12/31/91			Action: Hold or buy more.					

247

stocks. Again, the main reason we want to check prices is to look for price declines that could be an early warning of a possible dividend cut.

There do not appear to be any price problems with these stocks, at this time. They are all showing growth rates higher than the stock market indexes. In other words, they are outperforming the market. In fact, they are performing well enough to be considered growth stocks. Dividends are not calculated into the price increase, as income is our objective for these stocks; but if you added the dividends into the price performance, all these stocks would show growth and income better than 20 percent, which was our stated objective in the *growth* stock category.

A 23 percent average growth on an income portfolio of stocks is excellent. Price performance like this with income stocks strongly suggests that conditions are improving for the investment market. The price growth is higher than our goal for our higher risk portfolios of growth and total return.

Our income goal is closer than when we started, but not quite at the 7 percent return stated in our objective (Table 17.2). A return of 6.95 percent is very close to its objective and will likely be higher than 7 percent within the next year. The growth will be due to dividend increases.

The return is still quite attractive considering the fact that safe money investments (T-bills) have dropped below 4 percent. Our return on this investment will continue to increase each year as the dividends grow.

Table 17.2 *Portfolio Evaluation: Income*

Portfolio Evaluation							
Evaluation: Income 7% (Annual Dividends)							
	Annual Dividend		Portfolio Performance				Market
	Income	Yield	Invested	Current	Gain	Gain	Indu.
Date:	$	%	$	$	$	%	%
3/11/91		6.8	49,950				
9/33/91	2,544	6.8		52,550	2,600	5.2	3.7
12/02/91	3,412	6.8		58,600	8,650	17.3	1.8
12/31/91	3,412	6.8		61,675	11,725	21.3	9.9

Year-End Evaluation: Growth

We are looking for a 20 percent annual growth rate, which includes any dividends. At this point, we are counting four dividends as being received. Keep in mind this year-end evaluation is not a full 12 months. These stocks were purchased on March 1, 1991, so they still have two months to go.

We can see a pattern developing in the evaluations. The stocks continuing to do well are the ones that did well early on, and the underperforming stocks are still weak though they may be showing some improvement (Table 17.3).

Conagra Grows Despite Split

Even with a three-for-one stock split, Conagra continues to grow at a tremendous pace. The gain on the stock is 156 percent at year end. The P/E ratio is now at 26, up from 22, and from a five-year average of 14.8, which leads to some concern about the amount of anticipation building in this stock. It could be getting too expensive. If we do not see earnings coming in to fill the gap, we will sell some of the shares.

When a stock portfolio of any kind outperforms a lethargic market by this kind of a ratio we are tempted to wait for the proverbial other shoe to drop. It just can't continue to be this good or the market can't continue to be that bad. Somewhere, one or the other has to give. In a fast-moving, volatile market, it is usually the stock that gives and follows the rest of the market. When the market is lethargic, however, individual issues of stock will often map the way for the rest of the market to follow.

Lack of Corporate Earnings in General

The desperation at the end of 1991 was still directed at the lack of corporate earnings. Interest rates had fallen to their lowest point in many years and were continuing to drop even lower. Obviously worried, the Fed was doing everything possible to bolster the health of the economy. With an election only a year away, it was not a good time for a recession. Election outcomes are virtually always

Table 17.3 Year-End Stock Evaluation: Growth

Stock Evaluation					Growth Objective: 20%			Currently: 45.8%
				Year End 1991				
Stock Symbol & Dates	Qty #	Div $	Current Price	Begin Price	Return on Investment			Market Progress
					Divs $	Gain $	Gain %	
Conagra								ONE
CAG	300	$0.54	$35.500	$27.917	$131	$2,406	12%	Indu 8.9%
Dates Start: 3/1/91	Notes: Figures include 4 dividends; 2–3 split. Watch earnings. Note the growing P/E ratio.							Tran 18.0%
								S&P 12.6%
Today: 12/31/91	Action: Hold or buy more.					P/E 26		Avg. P/E 14.8
Albertson's								TWO
ABS	200	$0.58	$39.250	$38.500	$112	$412	3%	Indu 8.9%
Dates Start: 3/1/91	Notes: Figures include 4 dividends. Too soon to sell, watch earnings.							Tran 18.0%
								S&P 12.6%
Today: 12/31/91	Action: Hold or buy more.					P/E 21		Avg. P/E 17.3
Apple Computer								THREE
AAPL	100	$0.48	$56.375	$57.250	$48	−$40	−1%	Indu 8.9%
Dates Start: 3/1/91	Notes: Figures include 4 dividends. Showing improvement. Watch earnings.							Tran 18.0%
								S&P 12.6%
Today: 12/31/91	Action: Hold, prepare to sell.					P/E 22		Avg. P/E 13.9

Stock Symbol & Dates	Qty #	Div $	Current Price	Begin Price	Divs $	Gain $	Gain %	Market Progress
						Return on Investment		
Novell								FOUR
NOVL	400	$0.00	$60.000	$24.438	$0	$14,225	146%	Indu 8.9%
								Tran 18.0%
Dates Start: 3/1/91	Notes: 2–1 split. Watch closely; the price could collapse.							S&P 12.6%
Today: 12/31/91	Action: Hold/prepare to sell.					P/E 63		Avg. P/E 13.9
Syntex								FIVE
SYN	400	$0.92	$48.250	$37.625	$267	$4,517	30%	Indu 8.9%
								Tran 18.0%
Dates Start: 3/1/91	Notes: Figures include 4 dividends; 2–1 split. Watch earnings. P/E above average.							S&P 12.6%
Today: 12/31/91	Action: Hold or buy more.					P/E 26		Avg. P/E 16.3

251

affected by interest rates, but falling rates had not been helping the economy much up to this point. Some individual companies were beginning to show some hope.

Clear leadership was not evident, but individual stocks were holding their own, often reflecting previously established growth patterns, which is why it is possible to have a portfolio that is currently outperforming the rest of the market (Table 17.4). Although the current 45 percent is rather a phenomenal return, the likelihood is that the market will catch up eventually or the portfolio will lose some ground. For now, certain stocks in the portfolio are holding their value compared with the rest of the market. They are hot and likely to remain so for awhile.

Good Price Performance in Total Return

As with individual strong performance in growth stock, we also find cases of good price performance in total return stock (Table 17.5). American Home Products, a consistently strong stock, is still showing excellent performance with a 52 percent return since we purchased it back in March.

Table 17.4   *Portfolio Evaluation: Growth*

Portfolio Evaluation								
Objective: Growth 20%								
		Portfolio Performance						Market
Date:	Invested $	Current $	Gain $	Gain %	Dividend $	Total $	Gain %	Indu. %
3/01/91	46,625							
9/03/91		54,325	7,700	17.0	492	8,192	17.6	4.0
12/02/91		58,025	11,400	25.0	558	11,958	25.6	0.9
12/31/91		67,438	20,813	45.0	558	21,371	45.8	8.9

Table 17.5 Year-End Stock Evaluation: Total Return

Stock Evaluation				Total Return Objective: 12%				Currently: 26.3%
				December 31, 1991				
Stock Symbol & Dates	Qty #	Div $	Current Price	Begin Price	Return on Investment			Market Progress
					Divs $	Gain $	Gain %	
American Home Products								ONE
AHP	500	$2.60	$84.625	$57.000	$1,150	$14,963	53.0%	Indu 3.7%
Dates Start: 3/1/91				Notes: Figures include 4 dividends. Excellent performance. Watch the P/E, currently nearly 7 points above average. Need stronger earnings.				Tran 4.0%
Today: 12/31/91								S&P 5.9%
							P/E 20	Avg. P/E 13.2
				Action: Hold or buy more.				
Exxon								TWO
XON	500	$2.68	$60.875	$55.250	$1,340	$4,215	15.0%	Indu 3.7%
Dates Start: 3/1/91				Notes: Figures include 4 dividends. Notice that the P/E ratio is close to average. Stock is acting as expected. Above 12% annual objective.				Tran 4.0%
Today: 12/31/91								S&P 5.9%
							P/E 13	Avg. P/E 12.6
				Action: Hold or buy more.				
General Electric								THREE
GE	500	$2.20	$76.500	$68.000	$1,040	$5,290	15.7%	Indu 3.7%
Dates Start: 3/1/91				Notes: Figures include 4 dividends; Stock is performing well, but notice the increase in the P/E ratio. Stronger earnings are necessary to sustain the price growth.				Tran 4.0%
Today: 12/31/91								S&P 5.9%
							P/E 15	Avg. P/E 12.8
				Action: Hold or buy more.				

Exxon

Exxon has been slower, but is within the stated objective, showing a return of 15 percent by the end of the year. This steady growth is important, as we are unlikely to see much oil price strength in the near future.

General Electric

Look at General Electric. We were not happy with the performance a month ago, but now, at the end of the year, we are coming in ahead of objective. This is a respectable recovery in a short period. GE appears to have shown improvement with the market, proving it was worthwhile to hang onto a temporarily underperforming stock.

Compare with the Objective

We wanted at least 12 percent return for the year and we are showing a 26 percent return for 10 months, more than double our annual objective (Table 17.6). Some investment advisors might recommend selling when a stock objective is doubled because of the assumed increase in risk. The risk has only slightly increased here and selling at this point could be a serious mistake with these stocks.

Table 17.6 *Portfolio Evaluation: Total Return*

Portfolio Evaluation								
Objective: Total Return 12%								
		Portfolio Performance						Market
Date:	Invested $	Current $	Gain $	Gain %	Dividend $	Total $	Gain %	Indu. %
3/01/91	90,063							
9/03/91		98,063	8,001	8.9	1,755	99,819	11.3	3.7
12/02/91		100,751	10,688	12.6	2,765	103,516	14.9	0.9
12/31/91		111,001	20,938	23.2	2,765	113,766	26.3	8.9

These companies held their own in a market that was experiencing very little growth. Now, that a fair number of investors believe the market is giving signals of a coming economic recovery, is not the time to exit. A positive market should have an even more positive impact on these quality stocks, barring the development of individual difficulties. This is the time to hold on and even consider buying more stock.

The investment climate should remain favorable, with interest rates remaining steady to lower, until the election in the fall of 1992. Lowering of interest rates reduces the cost of doing business, thereby increasing corporate earnings. Increased corporate earnings attract stock buyers, and more buyers push the price of the stock higher.

Year-End Evaluation: Speculation

As stated in the beginning, although the stocks studied in this book are not being traded, some earnings-based selling points will be suggested.

Incredible Amgen

Amgen is still showing incredible strength, up 147 percent since our purchase last March. A lot of big investors are anticipating strong earnings to come in and fill the gap during the next few months. We must remember that the anticipation can retreat even more quickly than it appeared. For now, the stock appears to be stable.

Cray Back to Cycles

Cray Research appears to be back in a monthly cycle of trading. It was up nicely during the first part of December but has fallen slightly by the end of the year. The up-and-down movement here could be a return of that cycle from earlier in the year or could be end of the year sell-off.

Table 17.7 Year-End Stock Evaluation: Speculation

Stock Evaluation				Speculation Objective: 30%			Currently: 89.7%
			Year End 1991				
				Return on Investment			
Stock Symbol & Dates	Qty #	Current Price	Begin Price	Divs $	Gain $	Gain %	Market Progress
Amgen							ONE
AMGN	600	$75.750	$30.417	$0.00	$27,200	149%	Indu 8.9%
Dates Start: 3/1/91	Notes: Stock in well-defined uptrend. Hang on.						Tran 18.0%
							S&P 12.6%
Today: 12/31/91	Action: Hold or buy more.					P/E	Avg. P/E 41
Cray Research							TWO
CYR	200	$38.750	$41.250	$0.00	-$500	-6%	Indu 3.7%
Dates Start: 3/1/91	Notes: Better definition of the uptrend/Former resistance at $44.						Tran 3.9%
							S&P 5.1%
Today: 12/31/91	Action: Hold but watch $44 resistance.					P/E 12	Avg. P/E 12.6
Quantum Corp.							THREE
QNTM	150	$11.375	$15.583	$0.00	-$631	-27%	Indu 3.7%
Dates Start: 3/1/91	Notes:						Tran 3.9%
							S&P 5.1%
Today: 12/31/91	Action: Sell.					P/E 9	Avg. P/E 10

Speculation Still Depends on Amgen

The speculative portfolio performance (Table 17.8) is strong at the end of the year, still primarily due to the phenomenal price growth of Amgen. Our objective was to achieve a 30 percent annual growth rate. In 10 months, we have exceeded the objective with a 53 percent actual growth rate. If our speculative portfolio had only held Amgen during this period, we would be up 147 percent for 10 months. Had we been able to see into the future, this would certainly have been an excellent gain.

The fact is we cannot precisely see into the future, and therefore putting all your investment funds into one speculative stock is not a wise move. The small diversification here is a better and safer approach in most speculative situations. Diversification cut the return by more than half in this portfolio, illustrating why the underperformers need to be eliminated as soon as possible in a speculative portfolio. Next time, the opposite could just as well be true. Some diversification, even if it is only into three different stocks, provides portfolio protection from many unforeseen setbacks.

Table 17.8 *Portfolio Evaluation: Speculation*

Portfolio Evaluation					
Objective: Speculation 30%					
		Portfolio Performance			Market
Date:	Invested $	Current $	Gain $	Gain %	Indu. %
3/01/91	28,838	28,838			
4/01/91		35,850	7,012	24.3	−1.0
5/01/91		35,013	6,175	21.4	0.7
6/03/91		33,269	4,431	15.3	4.3
7/01/91		31,594	2,756	9.5	1.7
8/01/91		38,675	9,837	34.1	3.7
9/03/91		41,838	13,000	45.1	3.7
12/02/91		46,588	17,750	61.6	0.9
12/31/91		54,706	25,868	89.7	8.9

Key Ideas

Income stocks are doing well.

Year-end evaluation: Growth

  —Conagra continues to grow despite split.

  —There is a lack of corporate earnings in general.

We have good price performance in total return:

  —Exxon.

  —General Electric.

  —Compare with the objective.

Year-End Evaluation: Speculation

  —Amgen is still incredible.

  —Cray is back to cycles.

  —Speculation still depends on Amgen.

CHAPTER 18

Keep the Fast Horses and Shoot the Lame Ones

Varied Opinions on Selling

While all investors believe that there comes a time to sell certain underperforming stocks, nearly everyone seems to have a different opinion as to what factors to consider when selling a stock. Brokerage firms seldom make "sell" recommendations. Instead they will lower their opinion from "accumulate" or "buy" to a "hold" recommendation. The change to a hold opinion does not necessarily mean the investor should sell, but selling usually occurs when an opinion is lowered. On the other side, buying occurs if an opinion is raised to a more favorable level.

At times, a large number of big institutional investors seem to manage their portfolios based on changes in the analysts' opinions. As opinions are raised, the large investors buy the stock. As opinions are lowered, the stocks are sold. Most individuals are not able to respond fast enough to take advantage of analyst opinion changes, but it can be helpful to become aware of these changes and note them in your own portfolio evaluations.

December Sells and the Santa Claus Rally

A good time to look for end-of-the-year stocks to sell is in late November and early December. There are two reasons for this timing. One is that selling before the end of the current year allows investors to take maximum advantage of any tax losses. The other is the mid-December Santa Claus rally, which can put a few extra dollars into the end-of-the-year sells. Although it can be good to take a loss and be done with it, a nice rally lessens the blow. The Santa Claus rally doesn't always appear, but it is fairly regular in a favorable investment climate.

The Santa Claus rally is a market surge that frequently occurs during the month of December anytime in the three weeks before Christmas (see Figure 18.1).

As the 1988 graph shows, the rally first appears in mid-November and runs through the end of December. The rally is confirmed by the Dow Transportation average. In 1989, even after a correction that drops the Dow Industrial Average by more than 190 points in a single day, the rally again starts in mid-November, but this time loses steam in the middle of December. Because the Transportation Average really did not confirm the rally, it proved it to be rather weak.

In 1990, the short bear market hit bottom in mid-October and began to move the Industrials to higher levels. The Transportation Average does confirm the move, although weakly at times. A true extra rally appears in December, running through the end of the year.

The year 1991 shows Santa appearing at about the time everyone would give up believing in such things. Mid-December, both averages rally and continue through the end of the year to reach new stock market highs.

Adjusting a portfolio by deciding to buy or sell is always the most difficult part of investing. Analysis tells us a great deal about the market and individual stocks, but no amount of analysis can reliably predict the future. Careful stock selection can help reduce the number of necessary adjustments, but it does not eliminate them.

Sell the Worst Fundamentals

Some say, "Don't sell stock, sell fundamentals," which means sell the stock showing the worst performance in earnings, sales, and price growth, unless there is a solid reason to anticipate a positive

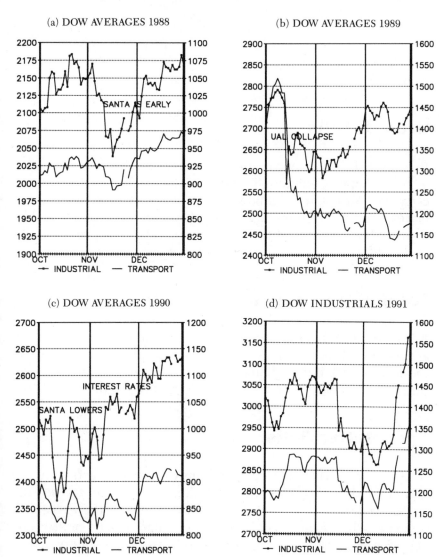

FIGURE 18.1   **Santa Claus Rally**

change in the next few months. High-performing stocks should be sold only if there are sound reasons to believe their performance will decline in the next six months.

These reasons should be based on earnings, earnings anticipation, or a special situation (such as a potential takeover). When you make the decision to sell a stock and buy another, you should take action as soon as possible, especially on sell transactions. Buying a new stock is a lower priority as no money is at direct risk. Maintaining a stock "buy list" can save time when an adjustment becomes necessary.

Growth Sells

Because it has not shown any significant growth for the past 10 months, Apple Computer is the most logical sell in the growth category. Although we know the primary problem is lowered prices to fight the competition, sales have not increased enough to improve the earnings situation. It is unrealistic to expect a significant improvement in earnings during the near future.

Total Return Stocks Are All Doing Well

All the total return stocks are above target and should not be sold at this time. There is some growing concern about the stability of the price of oil, but dropping interest rates can brighten the picture considerably.

Speculative Sells

In the speculation category, Quantum Corporation and Cray Research are dragging down the portfolio performance. If a sell decision is made at this point, these stocks would be the first to go. A partial sell of Amgen could also be in order because of its growing price but lack of growing value. An extreme amount of anticipation is coming into the stock.

Why to Sell

The two primary reasons to sell stock are to improve potential and protect assets. They don't include so-called profit taking, although it is covered under the category of protecting assets. Profit taking is a speculative activity that capitalizes on a recent price acceleration in the belief that the price will weaken and fall to a level at which it can be repurchased. Some individual investors claim to do well with this strategy and others do poorly.

When to Sell

An old stock market adage says, "Buy on weakness and sell on strength." Once you have made the decision to sell, make the transaction as quickly as possible. Delay can easily lead to frustration. It is better to wait for a rally and sell the stock on strength (at the market price) than it is to place a limit sell order and hope the price will rise high enough to execute the order. If your conclusions are correct, the stock could easily begin to drift lower in price and not be able to fill your limit sell order. Selling at market gets an immediate order execution. If you can do this on a price rally, all the better, but don't wait too long.

When Not to Sell

You should avoid selling on a temporary situation such as a market correction, only to take profits, well into a bear market, when you would do just as well to ride it out to recovery.

It all comes down to evaluating the situation, making judgments as to what is most likely to happen, anticipating the move, and taking swift action based on the decision.

Investing in the stock market doesn't have to be a total gamble. There will always be a certain amount of risk involved, but with care, attention, and some analysis you can stay on top of the situation and minimize the risk.

Rather than picking the "hottest" stocks in the market, it just makes more sense to set down clearly and precisely what you want in return for your investment and how you expect to get what you want. Set the objectives and make the stocks come to you. This method of setting clear objectives and modifying risk makes the stock selection process simple and easy to control.

While stock-investing objectives can be constructed differently from the four objectives discussed in this book, they should be applicable to most investors with only minor alterations in dollars invested and time frame.

The analysis forms in this book won't guarantee your results, but they will assist you in controlling the information, and that will improve your ability to select stocks that are most likely to achieve your objectives. These forms will simplify your analysis by making vital information readily available.

The fundamental and technical analyses presented here are abbreviated forms, using only the most important information relating to price growth and strength. Both systems of analysis have their strengths and weaknesses. Neither system will provide definite answers for you, but each provides good information to help you make those important investment decision, which is what stock investing is all about. Making sound decisions increases your chances of achieving your objectives in the stock market.

Key Ideas

There are varied opinions on selling.

Watch for December sells and the Santa Claus rally.

Sell the worst fundamentals.

Total return stocks are all doing well.

Why you should sell.

When you should sell.

When you should not sell.

CHAPTER 19

Points to Remember

Three Main Points

The basic points in this system delineate an organized strategy for being successful in stock market investing. Although the market never offers guarantees, the vast majority of stock price increases are based on anticipation of future growth. The future growth is anticipated due to the trends observed in the stock's recent history. The three most important factors in good organization are:

1. Set specific objectives.
2. Select good stock.
3. Evaluate performance and make appropriate adjustments.

Set Those Objectives Specifically

When you talk to brokers or friends who describe their investment objective as being to "make a lot of money," or possibly "to put my kids through college," be patient with them and say something like "Oh really? Well, that's nice." Then chuckle softly to yourself about how those objectives are much too unclear and general to be useful.

You will be amazed at the number of active stock investors who haven't the foggiest idea how to set up a workable stock investment objective. You might even have to teach your broker or advisor how to build an objective. If you find it necessary to do so, the effort will be worthwhile.

A well-defined stock investing objective will tell you what to look for, what to expect, and when to achieve the result. Anything less is more of a wish than an objective. Most individuals would rather put their investment money on an objective than on a wish. Save your wishes for the lottery.

Remember the Parameters

To be effective, a stock objective must have the following attributes:

- *Be Specific.* State the objective in terms that can be understood.

I am going to invest $50,000 in three significantly different growth companies, to expect an annual return of 15 percent for the next five years. Risk will be modified by selecting stocks with dividends between 1.5 percent and 2.5 percent annually. I will evaluate the portfolio at least quarterly, but watch it continually by checking prices every week.

- *Be Reasonable in Expectations.* Base them on observable performance.

We have to go to the market to define reasonable specific parameters. What kind of growth have these kinds of stocks been showing for the past five years?

- *Consider Risk.* Modify it to your comfort level.

The dividend parameter and the price tracking are our main risk considerations. Each time a dividend is paid, the risk is lowered by that amount. Price tracking will give you a picture of the strength or weakness of the current price trend. Other considerations such as debt, financial strength, and earnings growth stability can help you complete the picture of risk.

- *Have a Time Frame for Achievement.* Choose one year, two years, five years, and so on.

For growth or total return, a three- to five-year time frame is decent. The time period will cover one business cycle or possibly part of two cycles. While it is important to have patience for the stock growth, adverse earnings reports can change the picture enough to sell early.

- *Be Measurable.* If it can't be measured, how can it be evaluated?

"An annual return of 15 percent for the next five years" is certainly an easily measured parameter.

Classify the Stock

Any selection process based on sound logic is a system of elimination and focus. Get rid of those least likely to achieve your objective in reasonable safety and pick the best of the rest. If you have a different method of classification, fine—use it. Otherwise, the four classifications in this book will work effectively.

Stock Classifications

1. Income.
2. Growth.
3. Total return.
4. Speculation.

The classification of stock will focus your attention on only those stocks in line with your objective in terms of income, growth, total return, or speculation. Although you can mix the four basic types, that action will broaden the focus. In most situations, it will be more effective to stay with only one. Again, keep that focus tight.

Select Your Stocks with Care

When you go to the trouble to set a clear and concise objective, it will become only logical to select stocks that match the objective. Any stockbroker can tell stories of investors who claim to have an ultraconservative income objective and then want to buy excessively speculative stock. A few years ago, many retirees living on a fixed income, who tried to take a ride on the swings of Pan Am stock, ended up being taken for a ride instead.

In the selection process, form a clear idea of the kind of stocks you want in your portfolio and select those stocks for close analysis. Then determine which ones will be most likely to achieve your objective. The forms for the Stock Selector System can be helpful in implementing this procedure.

Study the Stock Market

Even a minimal amount of study of business trends, corporate earnings, and the stock market itself will give you some indication of market direction and strength. Television programs such as the *Financial News Network,* or *The Nightly Business Report,* or *Wall Street Week* can help you to keep abreast of the economy and the stock market.

Reading financial newspapers—*The Wall Street Journal, Investor's Business Daily, Barron's*—can supplement what you learn from watching television updates. More detailed information can be obtained from the *Standard & Poor's Stock Guide* (and other publications) or *The Value Line Investment Survey.* Such research materials can be of great assistance in your selection of stock as well as evaluation of performance. You can find the materials in the business section of a local library or you can subscribe directly.

Evaluate the Performance

Many investors mistakenly evaluate one stock at a time, instead of looking at the overall portfolio performance. They never see the full picture of strength and weakness. Looking at the full picture gives a complete perspective and can offer alternatives for doubling up. If two stocks are doing exceptionally well and others are doing poorly, sell the losers and buy more of the winners.

Take Action When Warranted

Taking action is difficult for nearly everyone. It is especially difficult when a decision has been based on a feeling rather than on a logical conclusion backed by analysis. An action can be pursued with confidence and ease when backed by a reasonable amount of comparative research. The full process is, do the research→analyze the information→make a decision→take the action.

Take fast, unresearched action only in an emergency, and keep in mind that many emergencies will be over by the time you are able to take action. If the Dow Jones Industrials drop 200 points in a day, it's probably too late to make a sell on the following day. If the emergency does not stabilize in the second or third day, the action can be taken. Just be ready to buy back when the market has more stability.

Knowing precisely when to buy and sell stock is difficult, but worrying too much about that fact misses a more important point regarding investing. The point of investing is to get an acceptable return on your money over a reasonable length of time. Timing for quick profits with buying and selling resembles playing the lottery more than it does investing. A long-term gain over a three- to five-year time span has a much greater chance of bringing acceptable profits.

Key Ideas

Three main points:

1. Set specific objectives.
2. Select good stock.
3. Evaluate performance and make appropriate adjustments.

Set objectives specifically.

Remember the parameters:

—Be specific. State the objective in terms that can be understood.

—Be reasonable in expectations. Base them on observable performance.

—Consider risk. Modify it to your comfort level.

—Have a time frame for achievement. Choose one, two, five years, etc.

—Be measurable. If it can't be measured, how can it be evaluated?

Classify the stock.

Stock classifications:

—Income.

—Growth.

—Total return.

—Speculation.

Select your stocks with care.

Study the stock market.

Evaluate the performance.

Take action when warranted.

APPENDIX A

Lotus 1-2-3 and WordPerfect Spreadsheet Setup

There are many ways to configure a spreadsheet or other information form. The setup suggested here is intended to be easy to use with minimal spreadsheet experience. As you become comfortable with the software and spreadsheet, you may want to use more complicated cell address references and formulas to fully utilize what a computer can do for you.

Screen Width

Setting up the Lotus 1-2-3 spreadsheet so that the width of the information exactly matches the side-to-side size of your computer screen enables you to see all the information from left to right. The screen width setup also makes a comfortable print size.

It Works Nearly Everywhere

Lotus 1-2-3 has a number of benefits, probably the most important being compatibility with other spreadsheets. What will work for Lotus 1-2-3 works in a similar manner for most other spreadsheets. In fact, Lotus 1-2-3 can be imported directly into many other spreadsheet programs and some word-processing software, including WordPerfect.

Cell Addresses

Lotus 1-2-3 and other spreadsheets use cell addresses as locations for either text or numbers. A cell address is a combination of the column letter and a row number (A1, B2, AB10, AC3, etc.). Cell addresses allow you to set up formulas which then perform formula functions that will automatically make adjustments as numbers are changed or added.

You can also add screens (other spreadsheet blocks of information) to reference stock market performance, then transfer that information to your stock performance data screen. All of this can be accomplished in the same spreadsheet file (see Table A.1).

At the top of the spreadsheet, we see the basic identification information, telling us this is a "Prospect Selector" with an objective of 7% annual income from dividends.

Step 1: Column Width—Adjust the column widths. **/ W C S** type in the desired number and hit **ENTER.** The Prospect Selector sample (Table A.1) indicates suggested column widths at the bottom of the spreadsheet. Continue the procedure for each column.

Step 2: Double Hash Line—In column A, row 1 (check the upper left corner of your screen to make certain it indicates A1) type an apostrophe followed by the double hash mark line all the way to column J. The line may have to be adjusted later for proper length, but it is easily retyped.

Step 3: Entering Text—Even though some of the text covers more than one column, the text for rows 2, 3, 4, and 5 are typed in cell B, the second column. The spreadsheet accepts virtually any amount of text you want to type into a cell and will spread it out across the page as necessary. This will cause difficulty only when text collides with information in another cell.

(For example: If you type additional text into the cell column C row 2, it will cover up part of the words "Prospect Selector.") It is important to be careful with longer rows of text and be sure to give them enough room on the spreadsheet.

Step 4: Single Dash Line—In column A, row 6, type an apostrophe followed by a single dash line all the way to column "J." Hit the **ENTER** key.

Table A.1   *Lotus 1-2-3 Spreadsheet Setup: Prospect Selector*

R										
O	(**Bold** items do not need to be entered in your spreadsheet.)									
W										
S°	COLUMNS >>>									
	A	**B**	**C**	**D**	**E**	**F**	**G**	**H**	**I**	**J**
1										
2			*Prospect Selector: Income*							
3			*Objective: 7% (dividend income)*							
4			*Source: Financial News Information*							
5			*(X means selected for further analysis)*							
6										
7	*Prospect*		*Annual Dividend*					*Price History*		
8	*Stock*					*Today's*		*12 Months*		
9	*Name*	*Symbol*	*$ Paid*	*% Yld*	*Rank*	*Price $*	*$ High*	*$ Low*	*% Change*	
10										
11	*Date: 2/28/91*									
12										
13	Alleg Powr	AYP		3.16	8.1	8	39.000	41	34	21
14	Atlantic En	ATE	X	2.96	8.3	9	35.750	38	32	19
15	Con Edison	ED		1.86	7.8	6	24.000	26	20	30
16	Cmnwlth Ed	CWE		3.00	7.8	7	38.500	39	27	44
17	Delmarva Pwr	DEW		1.54	8.3	10	18.500	20	17	18
18	Detroit Ed	DTE	X	1.88	6.4	2	29.375	31	25	24
19	MDU Resource	MDU	X	1.42	6.8	4	20.875	22	18	22
20	Ottertail P	OTTR	X	1.60	6.0	1	26.500	27	22	23
21	Union Elec	UEP	X	2.16	7.1	5	30.250	31	25	24
22	Utilcorp	UCU		1.52	6.8	3	22.250	23	17	35
23										
	W14	W6	W1	W9	W6	W5	W8	W6	W6	W8

(W14, W6, W1, etc. are Cell widths >>>)

° Row numbers and column letters are for example only. They appear automatically on your spreadsheet.

Row 13 Formulas:

Column	Formula
E	+D13/G13
J	+H13/I13-1

Step 5: Labels—Enter the information into the proper columns in rows 7, 8, and 9. Center the labels where possible by typing a carat ^ before the label.

Step 6: Line Copying—Move the cursor to column A, row 6 and copy the single dash line. **/ c ENTER** will copy the line, then move the cursor to row 10, column A; hit **ENTER** again and a copy of the line will appear in row 10. Also use this procedure to copy the double dash line in row one and place it in row 12.

Step 7: Entering Dates—Type in the date information in line 11. You can either use the date format in the software or enter the date as a label. When entering it as a label, type a quotation mark first. The mark will identify it as a label and will right justify the date.

Step 8: Column Format—Format the columns for the type of numbers they will contain. **/ R F C, F, P.** A prompt will ask you for the number of decimals; enter this information and hit **ENTER.** You will next be asked for a range to format; press the page down key a couple of times and hit **ENTER** again. Move to the next column and set its format.

Step 9: Data and Formulas—Type in the stock information and the formulas for column E and J. Use the copy function to copy the formulas to as many rows as you have stocks to examine. If the columns were formatted properly, you will not have to enter dollar signs or percent symbols. They will appear automatically.

Step 10: Line Copy—Copy the double dash line in row 12 and place it at the end of your list.

Step 11: Saving—Save your spreadsheet as a file. **/ F S** will ask you for a name up to 8 characters in length. Type in a name for the file and hit **ENTER.**

The Prospect Selector is now entered in Lotus 1-2-3. When your information is gathered, you can save this file under a new name and fill in the new information. Overwriting new information on the old data will retain the formats and cell width adjustments. Just be careful that all the old information is replaced with new or is erased.

You can erase information by **/ R E** (extend the highlight using the arrow keys) then hit **ENTER.** *Note:* See "Other Customizing Tips," at the end of Appendix A, for more about copying formulas, formatting, and other spreadsheet tips.

Stock Selector Setup

The Stock Selector form (Table A.2) contains both text information and numerical data. Although formulas can be used to calculate such things as dividend yields and growth statistics, there

Table A.2   *Lotus 1-2-3 Spreadsheet Setup: Stock Selector*

R
O   (**Bold** items do not need to be entered in your spreadsheet.)
W
S   °COLUMNS >>>

	A	B	C	D	E	F	G	H	I	J
1										
2	*Stock Selector: Objective*						*Research from Value Line*			
3	*Date: 2/28/91*		*Total Return: 12%*							
4										
5			*P/E*			*Average P/E ratio: 13.2*				
6			*Ratios*							
7							*5-Yr Average Annual Growth*			
8		*Current*	*5-Yr*		*Annual*	*Price +*				
9	*Stock*	*Price*	*Curr/Avg*		*Dividend*	*Dividend*	*Sales*	*Earnings*	*Price & Divs*	
10		*$*	*$*	*%*	*$*	*$*	*%*	*%*	*$*	*%*
11										
12	AHP	57.000	15	13.2	2.30	59.300	6.6	10.6	4.97	11.8
13	XON	55.125	14	12.6	2.68	57.805	11.4	3.8	14.26	18.4
14	GE	68.000	14	12.8	2.16	70.160	14.0	14.0	5.87	12.0

15
16   Notes: Base Price = $42.000
17   **AHP**   A leading supplier of pharmaceuticals/now bringing new products to market/ie:
18   birth control implant/Financial Strength A+/market weakness in come product
19   areas/long-term debt 66% of capitalization.
20 _____
21   Notes: Base Price = $37.125
22   **XON**   World's largest integrated oil company. Alaska oil spill costs have been
23   worked out, should not hurt bottom line/good stability in the company
24   due to balance of exploration and production/Financial Strength
25   A++.
26 _____
27   Notes: Base Price = $48.500
28   **GE**   One of the largest and most diversified companies in the world Several
29   businesses sensitive to recession/light recession ok Financial Strength A++/LT
30   debt is 12% of capitalization.
31 _____

W9	W9	W4	W5	W6	W10	W9	W9	W9	W9

(W9, W6, W10, etc. are Cell widths >>>)
(Total spreadsheet covers cells A1-I53)
° Row numbers and column letters are for example only. They appear automatically on
   your spreadsheet.

isn't much advantage. The number analysis will often be done separately, either on another spreadsheet or on a notepad.

Step 1: Column Widths—Change the column widths to bring the data to screen width. Cell widths used for this specific spreadsheet are shown just below row 29 as an example. The column width numbers do not actually appear in this location in a spreadsheet; they are on this page for illustration purposes only. Cell widths appear in the upper left reference corner of a normal Lotus 1-2-3 spreadsheet and only refer to one cell at a time, the one where the cursor is currently located.

Step 2: Double Hash Line—Starting in cell A1, type an apostrophe followed by a double hash line all the way to column J and hit the **ENTER** key.

Step 3: Entering Text—Move the cursor to row 2 and type the words appearing under "Text." "Location" tells you which column to begin the segments of text:

Location	Type in Text
Column A	Stock Selector:
Column D	Objective
Column G	Research from *Value Line*

Row 3 of the Stock Selector contains the date followed by Total Return.

Step 4: Single Hash Mark Line—Type in a hash mark line (———) in row 4. Begin the line with an apostrophe, identifying the line as a label and also to set justification to the left. Start the line in column A and run it all the way to J and hit the **ENTER** key. You might have to shorten it later by retyping.

Step 5: Entering Text—Type in the information in rows 5 through 14. The source of information (Column G, row 2) can be even more specific, such as *The Wall Street Journal,* February 28, 1991, or *Standard & Poor's Stock Guide.* In this example the information was taken from *Value Line Investment Survey.* Next we reaffirm that our objective is a 12 percent annual return on investment.

Step 6: Entering Information—Rows 5–9 are used for placing the information in each respective cell. The information labels the numeric data for the stock being analyzed. First, enter the name of the company symbol being analyzed (if you want to include a company's full name, include it with the notes, e.g., AHP is the symbol for American Home Products). In row 11, we put another dotted line.

Step 7: Use the Lotus 1-2-3 range format to get dollar signs and percent symbols. Also, this can set the number of decimal places to 2, 3, or zero. Columns can be justified to right, left, or centered with **/ W L R.**

Step 8: Save your Stock Selector Spreadsheet with an identity of its own. **/ F S** will ask you for a name up to 8 characters in length. Type in the name and hit **ENTER.** *Note:* See the "Other Customizing Tips," at the end of Appendix A, for more about copying formulas, formatting, and other spreadsheet tips.

Additional Information

Setting Column Widths

The Lotus 1-2-3 keystrokes for setting column width are:

/

Worksheet
Column
Set-Width

Type in a number (such as the number 9) and hit the enter key. The column will adjust to the number you entered.

Rows 12, 13, 14 have data for analysis: The "Base Price," which is the price we theoretically bought the stock at five years ago (remember to include the current year as one of the five) is with the Notes; the current price (here February 28, 1991); the dollar amount of the annual dividend ($2.30); then a figure that represents the sum of the previous two (formula: +B13+C13), current price plus the current dividend.

Range Format

The Lotus 1-2-3 "Range," "Format" (**/ R F**) screen allows you to set entire columns as dollars, fixed or percent. At the same time, you can dictate the number of decimal places you want the column to show. Prices are currency with three decimal places. Dividends only need two decimal places. Larger amounts of currency, such as dollar gain, don't need any decimal places showing.

Right Justify, Center, or Left Justify

In the examples shown in this book, dollar amounts and percents are right justified (**/ W L R**), text is usually left justified or centered, whichever you prefer. /W L R will ask for a range, which can be extended to any size you wish by using the arrow keys.

Individual cells are "left justified" when preceded by an apostrophe ', "right justified" when preceded by a quotation mark " and "centered" when preceded by a carat ^.

Formulas

The main reasons to use formulas in the spreadsheet are:

- *Accuracy.* Performing the math function once instead of several times lessens the chance of error.
- *Consistency.* Calculations are made the same way, causing less confusion.
- *Speed.* In most cases, formulas can be copied using the copy function on the spreadsheet. Copying is obviously much faster than retyping the formulas.

Entire columns can be copied at once, eliminating the laborious process of doing them all by hand. It is still a good idea to audit copied formulas and calculate them separately. Formulas can be entered incorrectly, or reference the wrong spreadsheet cell. Double-check all formulas the first time they are set up, to ensure accuracy.

Copying Formulas

Once a formula is entered, it can be copied with the copy function (**/ c**) and moved to the next row. The highlight for the copy function can be extended to cover several rows or columns by using the arrow keys. It might be necessary to "anchor" the highlight with a period, then use the arrow keys to extend the copy function. The use of the period depends on which version of the spreadsheet you are using.

The primary caution is to make certain the formula is referencing the correct cell address. It can be misleading and frustrating to get a bad formula. It is easy to check the formula with a calculator to make certain it is correct.

When first setting up a spreadsheet, before you have any numbers to input, using the number zero enables you to set up and copy formulas. If zero is not used and the formula references an empty cell address, the word "err" will appear. If the word "err" gets into the formulas, they will have to be reentered. Using zero keeps the formulas intact and gives zero for an answer until actual numbers are added.

Using a Fixed Cell Address

The formula automatically changes the cell address reference to the next row unless a fixing symbol is attached, such as a dollar sign ($). The dollar sign fixing symbol can be used when you want each formula to refer to the same cell address, such as with a beginning price or the number of shares currently owned. A dollar sign in front of the letter fixes the column. When placed in front of the number, it fixes the row. To fix both columns and row, use a dollar sign in front of both.

Digits and Decimals

Lotus 1-2-3 allows you to format the cells to differing numbers of digits to the right of the decimal. Prices are formatted with three decimal places, because prices are stated in eighths, which are best converted to three places. The annual dividend amount per share (column D) is two decimal points and the "$High, $Low, and %Change" are all zero decimal places.

The Stock Picks Selector (Table A.3) is an excellent place to use formulas. Multiplying the number of shares times the price, adding them up to make a total cost and subtracting that number from the total funds to invest is fast and accurate once the spreadsheet is established.

Stock Pick Formulas

The formula will then reference the new set of correct cells. Continue this procedure until you have all the cells requiring the

Table A.3 Lotus 1-2-3 Spreadsheet Setup: Stock Picks

R									
O	(**Bold** items do not need to be entered in your spreadsheet.)								
W	°COLUMNS > > >								
S	A	B	C	D	E	F	G	H	I
1									
2	*Stock Picks: Growth*					*Objective: 20%*			
3									
4	*Funds: $50,000*				*Actual Cost: $46,625*				*Leaves: $3,375*
5									
6	*Final Selection Based on Research*								
7									
8		Current Data	Averages				Next 5 Yr	X = Selected	
9	Stock	Current	P/E	P/E	Price	Analyst		Today's	
10	Symbol	Price $	Ratio	Ratio	Growth %	Forecast %		Date	
11									
12	AAPL	57.250	14	13.9	49.2	17.0	X	3/1/91	
13	Notes:	Low P/E high competition		Buy: 100		shares =		**$5,725**	
14									
15	ABS	38.500	23	17.3	46.2	18.0	X	3/1/91	
16	Notes:	Concern of market limits		Buy: 200		shares =		**$7,700**	
17									
18	CAG	41.875	21	14.8	22.0	18.0	X	3/1/91	
19	Notes:	Low growth history		Buy: 200		shares =		**$8,375**	
20									
21	NOVL	48.875	31	21.2	102.1	17.0	X	3/1/91	
22	Notes:	Rapid growth may slow		Buy: 200		shares =		**$9,775**	
23									
24	SYN	75.250	22	16.3	24.2	23.0	X	3/1/91	
25	Notes:	Low growth history		Buy: 200		shares =		**$15,050**	
26									
	W7		W10 W9		W9	W9	W10	W8 W9	

(W7, W10, W9, etc. are Cell widths >>>)

(Total spreadsheet covers cells A1-I26)

° Row numbers and column letters are for example only. They appear automatically on your spreadsheet.

Cell Address	Formula	Dollar Amount	Procedure to Copy
H13	+C12°F13 = $5,725		Place cursor in cell H13 hit
H16	+C15°F16 = $7,700		the following key combination
H19	+C18°F19 = $8,375		**/ c ENTER** move cursor to the
H22	+C21°F22 = $9,775		next formula cell and hit
H25	+C24°F25 = $15,050		**ENTER** again.

Actual Cost: (location F4) **+I13+I16+I19+I22+I25** = $46,625

Leaves: (location H4) **+F4-C4** = $3,375

same formula. Use a zero for price and quantity data if you are setting up the spreadsheet before obtaining the actual numbers. It is necessary to begin a formula with a figure (such as a plus or parenthesis) that tells the spreadsheet this is not a label.

The Stock Picks spreadsheet is primarily referencing the number of shares to purchase, the price per share, and the total dollars to invest. Other brief information, such as short cautionary notes can also be added.

Evaluation of Performance

The next three examples (Tables A.4–A.6) are combined in one spreadsheet file. They interact with each other to compute updated numbers. A setup like this will enable you to use the computer to quickly update your performance results. It saves time and helps to ensure accuracy, if the formulas are set up correctly.

Table A.4   *Lotus 1-2-3 Spreadsheet Setup: Evaluation (Screen 1)*

R O W S	(**Bold** items do not need to be entered in your spreadsheet.)								
°COLUMNS >>>									
A	**B**	**C**	**D**	**E**	**F**	**G**	**H**	**I**	**J**
1									
2 *Stock Evaluation: Growth*				*Objective: 20%*			*Currently: 14.6%*		
3									
4				*SEPTEMBER 1991*					
5 *Stock*			*Current*	*Begin*					
6 *Symbol*	*Qty*	*Div.*	*Price*	*Price*	*Divs.*	*Gain*	*Gain*	*Market*	
7 *& Dates*	*#*	*$*	*$*	*$*	*$*	*$*	*%*	*Progress*	
8									
9 Conagra									ONE
10 CAG	200	0.69	47.125	41.875	104	1,154	14	Indu	3.7%
11 Date:		Notes: (figures include 3 dividends)						Tran	4.0%
12 Begin:		. . . In our recommended list, because						S&P	5.9%
13 3/1/91		of consistent pattern of above avg. earnings							
14 Today:									
15 9/3/91		Action: Hold or buy more					P/E 14.7, Avg. P/E 14.8		
16									

Table A.4 *(Continued)*

R
O (**Bold** items do not need to be entered in your spreadsheet.)
W
S °COLUMNS >>>

	A	B	C	D	E	F	G	H	I	J
	Stock Evaluation: Growth				*Objective: 20%*				*Currently: 14.6%*	
					SEPTEMBER 1991					
	Stock Symbol & Dates	*Qty #*	*Div. $*	*Current Price $*	*Begin Price $*	*Divs. $*	*Gain $*	*Gain %*	*Market Progress*	
17	Albertson's									TWO
18	ABS	200	0.56	42.500	38.500	84	884	11	Indu	3.7%
19	Date:		Notes: (figures include 3 dividends)						Tran	4.0%
20	Begin:		. . . Financial Strength, relatively high						S&P	5.9%
21	3/1/91		shares will outleg market for 3-5 yrs.							
22	Today:									
23	9/3/91		Action: Hold or buy more					P/E 17.3, Avg. P/E 17.3		
24										
25	Apple Computer									THREE
26	AAPL	100	0.48	52.500	57.250	36	−439	−8	Indu	3.7%
27	Date:		Notes: (figures include 2 dividends)						Tran	4.0%
28	Begin:		. . . cut prices to win a bigger share of PC						S&P	5.9%
29	3/1/91		market/good earnings gains to '94-'96."							
30	Today:									
31	9/3/91		Action: Hold, prepare to sell					P/E 19, Avg P/E 21.2		
32										
33	Novell									FOUR
34	NOVL	400	0.00	33.750	24.438	0	3,725	38	Indu	3.7%
35	Date:		Notes: (figures include no dividends)						Tran	4.0%
36	Begin:		2-1 split						S&P	5.9%
37	3/1/91		". . . top choice for year ahead . . . rich P/E holds							
38	Today:		little appeal as long-term capital gain."							
39	9/3/91							P/E 34, Avg. P/E 13.9		
40										
41	Syntex									FIVE
42	SYN	400	0.92	44.125	37.625	268	2,868	18	Indu	3.7%
43	Date:		Notes: (figures include 3 dividends)						Tran	4.0%
44	Begin:		2-1 split; Long-term profits should benefit from						S&P	5.9%
45	3/1/91		additional new medications . . . should add 40 to							
46	Today:		60 cents a share by '91-96.							
47	9/3/91		Action: Hold or buy more.					P/E 23, Avg. P/E 16.3		
48										
	W8	**W6**	**W6**	**W8**	**W10**	**W8**	**W9**	**W6**	**W6**	**W5**

(W8, W6, W10, etc. are Cell widths >>>)

Row 10	Single Spreadsheet		Reference Spreadsheet	
Column	F	+C10/4°B10+previous	F	+P14
	G	(D10−E10)°B10+F10	G	+R14
	H	(F10/B10+D10)/E10−1	H	+S14
	I	Enter market gains	I	Indu +Y12 Tran +AB12 S&P +AE12

Table A.5   *Lotus 1-2-3 Spreadsheet Setup: Evaluation (Screen 2)*

R
O   (**Bold** items do not need to be entered in your spreadsheet.)
W
S   COLUMNS >>>

	L	M	N	O	P	Q	R	S	T
1	Stock Price Data		Albertson's			Symbol: ABS			
2									
3	Number of shares:								
4	Begin Qty.		200						
5	Split Qty.								
6	Split Qty.								
7									
8	*Dates:*					*% Annual*			*%*
9		*Div.*	*Stock*	*P/E*	*Total*	*Div.*			*Market*
10		*$ Pay*	*Price $*	*Ratio*	*$ Divs.*	*Income*	*$ Gain*	*% Gain*	*Gain*
11	*Split* >>>								
12	*Prices* >>>								
13	3/1/91	0.56	38.500		28	1.5			
14	9/3/91	0.56	42.500	23	84	1.5	884	11.5	3.7
15	12/2/91	0.56	33.750	20	112	1.5	−838	−10.9	0.9
16	12/31/91	0.56	39.250	21	112	1.5	262	3.4	8.9
17	2/4/92	0.56	42.500	23	112	1.5	912	11.8	12.5
18	3/3/92	0.64	42.000	22	144	1.7	844	11.0	13.1
19	4/1/92	0.64	43.500	22	144	1.7	1,144	14.9	11.7
20	5/1/92	0.64	40.750	21	144	1.7	594	7.7	14.6
21	6/1/92	0.64	39.375	23	176	1.7	351	4.6	17.3
22	7/1/92	0.64	41.875	24	176	1.7	851	11.1	15.3
23	8/3/92	0.64	42.750	24	176	1.7	1,026	13.3	16.7
24	9/1/92	0.64	44.000	24	208	1.7	1,308	17.0	12.2
25	10/1/92	0.64	44.000	24	208	1.7	1,308	17.0	11.8
26	11/2/92	0.64	46.500	26	208	1.7	1,808	23.5	12.1
27	12/2/92	0.64	48.625	26	240	1.7	2,265	29.4	12.9
28	12/31/92	0.64	50.500	27	240	1.7	2,640	34.3	13.4
29	2/1/93	0.64	49.125	26	240	1.7	2,365	30.7	14.5
30	3/1/93	0.64	52.750	28	272	1.7	3,122	40.5	15.3
	W8	**W8**	**W10**	**W5**	**W10**	**W6**	**W11**	**W7**	**W7**

(W8, W10, etc., are Cell widths > > >)

Row 14	Formulas:	
Column N	+M13/4°N 4+previous	(Note: Use the numbers **1,2,3,4** for March, June, September and December.
Q	+M13/N 13	Use a zero (no formula) for all other months. When starting a new year, be
R	(N14−N 13)°N 4+P14	certain to include all the previous dividends by adding + cell address to
S	(P14/N 4+N14)/N13−1	the formula:
T	+Y12 for Dow Industrials or +AE12 for the S&P 500	(P18 formula +M19/4°1°N 4+**P16**).

(Note: The asterisk ° sign is the multiplication function in formulas.)

Table A.6 *Lotus 1-2-3 Spreadsheet Setup: Evaluation (Screen 3)*

R
O (**Bold** items do not need to be entered in your spreadsheet.)
W
S **COLUMNS >>>**

	V	W	X	Y	Z	AA	AB	AC	AD	AE
1										
2	*Stock Market Data*									
3										
4										
5	*Stock Price Data >>>*									
6	*(Growth objective)*									
7										
8										
9	*Date*	*Indu*	*+/−*	*%*	*Tran*	*+/−*	*%*	*S&P 500*	*+/−*	*%*
10										
11	3/1/91	2909.90			1150.74			370.47		
12	9/3/91	3017.67	107.77	3.7	1196.58	45.84	4.0	392.15	21.68	5.9
13	12/2/91	2935.68	25.78	0.9	1199.58	48.84	4.2	381.40	10.93	3.0
14	12/31/91	3168.83	258.93	8.9	1358.00	207.26	18.0	417.09	46.62	12.6
15	2/4/92	3272.81	362.91	12.5	1443.25	292.51	25.4	447.23	76.76	20.7
16	3/3/92	3290.25	380.35	13.1	1443.01	292.27	25.4	412.45	41.98	11.3
17	4/1/92	3249.33	339.43	11.7	1381.17	230.43	20.0	404.23	33.76	9.1
18	5/1/92	3336.09	426.19	14.6	1359.49	208.75	18.1	412.53	75.82	11.3
19	6/1/92	3413.21	503.31	17.3	1376.12	225.38	19.6	417.30	47.06	12.6
20	7/1/92	3354.10	444.2	15.3	1341.41	190.67	16.6	412.88	42.41	11.4
21	8/3/92	3395.40	485.5	16.7	1314.76	164.02	14.3	425.09	54.62	14.7
22	9/1/92	3266.26	356.36	12.2	1240.23	89.49	7.8	416.07	45.60	12.3
23	10/1/92	3254.37	344.47	11.8	1260.45	109.71	9.5	416.29	45.82	12.4
24	11/2/92	3262.21	352.31	12.1	1366.01	215.27	18.7	422.75	52.28	14.1
25	12/2/92	3286.25	376.35	12.9	1426.85	276.11	24.0	429.89	59.42	16.0
26	12/31/92	3301.11	391.21	13.4	1449.21	298.47	25.9	435.71	65.24	17.6
27	2/1/93	3332.18	422.28	14.5	1517.50	366.76	31.8	442.52	42.05	19.5
28	3/1/93	3355.41	445.51	15.3	1484.66	333.92	29.0	447.90	77.43	20.9
29										

	W8	**W9**	**W7**	**W6**	**W9**	**W7**	**W6**	**W8**	**W6**	**W6**

(Cell widths >>>)

Column	Formulas:	
X	+W12−W$11	Type the formula once and use the copy
Y	+W12/W$11−1	function to duplicate as necessary.
AA	+Z12−Z$11	
AB	+Z12/Z$11−1	
AD	+AC12−AC$11	
AE	+AC12/AC$11−1	

Graph Capability

Organizing the spreadsheet with these three screens will also allow you to establish graphs of growth information. Numbers must appear in consecutive rows to make full use of a graphing capability. It is difficult for most individuals to get a feel for a trend by looking at numbers. A graph shows the trend at a glance.

An Important Word about Dividends

Dividend payments present a special problem to calculations. The dividend amount listed in the paper and other financial information is an annual amount.

A problem occurs because companies do not pay dividends at the same time. The problem is compounded when evaluations are not performed at the same times, such as monthly or quarterly. A real mess can arise if the stock splits three for two and further complicates a formula. There are two solutions to this dilemma, "standardization" and the "entering of values" instead of formulas.

Standardization

Standardization makes use of formulas at regular intervals—say you decide that dividends will be credited to the spreadsheet in March, June, September, and December. It matters not when they are actually paid, since we are concerned with performance rather than the actual banking function:

- Formulas are calculated to divide the dividend by four, then multiply it times the number of shares and add it to the previous dividend.
- The formulas are used only four times a year. The dividend amount is then simply repeated for noncredited months. If an actual dividend amount of $300 is credited to the spreadsheet in March, the number is repeated in April and May, and then is recalculated in June.
- The procedure will allow you to reference the dividend numbers in the formulas that calculate the gain in nondividend months.

Values instead of Formulas

For an even simpler solution, calculate the dividends separately from the spreadsheet and do not use formulas, just enter the actual amount; remember to add the former amount to the new payment. Again, it is necessary to put the same dividend amount into nondividend calculating months. Granted, you can calculate the dividends as they are paid, but trying to determine which dividend to count and in what time period to make the credit can be time consuming and frustrating. Either way, dividends are a special problem requiring attention and a decision.

Standardizing Dividends

For the spreadsheets here, we are standardizing to one dividend in March, June, September, and December. All other months are entered as values, not as formulas, using the total payments through the last dividend credit month. We know that all four dividends are paid by the end of the year, and it is performance of the annual dividend income and/or the price growth with which we are mostly concerned.

Multiple Spreadsheets

The following describes how to set up three different spreadsheets in the same file. The spreadsheets interact with each other and measure ongoing progress of the stock market and the growth stock portfolio. The spreadsheets then feed the data to the evaluation form.

Formulas listed at the bottom of Table A.4 are shown both for the Evaluation form by itself and for a multiple spreadsheet setup.

Multiple Spreadsheets in the Same File

Screen 1 (Table A.4) is set up much like the other spreadsheet formats with text and numbers, including some formulas. Two sets of formulas are listed:

1. Single Spreadsheet. If you want to set the evaluation file by itself, with nothing else added.
2. Reference Spreadsheet. For those who want the complete spreadsheet with all three screens.

The screens (Tables A.4–A.6) are set up side by side with one blank column separating them. The width of this column should be adjusted so as to not interfere with margins. A *width of three spaces* should be enough to accomplish this purpose.

Screen 2

The greatest advantage to Screen 2 (Table A.5) is the price tracking (column "N") and "Gain" tracking (columns "R" and "S"), which can now be easily placed on a graph. The formulas enable the spreadsheet to make the calculations of change. Placing the numbers on a graph shows us the progress of our growth.

Dividends

The goal here is to establish a format for growth evaluation. As stated earlier, some standardization is necessary even though it might not reflect actual happenings. Dividends can actually be paid out in any month, but we are standardizing our computation of them as follows: March = one dividend, June = two dividends, September = three dividends, and December = four dividends.

Make Adjustments for Splits

Make certain to adjust the amount of the dividend, the quantity of stock and the original price per share every time a stock splits. If a stock splits 2 for 1, the number of shares doubles, and the price and dividend are halved.

Stock Market Data

The next screen (Table A.6) shows the progress of the stock market, focusing on the Dow Industrials, Dow Transportation Average, and the listing of Standard & Poor's 500 Stock Index. This screen can be referenced by the "Market Progress" information in Screen 1 (Table A.4).

Information organized with this layout can also be easily graphed, either by itself or in combination with other data.

Stock market spreadsheet data is comparatively easy to set up and track. Here we are showing the figures on a monthly basis, but many investors track the stock market every trading day. Screen 3 (Table A.6) is useful as a referencing tool for Screen 1 (Table A.4) and also is another good candidate for graphing.

Comparing the trend of the market with the price movement of your individual stock can be most illuminating. Figure A.1 compares the trend of growth of Albertson's with the growth of the Dow Industrial Average from March 1991 to March 1993. It is easy to see that the growth tracked the market until July 1992; then Albertson's grew considerably faster than the Industrials.

Price Growth

It is also easy to graph the growth of the stock price. Table A.5 has the prices arranged to be graphed. The pattern is similar to the line established in Figure A.1, but most people want to know what it means in dollar growth as well as percentage growth. The following graph (Figure A.2) illustrates the growth of Albertson's

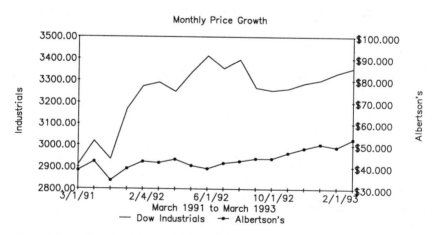

FIGURE A.1 **Performance Evaluation**

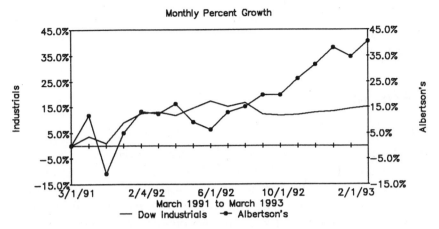

FIGURE A.2   **Performance Evaluation**

price over the same time period. It shows the sharp drop at the end of 1991 and the strong uptrend since July 1992.

Learning How to Graph

First read about graphing in the spreadsheet manual. Then just practice pulling up the graph function and setting various parameters until you arrive at an acceptable picture. Refer back to the manual as necessary, but it is the practice that will help you become familiar with the function.

From Lotus 1-2-3 Directly to WordPerfect Tables

When imported directly into WordPerfect (just pull the file up from the file menu), it is automatically set up in the "tables" format. There might be extra cells to the right and bottom, but they are easily eliminated with the "block" (F12) and "delete" key functions while in the table (alt-F7) format. While in the tables format, turn the block on and expand it through the columns you wish to delete. Hit the delete key and the prompt will ask you if you wish to delete columns or rows. Make the desired selection and the cells will be deleted. If you use dotted lines to make divisions in Lotus 1-2-3, these rows are unnecessary in WordPerfect and can be deleted.

Formulas

All formulas will be lost and converted to the values showing on the screen. If you want them as formulas, you will have to go into the tables format and redo them in the math function listed in the menu showing on the bottom of the tables mode screen (5). You will always know you are in the tables mode when the cursor fills an entire cell and the tables menu appears at the bottom. Text cannot be entered in the tables mode. Hitting the exit key (F7) moves you back to the text mode where you can type in information and data.

Every spreadsheet format has differences and similarities. WordPerfect basic formulas work much like those found in Lotus 1-2-3. It does not fix a formula reference to a specific cell address (using a dollar sign) as was done in Lotus 1-2-3. It does, however, copy formulas down or to the right for as many rows as you select. Entering formulas is a math function found in the "tables" format number 5.

Follow the screen prompts and either enter or copy a formula. You can also use the software copy function (Ctrl F4) to copy a formula from one cell address to another. Just make certain the correct cells are being addressed. It is also necessary to "recalculate" the new position (press 5, then 1).

Shrink Columns to Fit Screen

It will still be necessary to "shrink" some of the columns to pull the spreadsheet to screen width size. This can be accomplished by entering the tables format (hold alt and hit F7); place the cursor in the cell you wish to make smaller. While holding down the Ctrl key, tap the left arrow. The entire column will decrease by one space for every tap. If the column gets too narrow, some of the text will jog down to form a second line. Tapping the right arrow while holding the Ctrl key will expand the column again. Save often.

Storing Historical Data as Text

Data can be pulled into WordPerfect and stored as text without keeping the tables spreadsheet format. Storing the data as text has two advantages: It is more easily managed on the screen, and the printing process is considerably faster.

If you do not wish to use WordPerfect as a spreadsheet in the tables format, simply turn on the "reveal codes" (F11) and delete the tables code. The entire spreadsheet then appears as text and can be easily edited without the confines of the cells. Some cleanup is necessary to align the columns correctly, but moving the individual numbers with the tab key (it can be used since the information is no longer in tables) should straighten them, although you may have to reset the tab stops (shift, F8, 1, 8).

Removing the table code will result in a loss of the math calculation ability but still can be an excellent way to store data for historical reference. The easy of handling and speed of printing are definite advantages.

Portfolio Evaluation Forms

Portfolio evaluations for Income, Growth, Total Return and Speculation have significantly differing focal points; therefore, a model has been provided for each evaluation form, with suggested column widths and formulas (Tables A.7–A.10).

Building Stock Selectors in WordPerfect

The forms in this book are for purposes of organization. They hold the vital information necessary to make stock selections that achieve objectives. The forms were created in WordPerfect 5.1 in the *tables* section. The forms can be set up in various spreadsheet formats, with formulas to assist you in updating the information. The following describes the setup under WordPerfect 5.1 software.

The example will give instructions on how to build a table for the Growth Stock Selector. Although many of the other forms are different in design, the basics are all the same. You should be able

Table A.7   *Portfolio Evaluation: Income*

R								
O	(**Bold** items do not need to be entered in your spreadsheet.)							
W								
S	COLUMNS >>>							
	A	B	C	D	E	F	G	H
1								
2	*Portfolio Evaluation:*							
3	*Objective: Income 7% (Annual Dividends)*							
4								
5		*Annual Dividend*			*Portfolio Performance*			*Market*
6		*Income*		*Invested*	*Current*	*Gain*	*Gain*	*Indu.*
7	*Date:*	$	%	$	$	$	%	%
8	3/1/91			49,950				
9	9/3/91	2,544	6.8		52,550	2,600	5.2	3.7
10	12/2/91	3,412	6.8		58,600	8,650	17.3	1.8
11	12/31/91	3,412	6.8		60,575	11,725	21.3	9.9
12								
	W9	**W11**	**W6**	**W10**	**W10**	**W9**	**W9**	**W9**

(W9, W11, W6, etc. are Cell widths.)
(All row numbers, column letters and suggested widths are for reference only. They do not have to be entered on your spreadsheet.)

Column	Formula
F	+E−$D$8
G	+E/$D$8−1

Note: The dollar gain (column F) does not include dividend amounts. The most important category is column C, the Income received annually, since this is our objective with these stocks.

to build these forms even if you have not had experience with the tables format.

The Basic Growth Stock Selector

Bring up the screen format (Shift F8,1). Set the justification to left and hit **ENTER.** Set the right and left margins to zero and hit **ENTER** (actually they will default to about a quarter of an inch); hit **ENTER** again. Go into part 2 (should be able to just hit number 2) of the format section and set the top and bottom margins to zero; hit **ENTER** twice. Enter part 3 of the format section (hit number 3) and set the font to Courier 10 pt (it might already be set on this font). Times Roman 10 pt will allow more room for

Table A.8   *Portfolio Evaluation: Growth*

R									
O	(**Bold** items do not need to be entered in your spreadsheet.)								
W									
S	COLUMNS >>>								
	A	B	C	D	E	F	G	H	I
1									
2	*Portfolio Evaluation:*								
3	*Objective: Growth 20%*								
4				*Portfolio Performance*					*Market*
5		*Invested*	*Current*	*Gain*	*Gain*	*Divs*	*Total*	*Gain*	*Indu.*
6	*Date:*	*$*	*$*	*$*	*%*	*$*	*$*	*%*	*%*
7									
8	3/1/91	46,725							
9	9/3/91		54,650	7,925	17.0	492	8,192	17.6	4.0
10	12/2/91		59,506	12,781	27.4	558	11,958	25.6	0.9
11	12/31/91		78,723	31,998	68.5	558	21,375	45.8	8.9
12									
	W9	**W9**	**W10**	**W9**	**W6**	**W9**	**W9**	**W9**	**W9**

(W9, W10, W6, etc. are Cell widths.)
(All row numbers, column letters and suggested widths are for reference only. They do not have to be entered on your spreadsheet.)

Column	Formula
D	+C−B
E	+C/$B$8−1
G	+D+F
H	+C+F/$B$8−1

data. Hit **ENTER** until you are back to the word-processing screen.

Enter the Tables Format

Hold the Alt & hit F7; a screen prompt will ask if you want to set up: "1. Columns, 2. Tables or 3. Math"; hit number 2 for Tables. Set the number of columns at 9, hit **ENTER,** then set the number of rows at 25 and hit **ENTER.** You will probably need more rows for notes, but they can be added as needed.

You should now see a full grid with 7 columns and 10 rows (Figure A.3). Next we need to join some of the cells to make room for text.

Table A.9   *Portfolio Evaluation: Total Return*

R									
O	(**Bold** items do not need to be entered in your spreadsheet.)								
W									
S	COLUMNS >>>								
	A	B	C	D	E	F	G	H	I
1									
2	*Portfolio Evaluation*								
3	*Objective: Total Return 12%*								
4					*Portfolio Performance*				*Market*
5		*Total*	*Current*	*Gain*	*Gain*	*Divs*	*Total*	*Gain*	*Indu.*
6	*Date*	*$*	*$*	*$*	*%*	*$*	*$*	*%*	*%*
7									
8	3/1/91	$90,062	(w/o divs.)						
9	9/3/91		98,063	8,001	8.9	1,755	99,819	11.3	3.7
10	12/2/91		100,750	10,688	12.6	2,765	103,516	14.9	0.9
11	12/31/91		111,000	20,938	23.2	2,765	113,766	26.3	8.9
12									
	W9	W11	W12	W11	W10	W8	W12	W6	W6

(W9, W10, W6, etc. are Cell widths.)
(All row numbers, column letters and suggested widths are for reference only. They do not have to be entered on your spreadsheet.)

Column	Formula
D	+C−$B$8
E	+C/$B$8
G	+C+F
H	+G/$B$8−1

Make All Lines a Single Line

Hit the block key (F12), then hit the **END** key. Using the down arrow key, extend the highlight to the bottom of the table. Hit numbers 3, 7, 2, to make all the lines single. Move the cursor back to row 1, cell 1.

Row 1. Starting in the upper left-hand corner of the grid (use arrow keys to move the cursor), turn on "block" (hit F12). Use the right arrow to increase the size of the block by one section (see shaded area in Figure A.4). Next, hit the "join" command (number 7) and the letter Y for yes.

Move the cursor one section to the right. Turn the block (F12) on and with the arrow key expand the block through three cells. Hit the join command (7), then the letter Y. Move the cursor

Table A.10 *Portfolio Evaluation: Speculation*

R O W S						
	(**Bold** items do not need to be entered in your spreadsheet.)					
	COLUMNS >>>					
	A	B	C	D	E	F
1						
2	*Portfolio Evaluation*					
3						
4	*Objective: Speculation 30%*					
5				*Portfolio Performance*		*Market*
6		*Invested*	*Current*	*Gain*	*Gain*	*Indu.*
7	*Date*	*$*	*$*	*$*	*%*	*%*
8						
9	3/1/91	$28,850				
10	4/1/91		35,850	7,012	24.3	−1.0
11	5/1/91		35,013	6,175	21.4	0.7
12	6/3/91		33,269	4,431	15.3	4.3
13	7/1/91		31,594	2,756	9.5	1.7
14	8/1/91		38,675	9,837	34.1	3.7
15	9/3/91		41,838	13,000	45.1	3.7
16	12/2/91		46,588	17,750	61.6	0.9
17	12/31/91		54,706	25,868	89.7	8.9
18						
	W9	**W11**	**W11**	**W10**	**W9**	**W9**

(W9, W10, W6, etc. are Cell widths.)
(All row numbers, column letters and suggested widths are for reference only. They do not have to be entered on your spreadsheet.)

Column	Formula
D	+C−B$9
E	+C\$B$9−1

one more cell to the right and join the remaining four cells in the same way.

Row 2. Move the cursor to the second row, turn the block (F12) on, expand the block down two cells (shaded area shown below). Hit the join command (number 7), then press the letter Y. Continue this through the next four columns. Place the cursor in the sixth cell from the left. Turn on the block (F12) and expand the cursor by hitting the END key. Hit the join command (number 7), then the letter Y (see Figure A.5).

The table should now look like Figure A.6 (extra rows removed for illustration purposes).

FIGURE A.3

(Note: Extra rows were eliminated for this illustration.)

FIGURE A.4

Begin to Enter Initial Labels

At this point we will enter our various labels. Your table should look like Figure A.7. Hit the EXIT (F7) key to exit the table mode into the text mode.

Row 1. Start in the upper left corner. Type in the information "Stock Selector," hit ENTER and type in Date:. The words are too long for the space. Reenter tables (Alt F7); place the cursor in the upper left corner. Hold down the Ctrl key and tap the right arrow key once. This will stretch the column of cells to accommodate the words. Hit the Tab key, which will move the cursor to the next cell (SHIFT, then Tab, will move the cursor to the left). Also, the arrow keys or a mouse can be used to move to different cells.

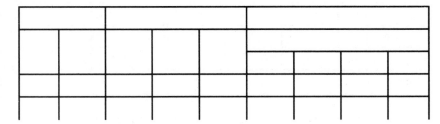

FIGURE A.5

FIGURE A.6

Row 2. Hit ENTER, then type in the word "Stock," tab to the next column, type "Current Price $," using the ENTER key and space bar to position the words. Proceed with the remainder of the text labels in a similar manner. The columns with a dollar sign should be left-justified and the columns with the percent sign should be right-justified. Justification can be accomplished in the TABLES mode (hold the Alt key and hit F7).

Move the cursor to the column you wish to justify; for example, in the cell under "Sales," turn on the block (F12) and extend the cursor down so it covers six rows. Hit the number 2 Format, then 1 Cell, then 3 Justify, then 3 Right. Move the cursor to the next column for justification and repeat the procedure.

Lines in the upper-right shaded area of Figure A.7 can be removed by moving the cursor to the cell above Sales; enter the tables format (hold Alt and hit F7), turn on the block F12 and expand the cursor down, then hit lines 3, inside 5, none 1. Move the cursor above Earn's and repeat the step. This keeps the cells intact but hides the extra lines.

Stock Selector: Date:		Objective: Growth			Research from			
Stock	Current Price $	P/E Ratios 5-Yr Curr/Avg $ %	Annual Dividend $	Price + Dividend $	5-Yr Average Annual Growth			
					Sales %	Earn's %	Price & Divs $ %	

Notes:

FIGURE A.7

All the forms in this book were created with this method. When you know the number of rows and columns and how to join or stretch them, creating a similar table for your own use should be an easy matter.

On some occasions, you may want to remove some of the lines but keep a cell intact to hold position. The "lines" command on the tables menu will allow you to hide lines but keep the cells.

Other Customizing Tips

Tabs. If you wish to use tabs within a table, use the "indent" command (F4), as the tab command will not work in tables. The tab command is used for moving the cursor from cell to cell.

Shading. In the TABLES format, the block command can be used to shade a group of cells at one time. Turn on the block, then extend by using the proper arrow keys. Hit the number 3-Lines, then hit 8-Shade, followed by 1-On. Shading can be a helpful accent when printing.

Copying. To copy a column of dollar signs, in the TABLES mode, turn the block (F12) on extend to cover the column you wish to copy, hold down the Ctrl key and hit F4. Hit a number 1 for block, then hit number 2 copy. Move the cursor to the top of the column you want to copy to and hit enter. The dollar signs will all appear in the proper cells.

Other Formats

Using the process described here should assist you in making any of the forms in this book. The format suggested should also allow the information to appear on the screen. Other formats will work, but may push the right margin off the screen. The forms are an easy method of controlling the most important information for stock selection. They can greatly simplify your personal stock investing and may make it more profitable.

Index